PROFESSIONAL DEVELOPMENT AND PRACTICE SERIES
ANN LIEBERMAN, *Editor*

Chartering Urban School Reform
Reflections on Public High Schools
in the Midst of Change

Edited by
MICHELLE FINE

Teachers College, Columbia University
New York and London

Published by Teachers College Press, 1234 Amsterdam Avenue
New York, New York

Library of Congress Cataloging-in-Publication Data
Chartering urban school reform : reflections on public high schools in
    the midst of change / edited by Michelle Fine.
        p.   cm.—(Professional development and practice series)
    Includes bibliographical references and index.
    ISBN 0-8077-3318-0.—ISBN 0-8077-3317-2 (pbk.)
    1. Education, Urban—United States—Administration.   2. High
schools—United States—Administration.   3. Educational change—
United States.   I. Fine, Michelle.   II. Series.
LC5131.C43   1994
370.19'348'0973—dc20   93-41347

ISBN 0-8077-3318-0
ISBN 0-8077-3317-2 (pbk.)

Printed on acid-free paper
Manufactured in the United States of America
99 98 97 96 95 94 8 7 6 5 4 3 2 1

This book is dedicated to Koray Maddox,
whose life and death at seventeen should
remind us all why we stay in the struggle for
social justice and democratic schooling.

From the Series Editor

The central task of the current reform movement in education is nothing less than building and transforming schools that are struggling to achieve democratic ideals. The purpose of the Professional Development and Practice Series is to contribute to this historic transformation by presenting a variety of descriptions of practice-oriented research—narratives, stories, cases of innovative work —that can lead to a deeper understanding of educational practice and how to improve it. At this time of important educational change, we need to be informed by the special knowledge of university- and school-based educators who are working in and with the schools to illuminate how and in what ways positive change can take place.

As new organizational arrangements and collaborative relationships are being forged and studied, old enduring problems are being looked at in new ways that are leading us to fresh insights. For example, the connections between teaching, learning, and assessment are being reexamined, and views of how teachers and students develop and learn are changing in a way that more actively engages them in their own constructions of knowledge. The authors in this series are attempting to involve us in a dialogue about action, participation, and change based on the best evidence. They have undertaken to struggle with the problems of practice and the challenge of rethinking the future of our nation's schools.

It is often true that the reforms of one era become the target of reformers of a new era. There may be no better example than the creation of the comprehensive high school. When it was created, it represented a move to provide students with a rich array of curriculum choices, as well as academic and vocational options. Today, with students increasingly alienated, dropping out, and in desperate need of a community that is rich both educationally and emotionally, large comprehensive schools seem an anachronism.

This book explores one aspect of the rebellion: the movement to create small, intimate school communities called "charters." The partnership that inspired them, the comprehensive changes that inform each charter, and the personal and collective struggles to institutionalize these new communities form the narrative structure of this book. Told from the perspectives of both insiders and outsiders, it has much to teach us, even as it involves us in the unfolding drama.

Ann Lieberman

Contents

Foreword

Chartering Urban School Reform is a progress report from a crucially important front in the struggle to restructure American public education. Although change needs to occur in virtually all American school districts, including those serving the wealthiest and most complacent suburbs, the success of the reform movement will be measured ultimately by its impact on our largest and most troubled urban districts. In one sense this may seem unfair, for it is in our largest cities that the job of the schools is most difficult, given the often overwhelming social and economic circumstances of students living in desperately impoverished neighborhoods. But these are the neighborhoods most in need of transformed schools, and it is in these neighborhood high schools that the Philadelphia Schools Collaborative has chosen to undertake its work.

When I arrived in Philadelphia in early 1990 to direct the education grant-making program at The Pew Charitable Trusts, the Collaborative was in its first full year of operation, working intensively in three high schools to create smaller, self-contained learning communities (charters) in which students and teachers would work together over a four-year period, and less intensively with 9th grade teachers in most of the other nineteenth neighborhood high schools. The core ideas of the Collaborative were familiar to me, for I had begun my career in education in the early 1960s as a high school English teacher on an interdisciplinary team in a school-within-a-school, and near the end of the decade had directed an experimental urban high school that was organized entirely into such teams. What was not familiar, however, and what remains unique today about the Collaborative is the breadth of its vision and the sweep of its ambition. The vision animating the work of the Collaborative is a system of secondary education organized around semiautonomous "learning communities" of adults and students, each with its own distinctive intellectual theme or focus, linked not only to outside resources and institutions in Philadelphia, but to national networks of schools and teachers pursuing similar goals. The Collaborative's ambition is that such learning communities, or charters, become the norm, not the exception or alternative, and that the entire administrative infrastructure of the district—central office, regional superintendents' offices, high school offices—be rethought and reinvented to support the work of charters.

The chapters that follow provide vivid testimony to the power of the idea of charters and to their potential to unleash intellectual energy and rekindle commitment on the part of veteran teachers in urban schools. The teachers and their university colleagues whose voices you will hear in *Chartering Urban School Reform* understand fully the yawning gap between their schools as they exist today, even after four years and roughly $11,000,000 in grants from Pew and the idealized vision of the Collaborative; but they have seen enough progress, and enough difference in the lives of real students, to know that there is no turning back.

Earlier this summer our foundation released the report of a panel of outside observers, led by Richard Clark, on the progress of restructuring in this school district. The report was sharply critical of both the school district and the teachers union, asserting that restructuring had lost ground during the last year, principally as a consequence of lack of consistent leadership and support from both sides. Following the release of the report we convened a day-long forum in which 75 parents, teachers, school board members, administrators, university and business partners, Collaborative leaders, and foundation staff came together to wrestle with the implications of the report and to begin to develop a plan of action to recapture lost momentum.

Despite major personnel changes, including the resignations of the superintendent, her top deputies, and nearly half the high school principals in response to a state early retirement incentive program, the early signs in this crucial fifth year of work in the high schools are promising. The school board president, interim superintendent, and new senior management team of the district have all reaffirmed their support for charters and for fundamental restructuring and have publicly committed themselves to the institutionalization of charters. As the search for a new superintendent gets under way, there is virtual unanimity among all parties that the principal task of the next superintendent will be the implementation of restructuring, *not* the development of a new reform agenda. And as Jan Somerville and Michelle Fine, the two founders and visionaries of the Collaborative, begin the process of transferring ownership back to teachers, parents, and community, new leadership from the teacher ranks and community has emerged to secure these reforms in the schools.

The process of fundamental educational reform is messy, slow, and difficult, and one becomes easily discouraged. The morning paper brings the predictable news from the National Education Goals Panel that after three years we have made little or no progress toward the ambitious goals set in Charlottesville by the president and governors. This will doubtless provide further fuel for those who advocate vouchers or other privatization schemes. Despite the absence of hard evidence of progress, however, I believe there is much to be hopeful about in American education—the movement for national standards, the development of alternative forms of assessment, the expansion of networks of reforming schools, the creation of the National Board for Professional Teaching

Standards, the growing number of states with coherent systemic reform polices and strategies. Finally, however, the fate of the reform movement will turn on whether the people at the heart of the educational process, teachers and students, are given the necessary leadership, support, and discretion to create meaningful learning communities in which all participants can flourish. *Chartering Urban School Reform* suggests the possibilities as well as the difficulties inherent in this vision of restructured schools.

Bob Schwartz
Program Director for Education
The Pew Charitable Trusts
October 1993

Preface

True to the spirit of messy, democratic, school-based reform, *Chartering Urban School Reform* grows out of collaborations among and between secondary teachers, university faculty, parents, students, consultants, and evaluators. Sharing a commitment to radically transformed public schools that provide rich academic possibilities for low-income adolescents, these writers tell stories of reform in varied dialects, narrated from diverse, sometimes discrepant, standpoints. As an editor filled with my own desires, defenses, and vulnerabilities, searching for clarity rather than unity, I consider the cacophony a virtue. Collectively, the writers have sought neither to tell a simple story nor to author a false coherence. Disharmonies will seem all too obvious, but at the heart of each chapter lies a commitment to sustained change, critical inquiry, and honest talk.

It is deeply ironic, therefore, that the names of the schools and the school district have been altered for this text. As per the determination of the district's legal counsel, all schools have been renamed. The district is simply represented as "the school district."

Such a narrative act may seem odd given that inquiry lies at the heart of this reform; given that this city's movement is nationally recognized and well covered in the press; given that our teachers, parents, and students have risked their voices, their collegial relations, their jobs and have taken the chance to believe—all in search of rich, democratic schools. This legal decision nonetheless speaks of the silencing that has grown inside, that surrounds and steals the breath out of public schools across the nation.

Like all public secrets, this one is designed to control and protect, and yet, ironically, it forces readers to imagine that there is much to hide. In its cloudy presence, hovering over text and schools, we are reminded that to speak at all, in the "public" sector of public education, requires incredible levels of courage exercised by educators, parents, and students taking risks and signing their names to their chapters. They are the true champions of public education. Willing to be accountable and honest, they deserve baskets of respect and have earned my deepest affections.

The chapters in this book speak through a commitment to urban school reform. In this spirit, we give boundless thanks to Diane Scott, who was the assistant superintendent for comprehensive high schools during the early years;

Helen Cunningham, originally of Pew Charitable Trusts; and Ralph Smith, who was the chief of staff for the school district during our earliest years. All spoke passionately and powerfully for what they believed. All have moved beyond the school district. We miss, deeply, their vision, integrity, and courage.

Thanks also are due to Janis Somerville, the genius and architect of the Collaborative in Philadelphia, and to Carol McIntosh, who, as always, has served as the exceptional one, holding together the pieces of a book (and my life) that, at moments, looked like it could fall apart. Praise, compliments, awe, and shared worries to all the teachers, administrators, parents, and students, as well as to the school district and the Federation of Teachers, who continue to struggle for public-sector reform.

Hoping for a better life for all children, better working conditions for all teachers, and more power for all parents, I look forward to someone else's editing of the next volume detailing the national struggle for democratic public schools. David, Sam, and Demetrius—thanks for sticking by me during my sometimes less than gracious days.

Michelle Fine

PART I

Framing a Reform Movement

Michelle Fine

The Philadelphia Schools Collaborative was born as a nonprofit organization committed to nothing short of the radical restructuring of the 22 neighborhood comprehensive high schools serving more than 40,000 students and the concomitant decentralization of the central district to support improved student outcomes, democratic governance of schools, and school-based decision making and management of resources. Janis Somerville, who was Director of Strategic Planning for the school district, took the position as Director of the Collaborative in 1988. I joined shortly thereafter when Jan and Ralph Smith, then Chief of Staff for the school district, prodded me out of Penn's Graduate School of Education. Finding the challenge impossible to resist, four years later I remain in the thick of a social movement that never ends.

The Collaborative set out to ignite a democratic reform movement of educators and parents, designed initially to reinvent existing neighborhood high schools. Early review of the data left no doubt that our work was cut out for us. In 1988, it looked like less than half of the typical ninth-grade class ever made it to tenth grade; in many schools more than 25% of incoming ninth graders were 16 or older, and 30% had been labeled as needing special education. Parents living in the district had so thoroughly pursued parochial and private school options that over one-third of all school-aged children were not attending public schools. Our task was to reinvigorate intellectually and professionally the educators who had survived typically 20 years in these anonymous and disempowering institutions, to reengage the students "left behind" who attended (and did not attend) these schools, and to organize the parents who were attached (and alienated) from these institutions of deep despair and not infrequent hostility. Simply stated, our collective work was radical, systemic reform—not one more "project."

Over four years the Pew Charitable Trusts invested more than $8 million, sponsoring public, data-driven talk; dinners, prep periods, and retreats; about "what is" and "what could be." Educators, parents, and students have visited one another's schools and other urban schools, witnessing the possibilities of rich urban education. They have fought and cooperated with one another, inventing strategies to transform urban schooling. Critique, analysis, trust, and inquiry have sat at the very heart of reform.

Our primary collective work has been to dismantle the urban high school as we knew it—large, anonymous, and filled with more cracks than safety nets—and to nourish, in its place, many small, intellectually intimate communities of learners called charters. Charters, as designed, are supposed to be controlled by the teachers who educate in them. Charters constitute ninth- through twelfth-grade heterogeneous communities in which teaching, learning, assessment, student supports, professional talk, parental involvement, and dreaming for the future are all supposed to happen. Charters are small schools.

In short, the Collaborative has become a nesting site, laboratory, living room, and safe space for dangerous talk and provocative practice. We have stretched into a public forum in which the undiscussable can be discussed, the unimaginable imagined, the inevitable interrupted, the undreamable tried, and the undoable done. You will hear in the pages that follow the multiple voices of students, parents, and teachers who have come alive, returned to the juices and passions that stirred them early in their days with public education. You will hear, too, the anger of students, parents, and teachers confronting poverty, racism, bureaucracy, and a 12-year federal, state, and local agenda committed to the abandonment of poor urban youths. In short, you will hear the visions and struggles of a multivoiced, contradiction-filled, painful, and delightful urban reform movement "in the midst of change."

The short biography of the restructuring in these urban high schools is worth knowing, if only to confirm that radical transformation within the public sector is eminently doable. Even in one of the most impoverished urban sites in the country, teachers, for the most part, have come back; parents, for the most part, want to be engaged; students, for the most part, seek deep connections with peers and adults and yearn for academic success. While the tensions have been many, the struggles seem endless, and the odds often appear insurmountable, the financial investment, overall, has been marginal to the budget of a large, urban district. The school-based transformations have been simply dazzling—and bureaucratic resistance daunting.

Chartering Urban School Reform represents the first installment in the autobiography of our reform movement, spilling from schools to streets to charters and back again. Our commitments have been to honest talk, courageous analysis, gutsy experimentation, and serious empowerment of educators, students, and parents. We have evidence, to date, that urban students are hungry for schools that nourish them intellectually and emotionally; that urban educators are committed to creating and attaching to such communities; that urban parents are eager to be engaged. But we have also learned that the stubbornness of bureaucracy is tough to anticipate and that the brutal inequities of the Reagan/Bush years have exacted an extraordinary toll on children growing up in poverty. We write, then, delighted with our bright moments, worrying aloud about our dilemmas. Surrounded, in the state and nationally, by cynical attempts at privatization and vouchers, we narrate our very different stories as educators, activists, researchers, parents, and students committed to radically democratic education for all in the urban public sector.

The chapters in *Chartering Urban School Reform* are designed to *reimagine* educational policies, practice, and research *for* school-based change. Written by "collaborators" of secondary and university faculties, the authors of these essays share the conviction that educational research can no longer afford to be merely *about* schooling but needs to be conducted *with* educators and students, *for* educational change, and always be *critical, collaborative,* and *creative.* Across chapters, authors reflect on how our practices, methodologies, ethics, epistemologies, and narrative strategies have been shaped by our desire to both incite and document reform. You will hear consensus, and you will hear conflict. All of this is built into a democratic movement for social change.

These chapters are all, by intent, "half done." A bit embarrassing, still vulnerable. We are all in the middle of ongoing tough and troubling conversations about change. Indeed, we might argue that neither restructuring nor inquiry is ever done. Instead of finished glossies and simple "how-to's," these chapters deliver disturbing and comforting reflections from researchers and practitioners struggling to create and document "what could be" rich educational communities, or charters, as urban high schools.

1

Chartering Urban School Reform

MICHELLE FINE

The work of the Collaborative was first begun in 1988 through a series of conversations between urban high school teachers; Jan Somerville, executive director of the Philadelphia Schools Collaborative; Ralph Smith, then chief of staff of the school district; Helen Cunningham, then at the Pew Charitable Trusts; and me, senior consultant. We tried together to imagine "what could be" ideal educational experiences for students and labor conditions for teachers within urban comprehensive high schools. In meeting rooms and in Jan's living room, after food and wine, we invented together images of small, intimate, and intellectually rich communities in which faculty would work closely and over time with one another and with a stable group of students. These teachers cherished the idea of working within interdisciplinary teams and with an ongoing cohort of students. They bristled, however, at the idea of creating these communities in "your existing schools, with your present colleagues." They shuddered when we noted that charters would begin in the ninth grade. One teacher gasped, "Ninth graders! They're all hormones and feet!"

Today, throughout the 22 public, comprehensive high schools in this city, over 90 charters exist, grades 9–12. All 22 comprehensive high schools have developed, at minimum, two charters a piece. Six schools are committed to fully charter. In these schools, all students and all faculty belong to a "community of learners." A full half of the charters have been "home grown," developed by interdisciplinary groups of teachers over the past three years. Charters are present-day versions of what we used to call "schools within a school," but they have quite specific criteria.

Anywhere from 200 to 400 students constitute a charter, with 10 to 12 core teachers who work together from ninth (or tenth) grade through to graduation. The charter faculty enjoy a common preparation period daily, share responsibility for a cohort of students, and invent curriculum, pedagogies, and assessment strategies that reflect a common intellectual project. Students travel together to classes and across their four years in high school. With teachers, counselors, and parents, they constitute a semiautonomous community within a building of charters. Charters result in diplomas and prepare all students for college and/or employment; the student body must be, by definition, heterogeneous.

Charters are not "programs" that meet once a week. They are not "transitional projects" for ninth graders or students in trouble. They are not pull-out, remediation, or advancement for students with special needs or with "special gifts." They cannot include only a common set of students, but must also have a common set of faculty who work together. No one school within a school should exist within a traditional high school (or it will be eaten, as we all know from experience). And charters should not be tracks, creaming students or teachers. They should, instead, work like small communities of adults and students, teachers and parents, counselors and university faculty, who nurture an engaging educational experience across four years and enjoy sustained and ongoing relationships, within and across generations, inside an urban public high school. The expectation is that charters will vary widely, but they share a commitment to neighborhood students, heterogeneity, active and student-centered pedagogies, and rigorous, if diverse, forms of accountability.

This reform movement was designed to engage existing neighborhood high schools in full transformation. We knew that all teachers, staff, and students, as well as parents, should feel attached to and engaged with such communities, grades 9–12. And we knew from existing evidence that such structures could surely support historically low-achieving students. As one teacher explained:

> More middle-class kids have the support and community and networks. These kids need it—and the charter delivers just that. A safe community in which they can learn, experiment, and be nurtured.

We recognized early that most of our resources would have to be invested in "resuscitating" the sense of possibility held by teachers, strengthening their discipline-based work, and facilitating their interdisciplinary work. It was, for some teachers, a chance of a lifetime. "This is why I entered education in the first place." For others, it was an assault on personal autonomy (i.e., "shutting my door"). "Create community with my colleagues and these students? Have you met my colleagues, have you seen these students?" Attitudes flourish between these poles.

CHARTERS IN CONTEXT

When we began this work, and even more so now, evidence had accumulated which documented that small educational communities, in our case charters, could enhance teachers' professional development, parents' levels of involvement, and students' academic and social outcomes (Wehlage, 1989).

It might be hard for a reader to recognize how different "life in the charters" is for students and teachers, relative to their median 20 years of "life in a comprehensive high school" in precharter days.

Before charters, most students in these high schools had six classes a year, were heavily tracked, were with different students in most of their classes, had different teachers every year, and belonged, emotionally, to no *unit*. Anonymity prevailed, and 45% to 55% of the typical ninth-grade class never made it to tenth grade—much less to graduation.

Teachers likewise were locked in an anonymous maze. They taught 165 to 180 students in a day, sharing them, as a group, with no one. Cut rates, discipline problems, truancy were extreme. Discipline and counseling responsibilities were separated from teachers' work. Classroom educators enjoyed what some called autonomy. They had, by all accounts, no power and suffered from extreme isolation. They rarely talked with colleagues at their school about their classroom work and were typically blamed for school failure.

> It was "do your own thing" before charters. Teachers rarely shared their strategies and programs. Meetings were all administrative, no pedagogy going on.
>
> In charters with colleagues, in department or interdisciplinary meetings, there's a lot more strategizing. There was no opportunity to talk to my colleagues before. There was no reason to talk to colleagues before. Teaching interdisciplinarily, it's compulsory. I'm certainly learning from colleagues, and colleagues ask me for help. Last week a teacher who has never in 35 years of teaching broken his class into groups, did so. He's not [even] in a charter. (Zach Rubin, teacher)

Most knew little about the personal lives of students, and for many this was just fine. Those deeply committed to students could choose "a few a year whom I know I could really make a difference with." Counselors worked through the alphabet, dividing students, A through Z, by the sum total of counselors available. Parents were invited to school either because their child was in trouble or because there was a large, schoolwide Parents Night, typically with terrible and embarrassing attendance.

Now, within charters, students still have six classes a year—but they may be taken two at a time, with deep concentration for 10 weeks; or there may be three per semester; or there may be four on-site at school and two in the community through internships and/or community-based projects. Students know the other students and faculty with whom they share a charter because they have an ongoing life (four or more years) together. In some charters, faculty have divided up all the students into "family groups" so that each student has one adult (teacher, counselor, aide, principal, janitor, and so on) with whom the personal connection is deep, sustained, and confidential over four years.

> Family groups are a forum for students to get the strength to help each other solve problems. They set the agenda. (Shirley Farmer, teacher)

As Renee Cohen, coordinator of the Trailblazers Charter, describes:

> Now, they [her charter students] chase me down the hall asking for help. They see me as their advocate, and they're ready to use me!

Teachers still have typically large urban loads, but they share their students over four years with their charter colleagues. Common prep times are spent discussing curriculum, instruction, and assessment issues; worrying about and delighting in individual students; planning Family Nights for "significant adults and children" in the lives of their students; strategizing about how to get Christina over the death of her father or Paul not to move down South or Mr. Rodriguez not to deprive Cantada of the charter trip to visit a college. Natalie Hiller, chemistry teacher, makes vivid her charter life: "It's put a smile on my lips and bags under my eyes."

Groups of charter teachers, with administrators and parents, are now involved in school-based policy making and in year-round, ongoing seminars of their own design. Within a tight accountability framework, some are studying and inventing authentic assessments. Others are integrating vocational and academic work. Many are creating interdisciplinary curricula, developing multicultural classrooms, infusing technology into instruction, and sharing a Seminar in Teaching and Learning with charter teachers from across the city. Modeled by Diane Scott, assistant superintendent for senior high schools (1991– 92), hard public talk—about racism, accountability, disengaged peers—has been legitimated. Within charters, as the following scene conveys, faculty are engaged in once taboo and still difficult conversations about the nature of learning and teaching in urban America.

> *MF notes*: There was a charter faculty meeting in ———. I had just been pulled aside by an administrator who was—astonished? pleased? worried? A group of charter students had just popped into her office raving positively about their charter but negatively about one teacher. One student put it this way, "We are ——— students. We deserve good teaching." She enters the faculty meeting.
>
> The teacher/facilitator for the day opens the meeting, discussing what he calls the slings and arrows of our charter:

We've been accused of taking lab areas. They say, You people want everything. You take all the labs, you drive other kids out of your charter. This isn't true! A number of students who were having trouble in our charter lobbied to leave, we resisted, monitored closely. We brought in more children, many of them ninth-grade repeaters and overage students. We did two days of work on rostering. We need data on how we are not creaming. Every time we are successful we have to hear, from our colleagues, that we are stealing the "best" students!

They then move onto talk about the "language of the contract we have established with students." We need time to ask ourselves, have we lived up to our end of the contract? Especially around how we are assessing students' work?

The conversation about assessment heats up—Let's talk about projects in the students' folders—how do we give humanities credit? If they do four projects they get 80 or 85? Three projects 74 or 76? Two projects 65? Only one they get a 50?

Another teacher: This is absurd! What are we doing? We are trying to change the system and conform to it at the same time!

Bob: This is emblematic of the system. Early failure means you never see progress. We need to set aside class time, and faculty time, to discuss portfolios and how we are going to assess student work within the contract we establish with them.

Let's end with something positive.

Ann: Kids are talking about their wonderful time in math!

Other math teacher: Kids are coming to math!

Social studies teacher: Several kids caught onto problem solving today.

Natalie: In my class kids passed a hat for goggles for the one kid to afford getting into the lab. They are really becoming a community.

Bob: I'm learning about their culture—they are educating me.

Marsha: We are educating each other.

Phil: We have to advocate for these children with the administration. One boy in my class was told he can't graduate. I have been here for 20 years, and never heard of this. So we need to advocate for our kids!

Three teachers stop me at conferences to announce, "I'm back! I was burned out and now I'm revived in my charter." At the same time, as might be expected, there are still many who resist, as one recently did at a citywide meeting of faculty:

It's no longer the principals, the administration that is making us work harder or more than we think we should. Now it's *peer* pressure. Those *damn enthusiastic teachers,* our peers, want us to do what they are willing to do. And I'm not willing, after all these years, to change my work!

Another teacher responded,

Hey, watch what you say! I'm one of those *damn enthusiastic* teachers, and I finally feel free to teach how, with whom, and with the beliefs that I have always wanted to.

Debates flourish within and across schools. Any kind of change is problematic. Democratic change is frustrating, loud, but possible.

Counselors at some schools, such as nurses and other student support staff, are redesigning their work to fit charters rather than serving alphabet fragments (e.g. A–G, H–K, L–P . . .) of a full school. For some, the shifts are already rewarding. One commented:

It's great to work with a group of teachers, and a group of students who share an intellectual project together. But it's a real shift. I'm used to L through Q in the alphabet.

Likewise, a teacher and charter coordinator describes:

Being in a charter, especially with the social work interns, has changed all of my work. So I, and other teachers, are being advocates for students. I am so delighted to hear my principal say, "Academics have to drive the rosters, not rosters driving the academics." That's a major change. One more thing: with charters, parents are really involved. We invited 22 parents in for a Family Night; 17 showed up.

Others worry that restructuring and charters are designed to "take away" their jobs. As charters become the primary unit for high schooling, questions are being raised by educators and parents about the need for many previously "essential," individuals who try to serve the whole school (e.g., Deans for Boys/Girls, disciplinarians, college advisers, roster or scheduling persons). So many of the once absolute functions needed in a large school are now being absorbed and transformed within the trusting relationships of charters.

At root, teachers' sense of themselves as intellectuals, as professionals, and as relational has been enhanced. Listen to an English teacher:

Finally I can teach students in ways that allow me to engage with them, and other faculty, and hold onto them for their entire secondary school experience.

Some request help. A history teacher who worked in a program for low-income, low-achieving, Chapter 1, overage students at her high school came to me two years ago:

> OK, Michelle, you told me you wanted me to get to know these kids. Now we do. And we know what is going on with them. The kid who used to flash the lights on and off in the back of the room isn't just a disciplinary problem, he's a young man with a crack-addicted mother, or he is homeless. These students have hard lives. Other than taking them home, I don't know what to do with them. You need to get me some help.

Some teachers admit that their involvement in charters has provoked a sharp shift in their perspective on students. Anne Bourgeois, math teacher and Federation of Teachers building representative for her high school, works in a writing-intensive, project-based charter that has allied with the Essential Schools movement. At a conference for charter educators, Anne spoke passionately to a citywide group of faculty about how teaching in a charter has transformed her view of herself as a teacher and her views of students as learners:

> I always thought of myself as a good teacher; but not always so creative. I have never enjoyed teaching as much as I do now. I am learning from my colleagues in the charter and, the most amazing thing, I never thought my students wanted to see themselves as students! We would all give the class away to the most disruptive students. Now the students tell Charlie to "shut up and let us learn."

Indeed, with these organizational changes, "regular" teachers have, over three years, collectively radicalized their sense of what is possible and therefore their demands. Those most engaged in charter life now say, "Allow us to work, as a stable educational community, with this group of students, parents, and with one another." For them that translates into:

> Don't bounce teachers out of the charter because the school has a momentary drop in enrollment, and don't appoint the next most senior person on the list to our charter. Teachers need individual and collective stability, we need time during the day to plan, reflect, and build curriculum, and we need to interview our peers to assure that they know, and we know, how we can live together as a community.

These issues would be central to the making of any community, but they have been, until now, considered almost impossible to raise, much less resolve, in a centralized urban school district. We can now appreciate how, over time, hierarchical, disempowering bureaucracies have kept teachers from seeing and hearing students' voices, parents' desires, and colleagues' strengths (Fine, 1991). Indeed, they have been unable to hear their own voices or see their own pedagogical power. But now—working as a team of teachers on the issues of organizational change, curricular development, instructional strategies, and assessment—many charter-based teachers report feeling "reinvigorated" and exhausted, ever-frustrated by constraints within their schools, and imposed upon by central bureaucratic policies and practices. And yet, because the focus on teacher/parent development has been so relentless and entirely school-based, teachers are already seeing differences in themselves and in their students. Concerns of education and labor are being addressed at once.

One charter leader explained how charters foster teachers' growth:

> Our idea was creating a safe place, an atmosphere of acceptance. There's no anonymity in a charter—that's why insecure teachers avoid them. Vulnerabilities hang out. That's where the charter is good because then vulnerabilities are accepted and teachers start developing strengths to start overcoming those vulnerabilities. In dealing with students holistically, as we can in the charter, we are dealing with teachers holistically as well. (Essie Abrahams, teacher)

Other teachers saw the same issue as an opportunity within a charter:

> You see someone with a rigid teaching style who's not yet open to a variety of kids' learning styles. But there's room for repair *through* collaboration. (Shirley Farmer, teacher)

> When we meet as a team and talk about students, we can brainstorm on how to handle problems. It makes a great deal of difference when I can say to that student, "Well your other teachers said *this* about you." We're working as a team and the students *know* that.

> I'm more aware of who their other teachers are and what they're doing. I tell students to *watch how their teachers teach*. That can help students study.

> Those meetings are really valuable. We discuss what we *can* do *for* students.

> It's better for individual teachers because theirs is not the only viewpoint on a student or class. They get ideas on how to handle a class because everyone has the same group. (Teacher)

Parents of high school students, who are the group most recently included in our reform work, comment that their relationships with schools have deepened because their involvement with charters allows them into the school not only to discuss a discipline problem, truancy, or a special education referral, but as increasingly less marginal members of the community. A mother of two boys, one of whom attends a charter, told me:

> When he was first in the charter, I thought "something new again." But then I saw him flourish, and the teachers took such an interest in him. And in me. They called me, and we worked together. The charter has given me something to connect to. Through it I became interested in the school and really, that was part of why I was willing to serve on the governance council at our high school. I feel like it is my school, now, too.

Based on preliminary evidence, parental involvement is increasing in quantity and deepening in quality through the charter school experience.

STUDENT OUTCOMES: THE LITMUS FOR REFORM

Charters are struggling to become learning communities that embody the very pieces of restructuring that we would consider essential to full school transformation: democratic governance and the creation of small intellectual communities with school-based, ongoing professional development, student-centered pedagogies, authentic assessment, deep parental involvement, and long-term relationships among faculty and students resulting in college entrance and/or work placement. Of the 94 charters, all are in the midst of trying to effect these transformations. A few, perhaps 10% to 15%, are exceptional. Most are still mediocre. All are very different from the others. None is worse than the full, anonymous bureaucratic school out of which it was designed.

Mapping a brief history of restructuring in our high schools, it is safe to conclude that over the period of implementation several things have occurred.

The number of comprehensive high school students has grown enormously. The citywide comprehensive high school population swelled from 38,885 in 1988 to 42,903 in 1992. For the ninth grade alone however, the numbers rose from 13,772 in 1988 to 16,561 in 1992, a full 20% increase. While 22% of schools lost enrollment or stabilized, 32% increased their ninth-grade student population by 10% to 25% and 36% increased it by 50% to 300%. This growth in ninth-grade enrollment reflects a demographic boom, an influx of immigrants and former parochial school students, a reduction in the dropout rate (as recognized by the state), and the return of substantial numbers of students, including "repeaters" who in prior years had failed to return to school.

The size of comprehensive high school faculties has not kept pace. During this same period, while the number of students increased by more than 10% (4,000 students), the number of teachers has remained relatively steady. In other words, in proportion to the increased number of students, there is a shortage of approximately 200 teachers.

Student outcomes improved consistently over time. Despite the rise in demand and cut in resources, student outcomes have improved and been sustained over four years. Evidence in Table 1.1 suggests steady improvements in attendance; course passage rates for English, history, math, and science; and rates of credit accumulation. Figures 1.1 through 1.3 display information on students who remain in high school, that is, who receive report cards at end of year and do not drop out; this number has increased, particularly for those repeaters who are most at risk.

Attendance figures are up slightly, the percent of students earning sufficient credits to be promoted has risen over time, and the percentage of repeaters—those who fail and yet return to school—is up. While steady progress is evident across all 22 schools, Table 1.2 demonstrates that schools which originally had the lowest levels of achievement improved most dramatically through-

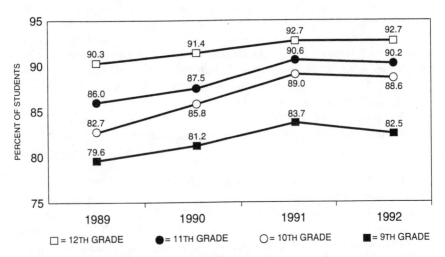

FIGURE 1.1 Percentage of comprehensive high school students receiving a report card—a measure of holding power.

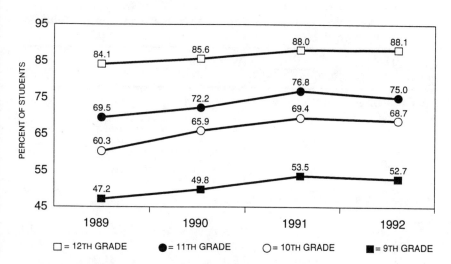

FIGURE 1.2 Percentage of comprehensive high school students promoted —a measure of academic progress.

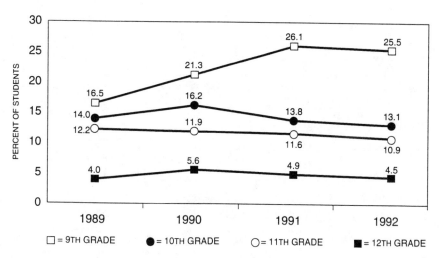

FIGURE 1.3 Percentage of comprehensive high school students who were repeaters.

TABLE 1.1 Outcome measures for comprehensive high schools, 1988–89 through 1991–92.

OUTCOME/ grade	Academic Year				Change
	1988/89	1989/90	1990/91	1991/92	
AVERAGE DAILY ATTENDANCE					
9th	—	67.9	69.7	70.1	2.2
10th	—	76.1	78.1	78.1	2.0
11th	—	78.8	80.1	80.4	1.6
12th	—	83.3	83.9	83.7	0.4
Total	—	74.6	76.1	76.1	1.5
PERCENTAGE PASSING MAJOR SUBJECTS					
English					
9th	54.3	58.4	60.4	62.4	8.1
10th	63.4	70.7	75.2	72.4	9.0
11th	74.8	77.8	80.4	81.0	6.2
12th	87.8	90.7	91.8	92.1	4.3
History					
9th	56.4	59.3	63.2	63.9	7.5
10th	62.4	67.4	71.8	72.3	9.9
11th	75.6	77.6	82.2	82.5	6.9
12th	90.6	90.4	92.1	91.2	0.6
Math					
9th	50.3	52.0	56.1	55.2	4.9
10th	59.3	65.6	68.2	68.0	8.7
11th	67.8	71.2	74.7	74.2	6.4
12th	84.5	86.4	88.3	88.3	3.8
Science					
9th	55.0	57.5	60.2	63.4	8.4
10th	65.1	70.0	73.0	73.9	8.8
11th	73.1	75.5	79.5	80.9	7.8
12th	88.7	88.4	90.1	91.1	2.4
CHANGES IN CREDIT ACCUMULATION RATES					
Percentage Earning Threshold Credits during 12-Month Academic Year					
9th	44.7	47.4	50.9	50.1	5.4
10th	50.2	56.0	61.8	60.4	10.2
11th	63.5	67.5	72.7	71.6	8.1
12th	78.7	79.9	83.3	82.4	3.7
Percentage Earning Promotion					
9th	47.2	49.8	53.5	52.7	5.5
10th	60.3	65.9	69.4	68.7	8.4
11th	69.5	72.2	76.8	75.1	5.6
12th	84.1	85.6	88.0	88.1	4.0

TABLE 1.2 Changes in outcome measures for comprehensive high schools, 1988–89 through 1991–92, by initial student achievement level of school.

OUTCOME/ grade	Initial Student Achievement Level of School		
	Low	Medium	High
CHANGES IN AVERAGE DAILY ATTENDANCE[1]			
9th	5.11	1.5	2.5
10th	5.61	0.8	−0.4
11th	1.96	2.2	0.4
12th	−2.84	2.7	3.7
CHANGES IN PERCENTAGE PASSING MAJOR SUBJECTS			
English			
9th	14.9	7.2	2.0
10th	13.4	7.1	4.5
11th	9.5	9.1	1.9
12th	6.3	6.8	−0.4
Social Studies			
9th	15.9	7.9	0.6
10th	15.7	11.4	9.9
11th	11.6	7.4	3.8
12th	7.1	3.4	−1.2
Math			
9th	8.2	4.8	1.3
10th	14.5	5.8	5.4
11th	10.8	8.1	1.2
12th	10.0	3.0	1.0
Science			
9th	14.7	9.1	1.3
10th	12.0	8.0	6.2
11th	12.2	8.2	5.8
12th	4.7	2.3	1.7
CHANGES IN CREDIT ACCUMULATION RATES			
Percentage Earning Threshold Credits during 12-Month Academic Year			
9th	10.6	4.0	1.0
10th	16.9	8.4	4.7
11th	16.6	8.0	1.8
12th	14.0	3.9	−3.4
Percentage Earning Promotion Based on Cumulative Credits Earned			
9th	11.0	4.1	0.8
10th	14.8	6.5	2.8
11th	12.2	6.2	0.2
12th	10.7	5.2	−1.4

[1]Data for Average Daily Attendance are for 1989–90 through 1991–92; all other data are for 1988–89 through 1991–92.

out the time of restructuring. Finally, as Table 1.3 reports, the percent of students taking the SAT has increased dramatically from 1988 to 1992: up from 12% to 84% depending on school, likewise for the PSAT, with a 6% to 74% increase, depending on school.

In sum, then, over the past three-year period, despite increasing demand from larger student bodies and decreasing resources from a diminished faculty allotment, schoolwide student outcomes have improved as a result of the reform work pursued in the comprehensive high schools.

The Impact of Charters

Charters are now numerous and, truth be told, their internal politics is more than a little complicated. There are still some schools in which charters look a lot like tracks, and a few schools in which only two charters exist. Yet a growing number of charters are designed to be heterogeneously grouped, and by September 1993, many schools were fully chartered. There remains, still, an uneven distribution of special education and repeating ninth graders who are rostered outside of charters. Beliefs in tracking, in the need for homogeneity, and in categorical groupings are more deeply embedded in schools than we anticipated. And so conversations about heterogeneity continue.

The educational research that bore most directly on development of charters came from Gary Wehlage's 1989 study of alternative schools and from Diana Oxley's 1990 analysis of "houses" in New York City's high schools. Oxley writes:

The in-depth analysis of New York City house systems [like charters] and review of the literature indicate the following features are critical to the success of house plans.

- Schools are organized into house units with no more than 500 students and a core teaching staff which instructs most, if not all, students' courses throughout their stay in school.
- Houses are divided into subunits containing an interdisciplinary teacher team and enough students to allow team members to instruct their required classload within the subunit.
- Student support staff are attached to each house, work exclusively with house students and collaboratively with each other and instructional teams.
- Extracurricular activities are organized within each house to give students more opportunities to participate in school life and to develop valuable skills not ordinarily pursued in the classroom.
- House classes, activities, and staff offices are physically located in adjacent rooms within the school building.
- Houses operate in a semi-autonomous fashion with the capacity to determine house policy, select staff, allocate resources, and discipline students.

TABLE 1.3 Students taking SATs and PSATs, by high school.

High School	Number of Tests Taken				% Increase
	1989	1990	1991	1992	
SATs[1]					
A	58	85	107	107	84%
B	44	60	77	113	56%
C	57	79	101	82	43%
D	11	7	20	27	45%
E	123	139	144	179	45%
F	86	254	112	122	41%
G	34	49	50	96	82%
H	68	86	67	96	41%
I	55	39	27	62	12%
TOTAL	536	798	705	884	
PSATs[2]					
A	—[3]	—	81		
B	69	92	189		73.9%
C	—	—	40		
D	15	31	56		73.3%
E	—	70	92		31.4%
F	51	46	45		
G	—	20	42		10.0%
H	—	70	95		35.7%
I	—	113	120		6.2%
J	—	—	56		
K	—	—	41		
L	—	—	126		
M	—	54	218	—[3]	403.7%
TOTAL	135	496	1201		

[1]As reported by the College Board, September 1992. Data include academic years 1988–89 through 1991–92.

[2]As reported by the individual high schools. PSAT exams are given in October of each academic year. Data include academic years 1989–90 through 1992–93.

[3]Data unavailable or no tests administered.

Quantitative analyses compared small and large schools with "weak house" designs to small and large schools with "strong" designs on both direct and indirect effects predicted on the basis of theory. Weak and strong were measures of faculty and student identification with the house. Findings indicated that house systems or houses with the more complete designs had more positive effects on staff and students than others. Well designed houses irrespective of school size outperformed weak ones in large schools on most measures, including students' relationships with peers, teachers, and support staff, extracurricular participation, sense of community, academic performance, and teachers' knowledge of students' all around performance. Well designed houses performed as well as the weakly designed house system of the small school on most measures and better than the small school with respect to sense of community and teachers' knowledge of student performance. (Oxley, 1990, p. ii)

As with the Oxley's New York City data, our initial evidence from those charters we would consider well designed is very encouraging. Students in charters outachieve their noncharter peers in the aggregate in terms of "survival," attendance, grades, and level of credit accumulation.

No doubt, to an urban-naive reader, the school and charter student achievement data at first glance tell a tough story of urban public high schools. Nevertheless, we see that students in charters tend to outachieve their nonchartered peers on a number of standard outcomes, including attendance and course passage (Table 1.4). Further, selected comparisons of demographically comparable students within charters (i.e., age appropriate, nonrepeaters) confirm the positive impact of charters. As Table 1.5 indicates, with selection factors removed, charter students who are on level have higher average daily attendance, higher course passage rates, and fewer suspensions than on-level students who are not in charters. In addition, while females outperform males across the board, charters seem to be equally helpful to young women and men, while slightly more powerful for African American and Latino students than whites.

THE POLITICS OF REFORM: ENGAGING EDUCATORS IN COLLECTIVE CHANGE

When we first began the work of restructuring, a fair number of individual teachers in the school district had already been engaged with professional development networks within and beyond the city (see Lieberman & McLaughlin, 1992). The challenge posed by restructuring was to import what had been their rich individual development work into their charters/schools. We sought to transform the conditions of teachers' workplaces *and* the sites of student learning by effecting sustained, collective, school-based transforma-

TABLE 1.4 Comparison of charter and noncharter students, total population.

	Charter	Noncharter	Charter Difference
ENROLLMENT	(n = 20,898)	(n = 18,905)	(n = 39,803)
9th Grade	52.0%	48.0%	4.0
10th Grade	55.6%	44.4%	11.2
11th Grade	51.4%	48.6%	2.8
12th Grade	50.0%	50.0%	.0
TOTAL	52.5%	47.5%	5.0
ETHNICITY			
White	16.1%	26.8%	−10.7
African American	66.9%	60.6%	6.3
Latino	12.5%	7.1%	5.4
Asian	4.3%	5.3%	−1.0
AVERAGE DAILY ATTENDANCE			
9th Grade	75.7%	67.6%	8.1
10th Grade	80.1%	74.8%	5.3
11th Grade	82.5%	77.8%	4.7
12th Grade	84.9%	82.9%	2.0
TOTAL	79.3%	73.5%	5.8
COURSE PASSAGE			
English			
9th Grade	62.7%	51.1%	11.6%
10th Grade	72.0%	62.8%	9.2%
11th Grade	77.5%	69.5%	8.0%
12th Grade	84.2%	82.5%	1.7%
TOTAL	70.7%	62.2%	8.5%
Social Studies			
9th Grade	62.2%	58.2%	4.0%
10th Grade	69.0%	64.6%	4.4%
11th Grade	79.8%	72.8%	7.0%
12th Grade	86.0%	84.5%	1.5%
TOTAL	70.8%	66.9%	3.9%
Math			
9th Grade	54.4%	51.9%	2.5%
10th Grade	68.2%	62.3%	5.9%
11th Grade	74.5%	66.3%	8.2%
12th Grade	83.5%	78.5%	5.0%
TOTAL	65.2%	60.3%	4.9%
Science			
9th Grade	64.0%	53.3%	10.7%
10th Grade	73.8%	65.8%	8.0%
11th Grade	77.8%	74.1%	3.7%
12th Grade	86.2%	83.7%	2.5%
TOTAL	71.4%	63.6%	7.8%

TABLE 1.5 Demographically comparable charter and noncharter students.

	ALL STUDENTS				FEMALE STUDENTS				MALE STUDENTS			
	Total	Charter	Non-charter	Charter Difference	Total	Charter	Non-charter	Charter Difference	Total	Charter	Non-charter	Charter Difference
Course Passage %												
English	74.7%	76.7%	71.3%	5.4%	80.0%	81.7%	76.8%	4.9%	68.7%	70.5%	65.8%	4.7%
Social Studies	76.1%	76.4%	75.8%	0.6%	79.8%	79.7%	79.9%	-0.2%	71.9%	72.2%	71.5%	0.7%
Math	68.6%	70.5%	65.5%	5.0%	71.5%	73.4%	68.0%	5.4%	65.5%	67.0%	63.2%	3.8%
Science	75.0%	77.2%	71.3%	5.9%	79.1%	80.7%	76.1%	4.1%	70.4%	72.9%	66.6%	6.3%
Average Daily Attendance												
9th Grade	79.8%	82.0%	75.7%	6.3%	80.1%	82.2%	75.7%	6.5%	79.5%	81.7%	75.7%	6.0%
10th Grade	83.2%	84.2%	81.4%	2.8%	82.7%	84.0%	80.2%	3.8%	83.8%	84.6%	82.5%	2.1%
11th Grade	83.6%	85.0%	81.8%	3.2%	83.3%	84.6%	81.3%	3.3%	84.0%	85.4%	82.3%	3.1%
12th Grade	85.3%	86.0%	84.3%	1.7%	85.4%	85.6%	85.2%	0.4%	85.1%	86.7%	83.4%	3.3%
Total	82.5%	83.8%	80.4%	3.4%	82.5%	83.6%	80.3%	3.3%	82.5%	83.9%	80.5%	3.4%
Percentage of Students with at Least One Suspension	16.4%	16.0%	17.0%	-1.0%	12.7%	12.5%	13.0%	-0.5%	20.5%	20.1%	21.1%	-1.0%
Ethnicity												
White	23.8%	17.1%	34.4%	-17.3%	22.6%	16.2%	33.6%	-17.4%	25.2%	18.2%	35.2%	-17.0%
African American	61.7%	67.8%	52.2%	15.6%	63.5%	70.0%	52.3%	17.7%	59.7%	65.1%	52.1%	13.0%
Latino	9.3%	10.8%	7.0%	3.8%	9.3%	10.1%	8.0%	2.1%	9.3%	11.6%	6.0%	5.6%
American Indian	0.1%	0.1%	0.1%	0.0%	0.1%	0.1%	0.1%	0.0%	0.1%	0.1%	0.2%	-0.1%
Asian	4.9%	4.0%	6.2%	-2.2%	4.3%	3.4%	5.9%	-2.5%	5.5%	4.8%	6.5%	-1.7%

Note: This table includes only on-level students. To test the contribution of charters on similar peers, this analysis removes students who are labeled as in need of special education and those who are repeaters or overage, looking only at "on-level" students in and not in charters.

tions leading toward improved student outcomes. This proved not to be such an easy task. These teachers had been remarkably energized by these already established local and national professional networks, but they were equally weary of trying to create school-based change. They were well socialized to a centralized, hierarchical system and accustomed to little freedom and no authority. They could not believe school-based change was possible—or that the process could be desirable.

In the school district, the shrinking pool of students meant that the last time a secondary English teacher or social studies teacher had been hired was 1972. Teachers had lived through installation of state-mandated graduation credits, centrally generated "initiatives," and piloted school-based projects; they had worked with the same colleagues (for 20-plus years) under disempowering structures; and they had often been bounced from school to school. Union–district relations had been deeply adversarial, although they had improved recently. Budget cuts by the state and the city were imminent, and the principals had voted to join the Teamsters Union during this administration. Teachers were spent.

So at those early meetings, when asked to imagine "what could be," teachers sought more freedom from district prescriptions, they envisioned "fewer overaged students" (this District had a promotion policy that resulted in 20% to 25% of ninth graders being substantially overaged), "more tracking," and "more special education placements." It was not that these teachers were ill informed about the best practices or harsh in their judgments about kids. They had fixed categories of experience, and from these they generated the only possible images of what could be—"more teachers and counselors."

The work of reform was clear. Committed to neither a top-down nor a naively bottom-up structure, the Collaborative worked with educators and parents, through ongoing critical conversations about practice, driven by their own experiences and those of other educators in similarly situated schools in the midst of reform. What we failed to anticipate, however, was the depth of "communitarian damage" that had infiltrated, divided, and defined the culture of their high schools. Even those principals and faculty who were individually energized and enthusiastic could barely imagine working with their colleagues to create rich educational communities. Few could imagine that the district would allow them the room for radical change, and fewer still could imagine a collective effort among colleagues sufficiently successful to produce improvements in student outcomes. The damage ran deep and wide. It took about two years to begin to melt what sounded like resistance (Sarason, 1990).

We were committed to transform *with*, not *despite* and not *around*, existing public schools. We would not set up alternatives, nor exempt a few schools with waivers from district–union processes. We were committed to systemic change affecting all. With teachers and parents this work has been terrific.

Each has a delicious vested interest in understanding the needs, strengths, and passions of students. Most, with support, are willing to stretch to get there. It took more than a short while to move out of "despair" and into a sense of possibility. But we had anticipated this after Debbie Meier warned us, "It's hard to fix a flat and drive a car at the same time."

Marshall Meyer and Lynn Zucker's book *Permanently Failing Organizations* (1989), however, told us more than we wanted to know about how *bureaucracies* resist change and in the process justify chronic failure. Meyer and Zucker argue that hierarchical and controlling organizations get used to producing failure and so generate ideologies and practices to legitimate and naturalize its inevitability (Fine, 1991). If you attend a typical urban high school graduation of 250 to 300 students, out of a school of 2,500 to 3,000, and ask why, you can hear defensive ideologies that explain why massive failure is unavoidable. Disempowered practitioners often collectively resist the notion that success is within reach. As Roberto Unger (1987) has written:

> Sometimes we conduct ourselves as exiles from a world whose arrangements exclude no true insight and no worthwhile satisfaction. But more often we treat the plain, lusterless world in which we actually find ourselves, this world in which the limits of circumstance always remain preposterously disproportionate to the unlimited reach of striving, as if its structures of belief and action were here for keeps, as if it were the lost paradise where we could think all the thoughts and satisfy all the desires worth having. When we think and act in this way, we commit the sin the prophets call idolatry. As a basis for self-understanding, it is worse than sin. It is a mistake. (p. 113)

In this district, the rate of school-based transformation has been astonishing. Three years into it, student data are cooking. Teachers are "back" in droves. Many principals are engaged. Parents are involved in unprecedented numbers. All are eager but often frustrated, trying to work collaboratively in ways that have been historically impossible within the confines of bureaucracy. They are connected to charters and struggling for the minimum of stability and security needed to build strong communities. We are now entering the next generation of dilemmas, struggles, fights, and indeed battles over how to *disestablish* and *reinvent*, a district that is committed to decentralized, neighborhood-based, autonomous, and accountable public schools.

Some of our dilemmas derive from the commitment to transforming systemwide "what has been" into "what could be," rather than peeling off a few motivated students, parents, or teachers into voucher schemes, new or alternative schools, or magnets. Many are profound dilemmas of organizational transformation in the public sphere. Dilemmas of bureaucracy emerge because charter-based educators and parents have interrupted the dehumanizing discourse of rationality and efficiency in bureaucracy by percolating visions of educational democracies and pressing for improved student outcomes. Quite a few are the dilemmas of working in the urban public sector in the 1990s, inheriting and combating a Reagan/Bush legacy that has fundamentally constrained the lives and dreams of low-income African American and Latino youngsters and their families. Below we review a sampling of these dilemmas, as they emerge within charters, schools, and the central district.

Dilemma One: Doing "What Is" While Doing "What Could Be"

In the midst of restructuring existing (not new) schools, educators live inside institutional schizophrenia. Teachers are caught between the radically new worlds they are inventing and the relatively untransformed bureaucracies that stand around them and in their heads. To illustrate: Two talented (math and English) teachers of a charter have been collecting portfolios from students, tracking "artifacts" of student knowledge, and working closely with social workers on students' emotional needs. Their students are overaged ninth graders—an academically discouraged group come alive. When it came time for mid-term grades, the teachers worried together and aloud. They decided that compared to themselves in the beginning of the year, these students had worked incredibly hard. But they could not, in good conscience, give them A's (for the most part) or F's. So they settled on C's. The student group was outraged and felt betrayed; morale and attendance dropped precipitously. Simply put, as one teacher reflected, "Giving C's knocked a hole in the program."

The work of creating charters within existing schools is markedly different from creating new schools, alternative schools, or privatized schools with eager, "willing" volunteers (students, teachers, and/or parents). Creating rich educational settings within existing bureaucracies, educators and parents must juggle the contradictions and invent educational possibilities in the midst of constraints and resistance. Trying to nurture educational communities amidst the crusty, fragmented organizations we have called urban high schools requires that parents and educators who are front-runners do double duty. They do "what is," create "what could be," transform "what has been" in their schools, and they press for systemic transformation. In the process, they offend almost every vested interest, and former friend, at some point. Once taboo, still heretical challenges arise regularly about the role of the central district, the need for school-based resources and decisions, the necessity for assistant principals, the schoolwide function of counselors, the standard practice of "bumping teachers," the right of teachers to interview/hire their colleagues, and so forth. The political reverberations are enormous, and the Collaborative remains the site for percolating, provoking, and protecting public talk about reform.

Dilemma Two: Autonomy versus Community

When this work was begun, I (like the other "university folk") was fundamentally ignorant about the realities of life inside secondary urban schools. I did not realize, for instance, that one of the only perks left in the "comps" was autonomy—getting to shut one's door. I also did not realize that few reforms in the past have asked educators to transform their individual and collective practices, as well as systemic policies and practices, in ways that would improve student outcomes. Among educators left in the comprehensive high schools, few would initially believe that full-blown institutional, collective change could be possible. Now, an ongoing struggle for faculty and students is how to create charters as rich communities that respect both collective work and autonomy of faculty and students. Less is more, community is good, work with your colleagues—this is quite a selling job, especially when incentive systems have changed little and until real flexibility or authority sits at the school site.

Dilemma Three: We Can Only Educate; We Cannot Deal with Their Personal Needs, Too!

Early on, this line was common among the educators with whom we worked. No longer. Working within charters has opened up the personal lives of students and of faculty. And there is no going back. There are good reasons that faculty became burned out or "callous" to students' lives. Educators today are picking up the pieces of a society ravaged by class and race stratification, and they are being held accountable for transforming students who carry the weight of the bottom of the social hierarchy into educated and optimistic citizens. In particular, high school educators inherit histories of academic defeat that they need to reverse. In this process, many educators, although certainly not all, have opted *not* to know the pains and struggles experienced by their students. "If I knew," said one very committed teacher, "what would I do?" Schools have long been established as fortresses against, not agents for, community economic development.

This dilemma, as it turns out, is also an opportunity. The emotional, social, and psychological issues of young adolescents now litter our schools, masked as attendance problems, acting out, discipline problems, or even learning problems. We now know, in charters, that the problems of "at-risk youth" can often be unraveled to reflect homelessness, family or community violence, learning difficulties, or cultural differences—the kinds of issues public education has traditionally shied away from. Young people import these issues into our schools. As one teacher noted:

> The students somehow understand that the bonus here is that we're not reverting to the old traditional "kick out" system. You can still work out

problems here. Here you have the opportunity to get ready. We're not going to abandon them.

The dilemma for those of us committed to reform is to figure out how to support educators who are willing, but understandably reluctant and ill equipped, to "take on" the lives of these youngsters. Teacher Emily Style paraphrased Mary Daly (1978):

> Then, with the rise of [charters] some [teachers and students] found each other, came to know each other in new ways. That was the beginning of our rough Voyage, which has proved—for those who have persisted—strange, difficult, unpredictable, terrifying, enraging, energizing, transforming, encouraging. For those who have persisted there is at least one certainty and perhaps only one: Once we have understood this much, there is no turning back. (p. 368)

This dilemma asks how we can create charters as safe places to discuss, even be educated through, social issues that feel like embarrassing "personal problems," so that students do not have to feel alone with the difficulties of living that so many have survived so well. The larger question—of charters as activist communities committed to local neighborhood development—still sits eager, on the cusp of our work.

Dilemma Four: Bottom-Up Change and Democratic Access to the "Best of Practice"

The Collaborative has been organized through the ideas and strategies of this district's educators and parents. But our commitment to accountability for student outcomes has also meant that we are invested in knowing and trying to provide broad access to the "best of practice." So, for instance, we have invited conversations about mainstreaming of students labeled in need of special education, heterogeneous groupings of students, racism, cultural studies, and teachers/parents' democratic participation in decision making. These are not all popular notions with either educators or parents (Oakes, 1988).

Given the research on the educational problems that derive from deep and rigid segregation and tracking, we knew that charters should be comprised of students of mixed achievement levels. Yet we heard passionate resistance, early on, from many educators and parents raised and practiced in the comforts of tracking and the "intimacies" of special education. Indeed, most schools exempted ninth-grade repeaters from their first year of restructuring, and many initially worked "around" special education. Bottom-up reform and the best of democratic practice are not always the same thing. But ongoing critical conversation and inquiry help.

We continue to struggle with how to get more educators and parents to imagine the virtues of heterogeneity, when indeed it looks like, feels like, and may indeed involve more work for the teachers, and less attention for the students. This is particularly tricky for principals of some schools that have become "last resorts" who want to establish, or protect, an elite track to attract "good" kids, or educators who have accrued enough seniority to place out of lower-track teaching, or educators working within special education, or parents of advanced-track students. Further, we wrestle with how to get federal and state regulations sufficiently pried open (e.g., Chapter 1, special education, Perkins monies, dropout prevention) so as to enable, and not constrain, the heterogeneous groupings of students. We have begun to move toward schoolwide use of Chapter 1 monies, integration of special education students and faculty, and school basing of federal Perkins monies for vocational education. But these shifts are slow, hard, and politically treacherous. And they could be done irresponsibly, with no accountability for monies or student outcomes. Finally, we debate how to get us all to shift consciousness so as to recognize that students are not born into a track but, indeed, develop over time into their own forms of intelligence.

Perhaps the best illustration of such thinking is embodied in one anecdote reported by a teacher working within a heterogeneous charter. She reports:

> My colleagues, especially those who aren't yet in a charter, say, sure your charter is doing well and has good student statistics, but you got all the middle-class kids in the school! Now, Michelle, you know there are no middle-class kids in this school. [Indeed, this is one of the poorest schools in the city.] But because of the work we do with the students, they start to look and act middle class (whatever that means) and then people accuse us of creaming! Now we have to haul out their eighth-grade records to demonstrate that these students were just like the other students—until they entered this charter, at least!

Dilemma Five: Autonomous, Democratic Small Schools Inside the Public Sector

This dilemma is the most profound. In the 1990s, it is no longer a mystery how to educate, and even educate well, low-achieving, low-income urban students—even those stuffed into the perverse box called "at risk." Collectively we have the knowledge, methods, and assessment strategies to transform our classrooms into engaging, critical, and creative sites of intellectual growth and personal development. What is a mystery in the 1990s is whether we have the political will to enable urban public schools, serving students of all colors and classes, to flourish. We have yet to imagine decentralized and democratic *districts* structured to support autonomous, community-based public schools.

Within this district's high schools, as in New York, Chicago, California, and elsewhere, small public high schools are emerging as relatively radical communities of teachers, parents, and students who feel they should have substantial decision-making authority and should be the site for distribution resources and flexible use of resources. At minimum they want to be *neighborhood-based, stable* (not have teachers pulled out in September or October of the year and returned in the spring), and *autonomous*. They want direct access to resources, and they want to determine how to use planning time, instructional review days, evenings, and summers as well as help students imagine their postsecondary plans. Some even claim that they should be responsible and *accountable* for student progress if the two prior conditions are met. These are not very radical demands for a community of educators, students, and parents.

Small schools, like charters, irritate, however, because they represent a fundamental interruption of rationalistic public education bureaucracy as we have known it. Charters' discourse of community, continuity, relationships, autonomy, and responsibility flies in the face of traditions of bureaucracy. These teachers do not want to be told how, when, where, and why to act. They do want, and deserve, resources that now sit centrally under layers and layers of supervision. They do seek connections with, and input from, other secondary faculties, universities, parents, corporate and community-based organizations. And they do want to remain public, democratic, accessible to all children, and accountable for improved student outcomes.

The jury is still out on *political will*—nationally, at the state level, and within local public school bureaucracies. As Asa Hilliard (1991) has argued:

> The risk for our children in school is not a risk associated with their intelligence. Public school failures have nothing to do with IQ, little to do with poverty, race, language, style, and nothing to do with children's families. All of these are red herrings. When researchers study them, we may ultimately yield to some greater insight into the instructional process. But at present these issues, as explanations of school failure, distract attention away from the fundamental problem facing us today. We have one primary problem: Do we truly will to see each and every child in this nation develop to the peak of his or her capacities? (p. 35)

If this round of reform fails, some form of privatization, "alternatives," independent charters (without collective bargaining), or elite "options" will prevail. Poor children will be abandoned, punished, and blamed. But many of us will know that the very public-sector bureaucracies that have claimed an interest "in all children" will be largely responsible—for their refusal to change to meet the needs of children. It is neither too expensive nor too late to transform the educational outcomes of urban adolescents—even those we have collectively placed "at risk."

REFERENCES

Daly, M. (1978). *Gyn/Ecology: The meta-ethics of radical feminism* (p. 368). Boston: Beacon.

Fine, M. (1986, Spring). Why urban adolescents drop into and out of high school. *Teachers College Record, 87*(3), 393–409.

Fine, M. (1987). Silencing in public schools. *Language Arts, 64*(2), 157–174.

Fine, M. (1991). *Framing dropouts: Notes on the politics of an urban high school.* Albany: State University of New York Press.

Fine, M. (1990a). Making controversy: Who's "at risk?" *Journal of Urban and Cultural Studies, 1*(1), 55–68.

Fine, M. (1990b). The "public" in public schools: The social constriction/construction of a moral community. *Journal of Social Issues, 46*(1), 107–119.

Foley, E., & Crull, P. (1984). *Educating the at-risk adolescent.* New York: Public Education Association.

Hilliard, A. (1991, September). Do we have the will to educate all children? *Educational Leadership,* pp. 31–35.

Lieberman, A., & McLaughlin, M. (1992). Networks for educational change: Powerful and problematic. *Phi Delta Kappan, 73*(9), 673–677.

McMullan, B., Leiderman, S., & Wolf, W. (1988). *Reclaiming the future: A framework for improving student success and reducing dropout rates in Philadelphia.* Bala Cynwyd, PA: Center for Assessment and Policy Development.

Meyer, M., & Zucker, L. (1989). *Permanently failing organizations.* Newbury Park, NY: Sage.

Oakes, J. (1988, January). Tracking: Can schools take a different route? *National Education Association,* pp. 41–47.

Oxley, D. (1989, Spring). Smaller is better—How the house plan can make large high schools less anonymous. *American Educator.*

Oxley, D. (1990, June). *An analysis of house systems in New York City neighborhood high schools.*

Sarason, S. (1990). *The predictable failure of educational reform—Can we change course before it's too late?* San Francisco: Jossey-Bass.

Swidler, A. (1990). *The good society.* Berkeley: University of California Press.

Unger, R. (1987). *Social theory.* Cambridge, UK: Cambridge University Press.

Wehlage, G. (1989). *Reducing at risk: Schools as communities of support.* NY: Falmer.

2

The Development of Schools that Practice Reflection

RICHARD W. CLARK

In December 1988, I made my first visit to this district on behalf of the Pew Charitable Trusts.[1] I went because Pew wanted my views concerning their participation in a multiyear, multimillion dollar grant to support systemic change in the city's neighborhood high schools. During that and subsequent visits, I have had the chance to observe classrooms, interview key players from the schools and central administration, read masses of materials, and talk with various other people who are not directly connected with the school system. After each visit I provided a written summary for Pew. However, my purpose here is somewhat different. I want to share, informally and anecdotally, what I have seen as one who, with no particular axe to grind, has had an unusual degree of freedom to poke around in the revitalization efforts being facilitated by the Philadelphia Schools Collaborative. In this chapter I share comments that reflect progress as of the summer of 1992. I share because I believe that the approach being taken here is unique and provides insights that can be valuable for others who would reform schools and because those who seek to emulate these pioneers need to be aware of some of the difficulties involved. I share because their work lends meaning to the concept of reflection.

THE WAY IT WAS

My first visits to these neighborhoods and schools overwhelmed me. A newspaper description of one school in the north part of town reminds me of my initial reactions:

> . . . the school is no oasis. The windows that were made to open are covered with bars, and the bricks are marred by graffiti. Inside, security guards and teachers armed with walkie-talkies patrol the halls.
>
> The children who attend are struggling with the crush of urban ills—drugs, drug dealing, gangs, unprotected teenage sex, pregnancy—and they don't leave their problems at the door.

"Make no mistake about it [school] is a tough school to be a student in
or to work at," said guidance counselor . . . (McLarin, 1992, p. A6)

The neighborhoods in which many of the schools are set feature bombed-
out and/or boarded-up row houses, empty storefronts, deserted car hulks, and
loitering men looking, without hope, at the world. The schools, for all of their
resemblance to maximum security prisons, were safe havens for children used
to life in the urban America of the late 1980s. They were not, however, places
noted for empowering either students or teachers.

One of my first memories of these high schools is of a teacher planning
group. Six teachers were gathered around the table in a high school library late
one afternoon. One said that during his 20 years in the city he had seen all
kinds of reforms come and go. Then, looking very intently at me, he said that
this was the first one in which they have asked teachers what really ought to be
done instead of telling them what was good for them. As a result, he said, "I and
the rest of the people you see here are willing to put in extra hours. Before this,
we would beat the kids out of here."

Shortly after that discussion, I met with a wily group of experienced senior
high principals. During our conversation, one chose to explain that he followed
the "three-year rule" when it came to dealing with innovations. I bit. I told him
I was not familiar with the three-year rule. "It's simple," he explained, "I wait
until the third year of a new project before getting involved. By then the district
has dropped the idea and gone on to some new thing, so at my school we don't
have to get involved in every fad that comes along."

There are early impressions of students to go along with these glimpses of
teachers and principals. One is of students walking down crowded corridors
with security staff, the principal and teachers telling these students to take off
their hats. The students remove the baseball caps, walk one step past the adult,
and defiantly jam the caps back on their heads.

Another early look at students related to attendance taking. Students in
these schools were attending school less than half the time; often, when they
did come, they were late. One school, apparently to teach the students a lesson,
rounded up all the latecomers at the end of the attendance period and sent
them to the auditorium, where they spent what was to be their first hour of
instruction for the day. There was an obvious connection between such
occurrences for students and the fact that I became accustomed to seeing no
more than 10 or 15 students in any classroom, even though teachers and
administrators assured me that teachers were routinely assigned classes of 30
and more students.

There are no early memories of dealing with parents. When I asked to talk
to some who were involved, the answer was, essentially, that none were involved. Schools told long stories of efforts to get parents to school—efforts that

included such incentives as meals for the parents and T-shirts for students. Schools described the multiple mailings and phone calls that along with the incentives succeeded in generating an attendance of fewer than 20 people at a session designed for parents of 400 or so ninth graders.

Early conversations with central administrators produced glowing support for the efforts of the Collaborative; after all, I was part of a process of deciding whether Pew should give money to support their efforts. In spite of such positive words, central administrators made few comments that suggested they had real faith in the ability of people in schools—principals or teachers—to produce necessary changes. Most made it clear that they were in their roles because, without their central guidance, people in the schools could not be trusted to make the needed changes. Moreover, the school-based people lacked the competency to do so without being told how. The same central leaders tended to emphasize that current efforts were exemplary in many ways—at least, that education in the system was not nearly as bad as people thought.

During these initial visits I also met with union leaders who were positive about the proposed grant, probably partly because they perceived that funding the Collaborative would mean more money in the pockets of their membership. The vision of the Collaborative was also consistent with the ideas being promulgated by their national president, Albert Shanker. Union leaders also saw another opportunity for influencing the direction of the district as they had been for several years through another inside/outside organization, PATHS/PRISM.

The superintendent stood out as a person with deep personal concerns for what was happening to the city's children, which could only be tended to if significant changes were made in the neighborhood high schools. Although a person with a reputation of being a dominating centralist, the superintendent made it clear that she was willing to risk criticism from her own staff and from elements of the community to further the strategy of "guided" decentralization that she, the Collaborative, and her chief of staff hoped would produce better student learning.

It was this set of conditions that Pew and the Philadelphia Schools Collaborative (PSC) faced as they began to develop their plans for revitalizing the district's neighborhood high schools.

THE PHILADELPHIA SCHOOLS COLLABORATIVE

The Collaborative is an inside/outside agency. The traditional approaches to private support for public education in this city contribute to people's understanding of it as an agency. Building on early initiatives in humanities and science education (PATHS/PRISM), career-oriented schools-within-a-school (high school academies), and the Corporate Committee to Support the Public Schools, the Collaborative is a 501(C)3 nonprofit group. Unlike these predecessors, it has an avowed purpose of institutionalizing change within the system.

The PSC director, Janis Somerville, has a significant part of her salary paid by the school district and has her office in the suite of rooms formerly occupied by a deputy superintendent. She is an insider, having been the superintendent's executive planning assistant, and an outsider, having spent most of her professional career in higher education administrative positions. She is joined by a senior consultant, Michelle Fine, whose base is in higher education, where she holds a tenured faculty position; but her heart is in public schools, where she passionately rejects the hopelessness expressed by others dealing with the day-to-day problems of schooling.

The Collaborative obtains its credibility as an external agency because it is funded largely by Pew and, therefore, able to function without bureaucratic restraints imposed on district projects or on change efforts funded by the federal government.[2]

Besides its key physical location in the district headquarters, the Collaborative maintains its position as a credible internal agency by the position of its director on the superintendent's cabinet, weekly meetings of the director and senior consultant with the superintendent, and the key role it has related to the joint committee responsible for overseeing the implementation of shared decision making/site-based management in the city. As the project has progressed, other actions have been taken to strengthen this internal power base.[3]

THE TASK OF REVITALIZING SCHOOLS

The Collaborative has helped provide teachers with a number of experiences that differ from their usual ways of working. Shared decision making/site-based management councils have been created to varying degrees in 19 of the 22 neighborhood high schools. As a consequence of teacher uncertainties and barriers raised by wary central administrators and union representatives, these councils offer as yet unfulfilled promises to teachers and parents for greater self-determination.

The change effort has also provided teachers with new leadership opportunities. Teachers have begun to serve as members of governance councils, had new and expanded opportunities to conduct staff development sessions, become leaders of "charters" (schools-within-a-school) in the high schools, and shared stories about the city's progress with educational leaders at a variety of national conferences. For example, chemistry teacher Natalie Hiller shared her views on national assessment with the superintendents and other leaders of the Council for Great City Schools. Grounded in weeks of collaboration with her peers in the thoughtful analysis of learning and assessment promoted by the Collaborative, Hiller's comments challenged these leaders to look past assertions of national reformers and remember the power possessed by teachers to determine the ultimate success of proposed panaceas. She began by telling the assemblage:

> It is with a bit of irony that I find myself positioned as the last speaker on this panel, because in many ways, as a teacher, I am the person who can create the most roadblocks and do the most damage to undermine whatever reform, whatever policies that come into existence. . . . As a person representing those who have the closest interaction with the students, I can guarantee you that I will have to be convinced that this national test creates the type of learning outcomes that I want for them or else when I close the door to my classroom, if I cannot define what this *manna* is, if I don't buy it—I can promise you I will not be serving it to my students.[4]

While this progress takes place, some teachers remain skeptical of the Collaborative and of their latest change efforts. These skeptics worry that a select group of teachers is getting benefits, such as out-of-town travel, that they are not getting. They worry that traditional positions, such as department head and roster chair, that have enabled teachers to escape from students to a myriad of quasi-administrative roles are being eroded by new approaches to leadership. They worry that new standards of teacher and student performance are being raised from the inside by their peers—worry because such standards are not as easily shrugged off as those which come from outsiders. They recall past glimpses of progress and worry that financial or political considerations will again interrupt and derail this latest effort. They hear mixed signals from central and school-based administrative leadership—signals that tell them their views are important and then make decisions that seem to contradict the message of their importance.

Some of these worries are about items that at first appear to be superficial. So what if some teachers get trips to Florida and Chicago while others don't? Unfortunately, within the highly "egalitarian" culture of schools such superficialities have sabotaged more than one earlier reform effort.

Some of these worries cut to the heart of what is unknown about teaching and learning. Recognition of the inadequacies of traditional means of assessing student progress contributes to awareness of the need for new ones. The ways in which such assessments are intertwined with the processes of student learning give teachers good reason to worry about fads in assessment. Like other solutions that come and go, some may be dangerous because they are oversimplified solutions to problems.

The Collaborative has built alliances among groups of teachers. In this regard they have discovered what predecessor change efforts have discovered before them—that it is easier to take individuals who are highly talented and committed and energize them than it is to spread the energy.

The Collaborative, committed to empowering people in the schools, must deal with the age-old question that faces change agents: when to go along with the proposals developed in the schools and when to require school-based efforts to satisfy their standards. For example, when and how should special education students be included in the subschools each high school is being asked to create? Given an a priori premise that tracking is bad and a tradition of separating students into homogeneous groups, how does Collaborative leadership insist on the teachers' arriving at the "right" answer? Given principals whose primary role has been managerial, how does one shift the role to that of an educational leader and make other needed changes without assuming the existing roles of principal?

Gradually principals have come to recognize that this may not be an effort to which they can apply the three-year rule. As funding has continued and the messages[5] from the superintendent have become more and more explicit, in the summer of 1992 it appeared evident that the Collaborative was in this one for the long run.

The creation of the high school office within the central administration may be the single act that has been most directly influential with the principals. Three years ago, high school principals reported to regional superintendents, each of whom had more than 30 K–12 schools to supervise. Most high school principals expressed the opinion that this structure did not allow them to share concerns with colleagues who had similar problems. In response, and with support from the Collaborative, the superintendent created a separate administrative office for the schools and placed one of their own, the Ida B. Wells principal, in charge as an assistant superintendent.

The new assistant superintendent found her closest allies in the leaders of the Collaborative. She also found that there were others in the central administration who were not ready to buy the new leadership strategies being advocated by the PSC. Her office became the source of much needed staff development for principals. It also became a focal point for conflict within the district concerning the central office role in school reform. Some of the conflicts surrounding this office have not been resolved, and their existence reveals the complexity of trying to modify long-established hierarchical behaviors.

Meanwhile, the need continues for extensive education for principals who were originally trained as managers and selected for their ability to maintain control within schools—and who are now expected to be instructional leaders who empower the people at the schools. This need has been met partially by assigning organizational development (OD) specialists to work alongside school leaders in the sites receiving intensive support from the Collaborative. The OD experts have helped create governance councils, aided in analyzing staff relationships, and helped schools set goals and define strategies for meeting goals. Their work has focused on developing leadership among charter coordinators and other teacher leaders as well as on helping principals with new roles.

The Collaborative has also sponsored a seminar for principals that parallels one developed for teachers to help them develop their inquiry skills. As teacher and principal leaders engage in critical examination of their own writings about what is happening in their schools, they gain an appreciation for the behaviors they need to help develop among the participants in their school communities.

Although the work of the Collaborative focuses on charters and the schools within which they exist, it has had to face the reality that schools are part of a larger ecosystem. Schools are not isolated islands. They cannot improve unless the larger system of which they are a part permits and supports their improvement. Goodlad (1987) and others write about the ecology of school renewal. The Collaborative has been living that story.

The federal government, whose investment through desegregation funds and Chapter 1 assistance is many times that available to the Collaborative from Pew, continues to inhibit change processes by placing restrictions on the use of funds. These restrictions concerning how money can be spent are complicated by layers of bureaucratic interpretations starting in Washington, extending through the state capital, and culminating in school district officials. Even getting officials responsible for such categorical funding to the table to discuss with other responsible parties a common approach can be a difficult task.

The district's central administration, like most, is populated with people who have risen through the ranks to a position where they hope to be able to tell others what to do. That is the model of leadership they have experienced. One is reminded of Cleveland's comments on the subject:

> There was a time, celebrated in song and story, when leadership was entrusted to "leaders." Their members were tiny, their information scarce, their expertise primitive, the range of their options narrow, the range of their power marginal, the scale of their actions limited. But they were at least in charge. (1985, p. 1)

Central administrators perceive that they are in charge, when in reality the nature of school systems leaves them relatively little influence. This creates an ecology for the schools that makes systemic change extremely difficult. To preserve their sense of being in charge, such leaders may constrict channels of communications, refuse to consult with others, build their own offices and domains, and initiate unrelated and/or contradictory initiatives of their own.

This district, like most large school systems, becomes littered with numerous "projects," some of which interfere with others without their proponents realizing that this is the case. The superintendent inherits the difficult and frequently misunderstood task of developing adherence to a common vision. If she plays this role too actively, people nod and say they knew she was domineering all along. If she hesitates, people fault her for lack of leadership. To the extent that she succeeds in diverting attention from herself as a charismatic leader and builds commitment to a common vision, people may begin to quit using perceptions of her shortcomings as excuses for their own inaction.

To deal with the ecology of the school, the Collaborative has initiated a variety of efforts. They lobbied state government for relief from restrictions and to avoid new problems from initiatives such as voucher systems. They have worked with the American Federation of Teachers (AFT) to bring together people who are engaged in similar initiatives in other urban districts around assessment of student learning, seeking ways to free students from the tyranny of inappropriate testing. They have pushed for continuing education efforts for central administration. They have had a hand in the restructuring of the central administration over and beyond the important creation of the new high school office. In the summer of 1992 they began working with a series of task forces that were intended to promote collaboration around their initiatives by administrators of categorical programs and by others with control over areas such as staff allotment, budgets, curriculum, and bargaining. Working with the Collaborative, the budget office has conducted several meetings designed to help school-based decision makers better understand financial documents. Such meetings are reassuring to school-level workers, who gain confidence from these efforts to address conditions that they see as limiting their work. Finally, PSC leaders engage in continuous dialogue with the superintendent to assure consistent messages from that office regarding the direction the district is taking in general and their work in particular.

Parents are another part of the ecosystem that needs attention in order to achieve systemic reform. The Collaborative and the schools have succeeded in recruiting parent members for governance councils and in providing training sessions for parent activists. At Wells High School parents are developing the capacity to assist that school and providing help to other schools wanting to improve the involvement of parents. Parents still perceive themselves as outsiders, but the number who are dealing directly with the schools grows steadily. Teachers still express doubts about the value of the parents' involvement and, with their principals, tend to think more of how to communicate *to* parents than *with* them. The teachers union worries that local school councils may come to be dominated numerically by parents in the same way they have in Chicago, although for now, the basic rules for the councils assure that parents will be in the minority. In fact, some have suggested that teachers' willingness to include parents to the degree they have may be related to fear of a requirement that parents be in the majority on councils as has been the case in Chicago.

The role of parents in the day-to-day life of charters is just beginning to be determined as various charters experiment with different ways of including them.

The local AFT is another critical component of the ecosystem surrounding the schools. This union's support with the district of shared decision making/ site-based management has been appropriately recognized by a citizens group as an exemplary practice of labor–management relations. Their support at in-service sessions, often by the active presence of the president, and their participation on the "joint committee" has undoubtedly encouraged participation by teachers who would otherwise be holdouts. The union has assigned key staff members specific responsibility for helping to implement approaches advocated also by the Collaborative. Their secretary–treasurer meets regularly with Collaborative leadership to resolve small problems before they become big ones.

Not all union activities support progress with school reform. By its very nature, the union contract with the district is a centralizing force. To the extent that it determines processes for staffing, identifies leadership roles such as department heads, or defines teacher responsibilities, the contract removes such decisions from the hands of the school governance councils and impinges on the daily life of teachers working in charters. By requiring schools to make decisions concerning change by super majorities of 75%, and determining that schools must have plans approved in advance before they can be entrusted with shared decision making/site-based management roles, the district and the union have severely restricted the power of people at the school at the same time that they claim to be granting more power. Thus, for example, we have an early example of a school succeeding in obtaining a two-thirds vote of approval for a plan but having the plan rejected. When a vote that is enough to amend the U.S. Constitution is not sufficient to change a structure within a school, the document requiring it may not be sufficiently enabling.

Teachers, principals, parents, and central administrators, looking for something to blame for their own inertia, use the union contract as a scape-goat. In such instances, people blame the contract for restrictions it does not contain.

Ultimately, of course, the success of change efforts is not determined only by the changes in the structure or processes at schools or by the modifications that are made in the ecology surrounding the school.

"Incidents" suggest some other dimensions of what is happening to students. A mother testifies that one of the charters provides a setting in which teachers take a real interest in her son for the first time since he entered the system. Students, who on a previous visit seemed unable to cope with anything academic, are engrossed in a biology lab that is clearly linked to a career interest in sports and physical education. A young mother's writing portfolio reveals considerable talent as she continues in school partially because of the nursery established for babies at her high school. Cross-age groups in one class discuss intelligently and in depth issues arising from their study of *Hamlet,* while another class examines with equal facility *Inherit the Wind.* A mixture of students from various cultural backgrounds grapple with the complexity of learning to speak and write Chinese. Students remain in the classroom speaking with teachers and with one another during break and lunchtime in the same school where, three years earlier, hall monitors had been driving them into the auditorium to sit out time because they were late to school.

Still, control of students receives much attention. Tracking is evident. Large numbers of students, particularly African American males, receive minimal challenges because they are special education students. Students not in charters seem detached from the school, and some students within charters testify that school has changed little for them. Pregnancy rates are high, driving teachers to tears as they try in frustration to reach the students before they have made decisions about their life that preclude economic or social success. Not all problems have been solved, but some signs of what schools might be like if they were solved are beginning to emerge.

Most hopeful are the beginnings of decision-making processes that offer hope for schools to become the center of change that the Collaborative is seeking for them to be.

REFLACTION

There is loose in the land a conviction that research must precede practice—that first someone develops a theory, someone else implements it, and *then* it is *done.* Sirotnik (1989) comments on this mistaken view of the change process as he talks about the dominant view of educational change, which he labels R,D,D, and E. He says:

> This linear model of "research, development, diffusion, and evaluation" essentially pits experts against practitioners. Those in the "know" are the scholars that generate the research and the experts that package and disseminate the findings in useable form and evaluate the use of these packages in practice. Those "in need of knowing" are the practitioners, the workers in schools, the consumers of new knowledge once it is appropriately distilled into in-service programs. School-based educators are seen as deficient in one or more skill areas and in need of retraining, rather than as professionals who reflect upon their work and upon ways in which they might do their work better. Schools are seen as places in disrepair and in need of fixing, rather than as messy social systems in the process of evolution. Changing schools then, becomes a process of programmatic intervention and installation—of applying remedies of research to the ills of practice.

> The school is an *object* to be changed, not a *center of change* . . . (pp. 93–94; emphasis in original)

Sirotnik's answer is to replace R,D,D, and E with what he calls "critical inquiry," a process that he acknowledges is similar to Dewey's problem-solving sequence. Such reliance on the intellectual prowess of the people on the spot has deep roots in American intellectual history. It is the combining of thought and action that Emerson saw as needed by people who would claim to be scholars. It is the reflective practice that Schön (1990) urges scholars to adopt. It is the behavior for which, according to Goodlad (1990), the teachers of this country need to be educated and are not. It is central to the efforts described by Lieberman and colleagues (1991a; 1991b) as they characterize recent efforts at urban school reform. It is the approach emphasized by Lieberman (1992) in her American Educational Research Association (AERA) presidential address in April 1992 when she said:

> I use the phrase "scholarly activity," despite the appearance that this seems to be a marriage of contraries or contradictions . . . and embrace of what appears to be two ideas that do not seem to fit comfortably together: Scholarship, defined as a "quality of knowledge and learning . . . which is systematic, attempting accuracy, critical ability and thoroughness," and activity, "requiring action, producing real effects as opposed to theoretical, ideal or speculative." (Webster's Unabridged Dictionary, second edition). The development of a synthesis from these seeming contradictions has important implications for scholarly work, and how we give voice to both activism and knowledge building. (p. 13)

Lieberman went on to discuss several specific forms of "scholarly activity," identifying "creating new frames and strategies for thinking about and taking action on these new learnings" as one example:

> Some scholars, going beyond thinking or studying about improving schools, are taking action based on broad comprehensive conceptions for changes, conceptions that, in many cases, include new voices and new ways of organizing work and understanding practice. Sometimes moving from theory and conception to action, sometimes from practice to conception or theory, sometimes creating strategies or documenting the conceptualization of strategies, they push the field forward, illuminating the possibilities and limitations for changing schools. (p. 19)

She cites scholars such as Comer, Goodlad, Gardner, Sizer, and Levin as examples, but in many ways the activist teachers and leaders of the PSC are engaging in this "scholarly activity." In fact a case can be made for saying that *it is the approach that is central to the work of the Philadelphia Schools Collaborative.*

As it is beginning to be played out in the PSC, it may rightly be thought of as "reflaction"—a combining of reflective thought and action based on that reflection. The teachers of Muñoz Marin High School describe it as "transforming ourselves: becoming an inquiring community." They acknowledge that they do not always do their planning based on reflective examination of data but stress that when they do they find that it "can be a means of melting resistance." As they describe some of the specific problems they have solved for themselves, they give their own brand of inquiry credit for helping them learn "how to use research to get 'unstuck.'" Most importantly, they acknowledge that the processes they are going through as professionals parallel those they want to help their students understand and be able to use.

Reflaction requires skill in inquiry. Teachers who take externally imposed curricula and teaching methods and attempt to use them as a novice cook would follow a recipe are unable to teach the diverse individuals populating their classrooms. Teachers who are able to inquire together can determine what actions are needed to deal most appropriately with their students because students in high schools experience the combined effects of several teachers, not the isolated impact of individual teachers. Teachers who have been taking part in Collaborative-sponsored learning seminars designed to strengthen their skills as action researchers have begun to recognize the power they have to solve the intensive and extensive problems they face. In a few instances subgroups within schools exhibit the capability to engage in reflaction as they examine how their students are succeeding and how they respond to different instructional offerings and as they consider alternatives and test the results of trying those alternatives.

Reflaction is hard work. Teachers who have five or six groups of students to meet with each day do not have time to do it well—even when they are willing to work the many extra hours that teachers in a number of the charters created under the auspices of the PSC have been willing to work. The Collaborative is trying to help teachers solve the persistent problem of how to rearrange time so that they can engage in the thoughtful practice that is needed. As they do so they run into regularities of district practice and restrictions on funds, such as those earned from summer school, that make extensions of school years difficult. Also, they run up against a major dilemma. If they arrange for external solutions, these approaches are likely to be rejected by those asked to implement them. If they leave problems to teachers to solve for themselves, they are apt to discover that teachers do not have the time to do so. The PSC has used summer and continuing education time during the school year to encourage collaboration among faculty members. They have also used grant funds to buy additional school-year planning time for individuals and small groups of teachers. Both of these solutions demand expanded school and school district budgets if they are to be institutionalized in the system. The search continues for solutions that are either so powerful that people will willingly pay more or so efficient that added funds will not be required.

Reflaction occurs at various levels. For systemic change to occur in this district, it must be the dominant approach by classroom teachers, teams working in charters, principals and their administrative teams, and the central administrators who support the school.

Reflaction requires substantial information. School district staff, working with the Collaborative and with Wendy Wolf of the Center for Assessment and Policy Development (CAPD), have been trying to develop a comprehensive student data base. The goal has been to have critical information about students online and to train individual data coordinators in schools to help decision makers interpret the information. Teachers, parents, and principals who have had an opportunity to work with the first group of coordinators report limited success. Teachers working to create charters have used data to help them demonstrate to the rest of the school that they do not have the elite student enrollment they are accused of having. Innovators have demonstrated to reluctant peers that student attendance and course completion are improving as smaller subschools give students a greater sense of belonging.

The learning seminars and other work sponsored by the Collaborative have begun to develop the ability of teachers to use qualitative information as well as to analyze numbers from a database. As ethnographic skills are developed and as school-based people learn to analyze and reflect, they obtain new insights into the way interactions among staff and between staff and students affect their success. Ethnographers have focused much of the early qualitative work on the teacher and the classroom as the unit of inquiry; they are just beginning to give attention to the charters and the schools.

THE WAY IT IS

School as we know it is doomed. And every attempt to improve—but fundamentally preserve—the present system will only prolong its death throes and add immeasurably to its costs, both financial and social. (Leonard, 1992, p. 24)

Optimism—at least about education today—is a fool's paradise. It leads to a disconcerting and potentially dangerous development: the conviction that education is in deep trouble but that the problems are mostly in someone else's schools. . . . Four years ago when David Kearns and I described the schools as a "failed public monopoly," we were accused of using strong, even intemperate language. But the events of the past four years have convinced me that our original charge was on target. . . . I believe it is time to end the monopoly, to end the exclusive franchise. (Doyle, 1992, pp. 513–514)

The foregoing are but examples of the many voices telling us that our public school system has failed. Solutions vary. Some, such as Leonard, offer a prescription of reforms. Others, such as Doyle and his colleague Kearns, offer vouchers to permit parents to choose private schools. Do we find despair for the future of public education or hope in new alternatives as we consider the status of the Collaborative's work in this district?

In this district many teachers continue to be excited that they are being given a real say in determining the improvements that are needed in their schools while a hard core of detractors resist change from any direction. Their union supports change but, like many other labor unions, worries that empowering individual teachers and faculties may hurt the union's ability to care for its membership. Principals acknowledge the presence of the change process but struggle to understand what it means for them as leaders. A new principal leadership academy has been created. Whether it will help with the change effort promoted by the Collaborative or seek to reinforce past practices remains to be seen. Central administrators continue to praise the efforts of the Collaborative while, by their actions, they show they are neither sure how their role should change nor clear whether the high school reform is an indication of a central change in district operations or just another in a long line of projects. As Doyle suggests, they may not be convinced of the need for change in their setting. Professional development activities have begun for this central staff. The superintendent continues to respond with written and spoken assurances that this effort at systemic change is real and that the Collaborative has her total support. Parents are getting involved, but not sure they are wanted. The leadership of the Collaborative has been instrumental in staving off a move in the state to create a voucher system. But what does all of this mean to students?

Significantly, teachers, principals, and parents at schools are engaging in *reflaction*. They are reflecting and taking action together as they work to create the schools the youth of this city need.

The tough questions of how to extend these promising beginnings remain to be addressed by Collaborative leaders as they fight to keep this effort on course. They know the theory concerning change of school systems. They know the strengths and weaknesses of the practitioners with whom they must work to achieve progress. They know they are faced with a difficult task. However, knowing that reflaction is hard does not always sustain people when they are in the midst of it. Unlike reform efforts elsewhere, the leaders of the Collaborative intend that their efforts will produce more than lip service about systemic change. They intend to institutionalize the capacity for change. This makes their task exceedingly difficult.

The leaders of the Philadelphia Schools Collaborative are committed to a revolution, even if many with whom they are working are still tinkering with the schools. They are "true believers" working with zeal alongside leaders, many of whom doubt a revolution is needed, let alone possible.

If the Collaborative is to achieve its ultimate goals, others will have to join the core of workers recruited thus far, swelling the number of those truly engaged in reflaction to a sufficient mass to overcome the bulky inertia that characterizes the schools they would revitalize. Meanwhile, while people elsewhere are talking and writing about how reforms should be made in urban schools, the leaders of the Collaborative engage in *reflaction. Like their peers they reflect. Unlike many of their peers, they act!*

NOTES

1. I brought to the work 20 years of experience as a school and central office administrator, experience teaching graduate courses in school administration and curriculum, work with school–university partnerships as part of the 14-state National Network for Educational Renewal, consulting experiences throughout the country on such issues as school-centered decision making, teacher evaluation, school district organization, collective bargaining, and CEO–Board relationships. While such experiences made me technically "qualified" to fulfill Pew's role as a critical friend to the Collaborative, perhaps the most relevant qualifications I had obtained from these earlier experiences were the convictions that schools need radical reform and that I knew much less about how such reform should proceed than I knew when I began my career as a high school teacher in the post-*Sputnik* era of reform at the outset of the 60's.

2. One of the often-told stories about the early days of the Collaborative narrates the success they achieved with teachers by being able to pass out checks at the end of a meeting rather than going through the paper work normally associated with district payments.

3. A detailed analysis of the work performed by the Collaborative during its initial years may be found in *The Philadelphia Schools Collaborative: An Assessment of Its First Three Years* (McMullan & Wolf, 1991). Mary Walton (1991) provided a journalist's perspective in her excellent review of the Collaborative's work in the magazine section of the *Philadelphia Inquirer.*

4. Natalie A. Hiller, remarks delivered to conference of Council for Great City Schools on "Images of Assessment and Accountability: National, State, and Local Perspectives," October 1991.

5. Such messages are no accident; they have been carefully crafted with the superintendent by PSC leadership. Special audiences have been arranged to assure appropriate settings for such remarks.

REFERENCES

Cleveland, H. (1985). *The knowledge executive: Leadership in an information society*. New York: Dutton.

Doyle, D. P. (1992, March). The challenge, the opportunity. *Phi Delta Kappan*, pp. 512–520.

Goodlad, J. I. (Ed.). (1987). *The ecology of school renewal, eighty-sixth yearbook of the National Society for the Study of Education*. Chicago: University of Chicago Press.

Goodlad, J. I. (1990). *Teachers for our nation's schools*. San Francisco: Jossey-Bass.

Leonard, G. (1992, May). The end of school. *Atlantic Monthly*, pp. 24–32.

Lieberman, A. (1992, April). *The meaning of scholarly activity and the building of community*. Presidential address, American Educational Research Association, San Francisco.

Lieberman, A., Darling-Hammond, L., & Zuckerman, D. (1991a). *Early lessons in restructuring schools*. New York: National Center for Restructuring Education, Schools, and Teaching, Teachers College, Columbia University.

Lieberman, A., Zuckerman, D., Wilkie, A., Smith, E., Barinas, N., & Hergert, L. (1991b). *Early lessons in restructuring schools: Case studies of schools of tomorrow ... today*. New York: National Center for Restructuring Education, Schools, and Teaching, Teachers College, Columbia University.

McLarin, K. J. (1992, April 13). A child shines amid the shambles. *The Philadelphia Inquirer*, pp. 1, A6.

McMullan, B. J., & Wolf, W. (1991, November). *The Philadelphia Schools Collaborative: An assessment of its first three years*. Bala Cynwyd, PA: Center for Assessment and Policy Development.

Schön, D. A. (1990). *Educating the reflective practitioner*. San Francisco: Jossey-Bass.

Sirotnik, K. A. (1989). The school as the center of change. In T. J. Sergiovanni & J. H. Moore (Eds.), *Schooling for tomorrow: Directing reforms to issues that count*. Boston: Allyn & Bacon.

Walton, M. (1991, October 6). Taking a new course. *Philadelphia Inquirer*, magazine section.

3

The Professional Development School as a Strategy for School Restructuring

The Millard Fillmore High School— Temple University Connection

MORRIS J. VOGEL
ESSIE ABRAHAMS-GOLDBERG

Contemporary school reformers have taken on a dizzying array of challenges. They have developed such diverse agendas as transforming teachers colleges, implementing curricular reform, promoting authentic assessment, empowering parents and communities, establishing school-based management, and allowing school choice. None of these agendas are necessarily mutually exclusive, but many reform advocates pursue their own interests with determined single-mindedness. The Philadelphia Schools Collaborative's comprehensive high school restructuring—of which the Millard Fillmore High School program is part—has instead taken an unusually broad and pragmatic approach to school reform. The Collaborative's inclusive approach has encouraged the professional development school at Millard Fillmore High School to evolve within the usually separate contexts of teacher education reform and high school restructuring.

One of the Collaborative's initial emphases was on linking schools in partnerships with outside entities that might bring their energy and skills to bear on restructuring. The idea of a professional development school was attractive to the Collaborative because it would involve one or more universities in the ongoing life of one or more comprehensive high schools. It offered an avenue through which university faculty and high school teachers could work as colleagues, with some presumed—but not thoroughly articulated (certainly not at the outset)—positive benefit to the high school. The Collaborative did not see itself testing or even carrying out any carefully defined strategy identified with the professional development school movement; indeed, after an early effort to pin down what seemed an evolving and elusive definition of the professional development school, the individuals most intimately involved with the effort this chapter describes studiously avoided the scholarly literature altogether.

The Collaborative made its original approach to Temple University*, part of the Commonwealth System of Higher Education, in the hope that its faculty (like the faculties of other such local institutions) might be an outside source of intellectual energy, willing to share disciplinary knowledge, time, and collegial fellowship with high school faculties. Temple was particularly interested in exploring potential school partnerships because it had joined the Holmes Group and its College of Education was rethinking its teacher preparation program. The college was moving toward a five-year program in which the school district master teachers would figure importantly. It was clear that both Temple and the schools with which it might be paired stood to benefit from a partnership. Thus was born the Millard Fillmore Professional Development School.

We have discovered that the relationship brought to the Fillmore program nearly all the benefits we had imagined it might. We have developed an intellectually challenging curriculum, and, even more importantly, a process through which teachers continuously explore and develop ambitious new curricular possibilities. Teachers in the program have assumed new responsibilities; they have expanded their sense of professional role. And, most importantly, students in the program are excited about school and are succeeding in schoolwork.

But we have also encountered a significant downside in the relationship. When we began we knew that we needed to figure out how to make a school work; now we need to think about making a school of education work as well. And we also need to manage a relationship between partners who remain unclear about the roles they are playing in one another's activities.

Background

The city's first professional development school (PDS) opened at Millard Fillmore High School in September, 1990, with two distinct yet complementary missions. Originally called the Lab School by Fillmore teachers and students, the PDS is implementing a program that supports student success; it proposes, at the same time, to create at Fillmore a center for the education of would-be teachers enrolled at Temple University. Uniting these missions is the core vision of the PDS: It is a community of learning based in a full partnership between Fillmore High School and Temple University, a partnership in which high school teachers and university professors work as equals in transforming education in both settings. We can, based on three years of experience, report significant success in both aspects of the PDS mission. We should also note that we have not been fully successful in realizing the promise of our partnership as it relates to teacher education, though we remain hopeful.

The PDS differs from other charters in the depth and scope of the university–high school partnership that is its distinguishing feature. The partnership is meant in part, at least, to redress an unfortunate reality: Teachers whose training is in traditional colleges of education, whose careers have been circumscribed by assembly-line work rules, and whose programs have been codified in districtwide standardized curricula, are often not in a position to exploit the new possibilities that restructuring promotes. In narrow terms, the university connection represents a source of outside intellectual energy for the restructuring of the high school.

University faculty have assumed responsibility for working with teachers—as advisers and resource people—in the PDS. A co-author of this chapter (Vogel)—a professor of history at Temple University—has led ongoing subject-matter seminars directed toward the evolving curricular interests and needs of the Lab School teacher team; faculty from other universities, as well as Temple, have participated in this seminar both during the school year and in summer institutes. These university faculty model collegial relationships for their high school peers, thus helping transform authoritarian high schools into communities of learning.

On one level, then, this collaboration represents a generous impulse: Temple's assumption of its responsibility as a public university. But this is a genuine partnership, not a one-way relationship, because Temple needs this program as well. The Fillmore PDS is an essential component of the new five-year B.A.–M.Ed. teacher preparation program that the university has developed in response to the current teaching reform movement. The new program coexists with a traditional four-year B.S. in Education.

The new program requires Temple students preparing for teaching careers to complete a major in the College of Arts and Sciences and a minor in the College of Education, the latter rooted in a set of highly structured experiences in the professional development schools associated with the university. (Temple is also working with a PDS at Hill High School; it is planning a similar program at Wells High School.) Coursework in the minor builds on the student's clinical experience in the PDS—an experience for which school district master teachers assume complete responsibility—and on the major, focusing the student's attention on strategies of inquiry (which are, after all, at the core of the disciplined study that characterizes the arts and sciences) and pedagogy. Coursework in the minor also considers schooling in broad terms, contextualizing it within a range of economic, political, and social issues. The PDS and its master teachers also co-teach selected arts and sciences courses and courses in the education minor, assuming important roles in the education of university students preparing for teaching careers. Students complete requirements for teaching certification and earn an M.Ed. through a fifth-year internship in which the PDS is also to play an important, though not yet fully defined, role.

Planning

Temple University began planning the reorientation of its teacher education programs in 1987. The university developed a preliminary proposal requesting Carnegie Corporation funding for this initiative in early 1988; that proposal laid out the approach that continues to inform the Temple program today. Given the complete absence of high school input in the formative stages of this planning process—and the university's uncertain commitment to the new program represented in the continuation of the much larger 4-year program—the relative success of the Temple–PDS relationship should be more surprising than the difficulties thus far encountered.

A one-week institute formally initiated high school involvement in the PDS during July 1990. The institute introduced the idea of having teacher teams plan interdisciplinary curricula. Purely so that we could have a starting point, we selected the idea of modernity as our intellectual focus for the week. The goal was to see if we could organize ninth-grade curricula in which students examined the origins of the contemporary world—their world. We read Shakespeare and talked about early capitalism; we read about the Industrial Revolution and talked about both romantic poetry and technology; we read Darwin and talked about biology, imperialism, and racism. Some of the sessions brought together the group as a whole—about 30 teachers from Fillmore, Wells, Hill, and DuBois High School—with university faculty members for a series of conversations. In other sessions, the group broke into disciplinary teams—English, math/science, and social studies—to try to reach consensus on how to approach each discipline within an interdisciplinary, theme-oriented curriculum. In other sessions teacher teams from each school met separately to try to outline a year-long program.

The Fillmore team was the most successful. It included three teachers—of social studies and environmental science as well as the English teacher (Abrahams) who co-authors this chapter—several department heads, and the union building representative. The team's composition was nearly ideal; it brought together the teachers who would actually be responsible for implementing the program—with the exception of a math teacher—and individuals whose support would be essential as the program was introduced in the school. The teachers meshed as a group collectively responsible for an ambitious intellectual program, and they developed a literature-driven curriculum that incorporated environmental science, world history, English, and (in organizational terms only) algebra. They divided the year into large topics: what makes a human human (and early hominids); the hero (and Africa); the antihero (and the Industrial Revolution); the community (and China/Japan); and inhumanity (and modern political oppression). The curriculum built only partially on the content introduced in the institute; the teachers knew that they themselves had to learn a great deal to carry it off.

Fillmore teachers at the institute were in effect building a charter from scratch; they built it around content, an interdisciplinary approach, and a collegial intellectual engagement. Wells teachers came from its Motivation Program, a preexisting school-within-a-school that already had its own focus: student achievement and the enrichment of traditional courses. They found the institute's approach uncongenial and their school dropped out of the PDS program. They subsequently decided to reenter after some Motivation faculty spent several days observing the Fillmore Lab School summer institute in July 1991.

The origins of the PDS emphasis on an interdisciplinary approach are shrouded in the mists of time. The idea appears in Temple's original Carnegie proposal (1989), although its presentation there is substantially less ambitious than the concept developed in the 1990 summer institute. It was clear by that point that several considerations supported an interdisciplinary strategy. For one, the PDS depends on teacher teams, operating collegially. If teams are to exist in more than name, they require that members engage in collaborative effort. Team members are collectively concerned about the students they share; team members dealing with the same intellectual content in their classes will also need to share intellectual interests. Teachers must talk to one another across disciplinary boundaries to do this; an interdisciplinary approach is thus essential if professional development schools are to be shared communities of learning—for teachers as well as students.

Further, an interdisciplinary approach by its very nature supports innovation. There is no standardized interdisciplinary curriculum in this district to fall back on. The experience at Fillmore's Lab School demonstrates that teachers bringing their diverse disciplines to bear on the exploration of a single broad topic can develop creative approaches to their subject matter. Whether it is a specific approach or the fact that teachers invest deeply in it as its creators, the result is a greater likelihood of positive student response. Finally, an interdisciplinary approach requires teachers to leave the safety of their learned subject areas, encouraging them, in an atmosphere of mutual support, to present their disciplines not as bodies of fact but as modes of inquiry, as self-conscious ways of learning and hence of teaching.

An interdisciplinary approach is not a universal answer to the problems of urban schools. It does not involve the substitution of one standardized curriculum for another. It is rather a rubric within which teacher teams can develop programs suitable for their students. Teachers work with arts and sciences faculty in exploring their interdisciplinary themes and in filling them out with curriculum specifics. The curriculum developed is subject to constant revision through the same process that created it. The essential product is a process.

Implementation

The summer institute ended with an ongoing curriculum planning process in place for three teacher teams, but without any clear sense of what might happen next in terms of developing a PDS. Temple had still not received word from Carnegie on its proposal, and institutional considerations seemed to require outside funding before Temple proceeded with its new teacher education program. Fillmore's principal, one of the district's most experienced principals, responded to this uncertainty by simply implementing the PDS unilaterally and immediately.

The principal took several actions to implement the Fillmore PDS in September 1990. He block-rostered four ninth-grade classes (totaling 125 students) into the program. He appointed two teachers—English teacher Essie Abrahams-Goldberg° and social studies teacher Zachary Rubin°—program coordinators and reduced their teaching loads even though the contract between Temple and the school district that would pay for this was still unsigned, the positions had not yet been formally advertised, and the method of selecting program coordinators (who would also be adjunct faculty at Temple) was not yet decided. He also set aside a large room as a home for the PDS and promised an outside telephone line, a computer, and $1200 in seed money. Fillmore was, in the principal's words, ready to follow the Japanese model of "building the plane while we fly it."

As the 1990 school year opened, the building's rumor mill had it that the Lab School was not going to get off the ground. At 10:30 A.M., on the first day of school, the principal summoned Abrahams, Rubin, and two other teachers (one who had been part of the summer institute and one who had not) to a meeting in his office. The program would go forward. Two teachers had not applied for the program; they were assigned to it. The principal would later assign another English teacher (two classes), a history teacher (one class), and a science teacher (one class) to the PDS.

Looking back on the start of the 1990–91 school year, Abrahams and Rubin recall feeling somewhat like protagonists in a fairy tale or myth who had just been given an impossible task. Both experienced teachers, neither was certain how to transform their curriculum outline, their amorphous relationship with Temple, and their new office—an almost empty room with fading paint and cracked cinderblock walls—into a PDS.

The Setting

Teachers and administrators had long considered Fillmore, a traditionally "white" school, a plum assignment, a school to which teachers transferred "up the boulevard" after service in more challenging settings. Twenty years ago, the school spread its 3,500 students across four shifts. Today, one shift serves fewer than 1,700 students. Enrollment dropped as the neighborhood aged and more affluent residents left Mayfair, Fillmore's neighborhood, for suburbia. The school's population changed as well. The neighborhood's new residents were generally less well-to-do than the families they replaced; magnet schools introduced to encourage desegregation stripped the best students from Fillmore as they did from all comprehensive high schools in the city; and voluntary busing increased the school's minority population.

As its size declined and its population changed, Fillmore's teaching staff and its academic offerings contracted. German and Latin were dropped when teachers retired; a physics teacher was dropped after 23 years at Fillmore. Only one art teacher, one instrumental music teacher, and one vocal music teacher remain. Faculty morale suffered as well. Many teachers complain that few "good kids" are left. Most sigh for the students of yesteryear, of 10, 20, and 30 years ago. There is an irony here: Abrahams notes that she has heard this lament from the time she arrived at Fillmore in September 1969: "talented teachers telling me about the wonderful students we once had."

Fillmore's faculty has also changed. Like other high school faculties, it has aged; it has also not welcomed new blood in years. In earlier days, teachers talked during lunch about books or plays or shows. Conversation in the building now seems more limited to personal issues, gossip, complaints, and retirement dates. Power struggles rack some departments; winners get the best rosters and the most periods released. There is little talk in the faculty lunchroom about lessons that work or fail, articles in education journals, or trends in academic disciplines.

The Original PDS Staff

All but one of the teachers in the program were veterans. Abrahams had taught for 22 years, 21 of them at Fillmore High School. She had become active in teaching reform through the Philadelphia Alliance for Teaching Humanities in the Schools (PATHS) and was a teacher-consultant for the school district through Susan Lytle's* Philadelphia Writing Project. Abrahams had also worked on staff development at Fillmore; she was interested in the professional growth of faculty. She had slowly transformed her classroom from a highly structured teacher-centered room to a more student-centered, active learning format.

Rubin's 19 years in the system had been spent mostly at Fillmore, but as the most junior member of the department he had been dropped from the staff six times and had therefore worked at a variety of schools. Many think him one of the brightest and best-read teachers at Fillmore; he had worked on several PATHS projects, including a science-and-society institute with Morris Vogel and the two-year world history curriculum. He is also a member of the American Federation of Teachers building committee. Rubin wanted to work in the Lab School because he recognized that "students spend 10 months in my classroom, but don't really learn history." He wanted a setting that would let him share his love of the discipline.

The other teachers were fine traditional teachers, long committed to their work. Some now described themselves as burned out. One had been dropped from Fillmore six times in the 19 years she had taught in the district. She had become involved with the Environmental Science and Horticulture Academies during her current tenure at Fillmore. When first approached about the idea of working in an innovative program, she confessed her reluctance. During the fall, she finally confided the extent of her burnout to Abrahams. Drawn into the fold by the opportunity to explore alternative assessment, she was lured by the promise of fulfilling lifelong professional goals.

> "You mean," she said, "I never have to give another test?"
> "You never have to give another test."
> "I can work from projects?" she asked. "I can do everything I've always dreamed of doing?"
> "Yes," we assured her, "you can be the teacher you always dreamed of being."
> With those words, she was off and running.

Another teacher had recently come to Fillmore when his former junior high school lost its ninth grade. He was awaiting final ruling on a grievance he had filed to allow him to follow his students to another high school. He saw himself as a traditional math teacher who believed in teaching his subject from the text, although he recognized the need to use word problems for enrichment. He met the needs of the Lab School's interdisciplinary agenda part way by offering to spend class time on math skills, such as graphing, that would help the science teacher with her subject.

Three other teachers with very diverse pedagogical styles and beliefs received partial loads in the Lab School through impressment. One was viewed as disaffected and expressed his frustrations by blaming students. Another had come to teaching late in life and was relatively inexperienced in the classroom. The assignment of disaffected teachers by department heads would remain a problem for the program in subsequent years as well.

The last slot was filled by an unknown. No one in the English department wanted to work in a new program in a position that required closely cooperating with other teachers, learning new material, developing a new curriculum, and meeting after school on a regular basis. One teacher, relatively new to Fillmore, tentatively consented to enter the program until she learned that she would have to forsake the curriculum she knew well and the 30-year-old textbook she "loved" to work with new materials. Perhaps next year, she volunteered, when she was not taking so many courses and working her second job. The fortuitous resignation of an English teacher on the first day of school meant that a replacement would arrive at Fillmore on October 1. That teacher, completely new to the school but not to teaching, became the final member of the team. Substitutes filled the vacancy until she arrived.

Variation in the level of teacher commitment posed some difficulties for the Lab School team, but it allowed the Collaborative to test one of its assumptions about the utility of charters. Restructuring seeks not only to engage the most motivated teachers, but also to involve every high school teacher in the district in a teacher team. The intent is to use collegiality and peer pressure as strategies for reaching unengaged teachers and transforming schools.

The Seminar

During the first two years, the Collaborative funded a biweekly, credit-bearing, Temple University seminar for the Lab School team; university professors expert in various content areas and a consultant on innovative teaching techniques—sometimes paired and sometimes one at a time—assigned reading and led discussions. Teachers regarded the seminar, which met in the PDS office at Fillmore, as a special perk. Teachers set the agenda.

Some of the seminar's early meetings focused on active learning. Pat Macpherson*, formerly an English and writing teacher at Germantown Friends School* and now pursuing a writing career, met several times with the group to work on active learning strategies and to facilitate group dynamics. Macpherson encouraged each person to participate and made even nonvolunteering teachers feel comfortable. Outside presentations on content tended to focus on Asian history and culture. The curriculum outline they had developed called for the Lab School to spend one marking period in the spring on Asia. University faculty engaged the group in conversations about their research in such subjects as Chinese science, the Japanese family, Korean Americans, and Chinese history and values.

By mid-October, the seminar had attracted a young, dynamic teacher in Fillmore's Hearing Impaired Program. She was the first outsider to attend; she has initiated still-ongoing efforts to develop a similar interdisciplinary program in her department. A French teacher who taught a number of Lab School students and a history teacher who taught none also began attending the seminar in the spring. In the next year, the history teacher taught one course in the PDS and became full-time faculty in the third year. The French teacher (who was only teaching at Fillmore for the year) successfully recruited his department head for the next year. The teachers also decided to invite the Fillmore student teachers assigned to their program to the seminar; they thought student teachers would find it useful to see professional teachers still learning their craft. These student teachers were enrolled in Temple's traditional four-year education B.S. program.

Humanitas

In early November, Vogel and Abrahams spent a week observing Humanitas, a Rockefeller Foundation–supported interdisciplinary humanities program in the Los Angeles public schools. Humanitas promotes school renewal much as PATHS does in this city; but it is particularly innovative in bringing teams of teachers for week-long visits to two high schools with strong interdisciplinary charters. Visiting teachers observe Humanitas classrooms, discuss teaching in structured seminars, and plan programs for their own schools with the assistance of Humanitas teachers.

Abrahams returned to Fillmore realizing that teachers who were uninvolved in the planning of a curriculum were unlikely to take the risks required to implement it. Teachers already owned the standardized curriculum in which they had invested much of their careers; they also had to own innovation in order to feel validated. Watching Neil Anstead°, Humanitas coordinator at Grover Cleveland High School°, she better appreciated that her role included supporting teachers through change.

Evolving the Curriculum

The Lab School had concluded its first major unit of study by this time without significant collegial interaction among its teachers. Students had no sense that they were in a special program. Nor was classroom experience fully living up to teachers' expectations.

Abrahams's Los Angeles experience helped her convince the teacher team to take greater risks on the next curriculum unit, Africa. One teacher in particular was an important contributor here; she had spent time in Liberia with the Peace Corps. But Abrahams and Rubin had to do a great deal of outside work. Rubin borrowed a dilapidated set of Chinua Achebe's *Things Fall Apart* (suggested by Los Angeles teachers) and other source material from a colleague; Abrahams spent time researching. Collaborative money purchased the African Writers' Pack. (After the unit succeeded, the English Department bought two class sets of *Things Fall Apart*.) Collaborative support also allowed the photoreproduction of class sets of African short stories. Humanitas teachers had stressed the importance of giving students consumable texts to mark up so that they might make their own meaning of the materials.

The Africa unit was also planned with a collective culminating activity in mind. This was an African jam, featuring papier-mâché masks that students read about and constructed in English class. The jam was held in the library before winter break. Every one had something to contribute. There was a show-and-tell of a teacher's time in Liberia. Students donned traditional African attire and related the tale of Gustavas Vassa's capture and enslavement. History classes acted out scenes from the life of Mansa Mussa, a West African king. A support teacher shared objects her daughter had brought back from Africa. Students in English classes presented an orchestrated and choreographed choral reading of *Lord of the Dance*, a piece about the mask in traditional and modern Africa. At the end of the program, Macpherson announced the winner of the mask competition and awarded a $10 prize. By the time refreshments were served, it was clear that something magical had taken place. Students felt part of the community; so, too, did faculty.

THE TEMPLE UNIVERSITY CONNECTION

The student teacher program linked the PDS to Temple's College of Education. The link was initially tenuous; Fillmore's teachers and the College were unable to make their different needs clear to each other. By the end of the second year, Fillmore had defined the paradigm for teacher preparation in the PDS, a case of practice leading theory.

The student teacher program highlighted differences between the College of Education and the PDS. Embracing the Collaborative's philosophy, the PDS committed itself to working with all teachers. It assigned student teachers to both more and less engaged staff members in the belief that all teachers who mentored student teachers would themselves develop professionally. Teachers more marginal to the charter were encouraged to devise projects for student teachers to implement; other teachers worked in more reflective modes, thinking aloud with student teachers as they modeled lessons. This approach was not entirely successful. Student teachers—like most high school students—can readily recognize unengaged teachers. In one case, a student teacher's disdain for a teacher grew over the semester. In other instances, students began to imitate a lack of investment, perhaps without realizing it. The PDS was willing to accept these risks both because of its own agenda and because it thought it useful to expose student teachers to a range of techniques and competencies.

Another difference involved the supervision of student teachers. The College of Education's original approach was to place authority over its student teachers in the hands of a main campus supervisor who made six brief visits to the school each semester. Cooperating teachers theoretically exercised day-to-day supervision, but essentially turned classes over to student teachers as quickly as possible. The first semester the PDS operated, the two students assigned to the school were supervised by a graduate student totally uninterested in the PDS. Her notion of supervision was limited to filling out College of Education checklists. She met with Abrahams once for approximately two minutes— long enough for introductions and polite small talk.

Frustrated by the university's apparent lack of interest in the program, Abrahams unilaterally established a weekly practicum for the next set of student teachers. Although she was concerned about usurping the role of the university supervisor, she went ahead, buoyed by the enthusiasm and support of the second-semester Temple supervisor. Abrahams and Rubin led the weekly discussion; cooperating teachers looked in, as did the principal and observers from other schools developing similar programs. The Temple students shared observations, posed problems, accepted advice, and considered such issues as learning styles, assessment, and creating curriculum during free-flowing discussions. The College of Education ultimately adopted this paradigm for its other PDS sites. The success of the Fillmore program also led the university to place its student teachers in schools as members of groups, not as isolated individuals. The university has not yet accepted the suggestion of PDS teachers that their practicum count as a credit-bearing course.

By the end of the first year, the College of Education had agreed that the PDS coordinators would formally take over the supervision of student teachers. One student teacher found it somewhat awkward that the individual issuing his grade also saw him regularly in class. Yet this is precisely the strength of this approach. Supervisors who are on site have a much better understanding of the classrooms in which student teachers are working, and a better sense of the issues they confront, than do university-based supervisors. Supervisors who are part of a school faculty can also offer more sensitive and more ongoing support to colleagues who take on responsibilities as cooperating teachers.

Student Teachers and School Transformation

Student teachers brought new blood into Fillmore's faculty. College students were new—and generally appreciative—colleagues; their arrival brought new conversations, and even some new approaches. Even a teacher who was disappointed that Temple's education students brought "traditional methods of teachers as authorities" with them commented that student teachers were freeing agents. Another cooperating teacher was able to develop her more "outlandish" ideas with the assistance of a collaborating adult in her classroom. She risked teaching *Lord of the Flies* through a variety of activities, including a simulation between hunters and the hunted.

Student teachers are also cross-pollinators, carrying ideas from one classroom to the next. One of the first student teachers regularly brought teaching strategies from a nontraditional English classroom to a traditional one. By the second year of the PDS, one cooperating teacher came to depend on her student teacher modeling lessons for her.

But the presence of student teachers does not guarantee classroom transformation. Teachers have to reflect on their own practice before they can embrace change. And if unengaged, teachers lack the commitment or the interest to reflect on their work.

Slow but Steady Progress

The pace at which good things happened in the PDS accelerated in the second half of its first year. A promised phone line appeared, as did the program's computer; the latter enabled Lab School teachers to shift their energies more fully out of departmental offices. February also brought additional Collaborative funding for teacher development.

Vogel meanwhile had obtained a small grant of $2,000 for a peer-tutoring program. The money paid more successful students an hourly wage to work with students who needed help; it also paid student teachers to supervise this after-school program. The program ran from February through April; it was an amazing success. Student performance improved and student tutors received recognition for academic achievement from teachers and students alike.

The excitement of February spilled into March. Teachers began to meet weekly. Even the least engaged teacher grew more talkative and began sharing his experiences. Teachers stayed later and later at sessions, sometimes remaining beyond 4:00 to discuss ideas with guest speakers. Abrahams and a colleague visited New York's Central Park East High School in mid-March. It was the first time these two women had spent any considerable length of time together. The other teacher noted that

> the experience in New York just made me realize that we were on the right track and I think there were a couple of points that allowed me to refine what I was doing. I was tickled pink to find we were doing it successfully with 33 random students [in each class] and they were doing it with 15 self-selected students. We were making it work with kids that some people treat as leftovers.

Planning Year 2

In mid-spring the Lab School gave an open house for the Fillmore faculty in order to recruit the additional teachers required to staff the program as it expanded into tenth grade. Teachers stuffed neon yellow invitations in every mailbox, announced the event in the school's dailygram, and offered refreshments, but only three people attended. Of those three, two became involved in the program. Complicating recruitment was the problem of how many teachers the central office bureaucracy would assign to Fillmore (the faculty allotment) for the following year, which would not be announced until early June.

Though Abrahams and Rubin were anxious about the next year, the Lab School teachers mounted an interdisciplinary, multimedia presentation for parents and students at the mid-May incoming freshmen open house.

Fillmore's principal announced the next year's allotment at a faculty meeting in late May. The mood in the auditorium was somber as the principal explained that 16 teachers, two counselors, and one nonteaching assistant would have to be dropped. This was also the day of the Lab School's last session with Pat Macpherson. When Abrahams walked into the program office, she was faced with the prospect that she would be the only member of the group returning next year. Though dispirited, the group decided to proceed with the session on active learning.

In spite of uncertainty, the group continued to reflect on the past year and plan for the next one. A set of teachers presented a workshop on alternative assessment to a citywide meeting of teachers, administrators, and parents on June 1. One of the early recruits found the opportunity to speak about her experience exciting: "It helped cure the burnout, it made me excited about teaching again. When you find something that works, it's almost your obligation to share it." Alternative assessment allowed her to rethink her practice and repackage what she had learned in her experience. She had grown professionally during the year.

The Collaborative agreed to underwrite two week-long summer institutes for the Lab School. The first planned an interdisciplinary tenth grade; the second revisited the ninth-grade program. Both integrated new teachers into the Lab School. Vogel wanted the teachers to think about a biology-driven tenth grade. Teachers thought this might work, and two met with Vogel and a Temple biology professor in early June to begin planning the tenth-grade summer institute.

The Lab School needed to add enough new faculty to teach four new classes of ninth graders and handle the tenth graders who continued in the charter. But when positions in the charter were posted in June, no one applied. It was as if nothing had changed, but that clearly was not the case.

One teacher from the PDS applied for and received a position as program director in the Environmental Science Academy, her first love. She left the Lab School reluctantly, remembering that one of the things she enjoyed about the program was its interdisciplinary nature: "I began to appreciate other disciplines as they related to mine. In science, we tend to have tunnel vision and don't see how other people deal with the same material." Despite her departure, she consulted with Abrahams on science teachers who might be appropriate for the Lab School and worked closely in the summer institute with the incoming biology teacher. Although the teacher who had a grievance pending had "won" and was leaving, he checked with Abrahams on a daily basis to find out who would teach math in the program. He felt that the program had too much energy invested in it to allow it to fail.

Teaching assignments were not announced until the final day of the 1990–91 school year. The math teacher who had attended the open house would teach algebra I as part of the ninth-grade team; she was excited by the challenge of integrating her discipline into a broader curriculum. But one teacher assigned to teach tenth grade was entirely unwilling to engage in collaborative effort. He refused to attend the summer institute, vowed never to meet with team members during the year, and announced he would not deviate from the school district's standardized curriculum.

Another teacher in the original team refused to teach ninth grade again. He had "33 years in the system and nothing to show for it. No time off. No special compensation." His place has been filled by an excellent social studies teacher who had helped develop the PATHS world history curriculum. She signed on after the summer institute. Rubin survived the cut in Fillmore's complement; he found the program "invigorating." It was "change, something out of the ordinary. The novel is always more interesting." Yet another teacher applied to another program, but after being accepted decided to rejoin the Lab School. Two foreign-language teachers who joined voluntarily participated in the tenth-grade summer institute, working to integrate Spanish II and French II into the new biology-driven curriculum.

Considering Success

The program worked at Fillmore. The Lab School enrolled 125 ninth graders in four block-rostered classes in 1990–91; 110 of these students returned as tenth graders for the 1991–92 year. While no data allowing exact comparisons with other Fillmore students are available, experience suggests that 70 to 80 students would have returned under normal circumstances; indeed Fillmore's roster office was doubtful about filling the three tenth-grade classes for which teachers in the charter had planned their second year. The first year's ninth graders successfully followed an innovative, biology-driven, integrated tenth-grade curriculum. And a second group of four ninth-grade classes pursued a revised version of the literature-driven program taught the first year. The program has now completed its third year. Over 100 of our first students completed the eleventh grade in a curriculum that integrated English, American history, Spanish III, and French III during the 1992–93 school year. Class work for the year emphasized the theme of diversity as an organizing principle of the American experience. The charter enrolled its third cohort of students in the ninth grade, studying a curriculum that teachers have revised yet again; the charter's second cohort worked with a revised biology-oriented curriculum. As of this writing (summer 1993), we have planned an ambitious twelfth-grade curriculum for our first cohort, and revisited—yet again—the ninth-, tenth-, and eleventh-grade programs.

Fillmore's teachers are, after all, about the business of transforming education. But they are relying on more than extremely high student attendance and
retention—unprecedented though those are in Fillmore's recent history—in de-
claring success. Teachers comment regularly on how they continually raise expectations and find that students meet them; on how students bring excitement and
interest to the classroom; on how Lab School students are better at collaborative
work than Fillmore's more advantaged Academy students; and on any number
of other indicators best determined qualitatively by classroom teachers.

Matching the record of student success as an achievement of the PDS is the
community to which the PDS effort has given rise. Fillmore's teachers have
developed a collegial environment within which they and students alike share
membership in a community of active learners. They have found a way to integrate new teachers into a charter. They have created a process through which
the program continues to evolve, revising old curricula and creating new ones.

The program's connection with Temple's College of Education was perhaps less successful. Temple's students reported uniformly positive experiences in their Lab School field placements. But the College of Education alter-
nated between paying no attention to Fillmore and demanding that Fillmore
(and other PDS) teachers holding university adjunct appointments assume the
far-reaching responsibilities on the university campus listed in the original
Carnegie proposal. The original proposal did not, of course, foresee the enormous commitment in time and energy that teachers would have to invest in the
high school component of the program. It may have been naive to expect too
easy an integration of university and high school. It is unfortunately not clear
that the College of Education has the flexibility to recreate a program already
committed to paper even as that program evolves.

The Lab School team is sanguine about the first three years of their charter. They expect to continue evolving. They expect it to be an important model
for the transformation of district high schools, and they hope that it can play
a large role in reorganizing teacher preparation at Temple University. They
believe that the program has implications for the national school reform movement.

NOTE

Please note that in keeping with the worst traditions of 1950s social science, all city,
school, and individual names are pseudonymous unless marked*. The Philadelphia Schools
Collaborative* operates in a large industrial metropolis of one and one-half million residents, midway between New York and Baltimore.

4
Charters and Restructuring

BERNARD J. MCMULLAN

This school district began a process to examine ways in which comprehensive high schools could be strengthened to better serve students and ensure improved student performance. The characteristics of the district's comprehensive high schools closely mirror those of typical comprehensive high schools throughout the nation—large and impersonal, with high rates of failure, high dropout rates, and a scarcity of effective programs serving large groups. Further, options for innovation were constrained by limited school and district resources, highly prescriptive graduation requirements established by the state legislature, a standardized curriculum implemented several years before in an effort to remove some of major inequities in education that existed across schools and classrooms, and a conservative administrative approach to handling categorical funding support.

In its initial discussions about improving comprehensive high schools, the district placed a strong emphasis on students who were most at risk—that is, those with a high likelihood of dropping out. As part of its effort, it commissioned a synthesis of national dropout prevention research and programmatic initiatives. The report, *Reclaiming the Future* (McMullan, Leiderman, & Wolf, 1988), identified a series of guidelines for restructuring high schools that would simultaneously improve the performance of all students as well as reduce the district's burgeoning dropout rate:

- Deliver education in small, intensive units with low ratios of teachers to students and many opportunities for personal contact. (Wehlage, 1983; Hess & Lauber, 1985; Hamilton, 1986; Bennett, 1987)
- Develop high teacher expectations, reinforce student self-worth, and set clear standards and hold students to them. (Goodlad, 1983; Wehlage, 1983; Hamilton, 1986)
- Use a wide range of instructional techniques, including individualized approaches and state-of-the-art instructional methods (e.g., cooperative learning, computer-assisted instruction, mastery learning approaches) to upgrade the general quality of instruction and reach individual students. (Carroll, 1989)

- Meet the broad range of needs of youth with multiple disadvantages or risk factors. Provide integrated remediation with components to meet health and social service needs. Develop holistic, comprehensive programs combining social and academic activities. (Oakes, 1985; Wehlage & Rutter, 1986)
- Incorporate sustained adult contact into programs. The first option is to have this sustained contact be with teachers. Other options are to use counselors, community workers, parents, and businesspeople. (Wehlage, 1983)
- Establish purposive partnerships with the outside community (parents, community organizations, private-sector business, colleges and universities, and social service deliverers) as a way to expand resources available to the school, to build a broader constituency for public education, to empower parents and the community, and to create access to opportunities (jobs, postsecondary schooling) beyond the schools. (Education Commission of the States, 1983; Marburger, 1990)
- Build in incentives, such as jobs, for attending and performing well in school.
- Remove barriers to attending school: provide as necessary child care, income-producing opportunities (work–study and part-time jobs), flexible hours, transportation, and so forth. (Oakes, 1985; Fine, 1986)
- Change policies having unintended or perverse effects: methods of accounting for student enrollment, suspension, grade retention, withdrawal, teacher assignment, and so forth. (Powell, Farrar, & Cohen, 1985; Fine, 1986; Wehlage & Rutter, 1986)
- Identify at-risk youth early—both early in their school careers and as early as they manifest signs of poor performance.

The guidelines proposed in this report became central principles for the Philadelphia Schools Collaborative and initiatives designed to restructure the district's comprehensive high schools. Combined, they constituted a prescription for developing broader, systemwide changes that would make schools more hospitable for all students, not just those considered to be at risk.

THE MOVE TO CHARTERS

The Collaborative's strategy for restructuring required a transformation in three essential and interrelated elements: classroom pedagogy, school organization, and the institutional environment in which restructuring occurs. Restructuring would require progress in each of the elements and further assumed that each element would be necessary, but not sufficient, for restructuring (Sizer, 1984; Passow, 1990; Brown, 1991). At base was the development of charters.

The most critical objective for advancing restructuring through charters is that it provide a clear opportunity to *transform* teaching practice by providing teachers with an opportunity to experiment with different approaches and with the control over time, resources, and policies needed to ensure that such experiments can occur. Through its efforts, the Collaborative has used professional development activities to help teachers understand and adopt the approach that they feel is most appropriate for their students but did not seek to press for a single, particular model.

Development of charters within the district has been rapid. When the Collaborative began in 1988, most comprehensive high schools had few or no programs that met the characteristics of a charter as just described. The major programmatic exceptions within comprehensive high schools were 12 programs supported by the High School Academies, nine Motivation Programs,[1] and a handful of other programs widely scattered across schools. Overall, there were fewer than 30 such programs. The bulk of the programs that existed tended to serve a very restricted band of students—using selective screening strategies and applying strict performance standards for continuation in the program. In retrospect, it is likely that fewer than half of the programs existing in 1988 would have been certified as charters as presently defined.

In the years since the Collaborative began, the most notable change in the instructional organization of comprehensive high schools has been the emergence of charters. During the 1990–91 school year, the number of charterlike programs within them had grown to just under 50. By September 1991, more than 80 programs had been designated as bona fide charters by the Collaborative and the Office of Senior High Schools and eligible for additional allotment support.[2] In addition, a score of additional initiatives, labeled transitional programs, that do not meet the full definition of a charter, but were developed and approved as renewal vehicles within their schools, had also been launched.

Further, charters are now a fixture at every comprehensive high school. Each school has at least two charters; the maximum number of charters slated to open in September 1991 was seven. The distribution of the number of operational charters across schools by the opening of the 1991–92 school year is displayed in Table 4.1. Table 4.2 presents the type of charter expansion during the period. The restructuring process has resulted in a net increase of 50 charterlike programs since the 1988–89 school year.

Growth of Charters

Approximately 40,000 students are enrolled in these 22 comprehensive high schools. We estimate that no more than 4,600 students were served by the 30 or so charterlike initiatives extant in comprehensive high schools in

TABLE 4.1 Distribution of charters across schools.

Number of charters within schools	Number of schools
2	4
3	8
4	3
5	4
≥6	3

1988. The bulk of these students were served by Academies and Motivation Programs.

Accounting for students assigned to or affiliated with charters during the school year did not become routinized across all comprehensive high schools until the 1991–92 school year. However, based on data available for the 1990–91 school year, it is reasonable to estimate that between 7,000 and 7,500 students were served in charters across all comprehensive high schools during that school year. Results for the 1991–92 school year indicate that of the 40,500 students enrolled in comprehensive high schools during the school year, 13,331, or 32.9%, were affiliated with the 80 or so charters open during that year.

As noted above, the movement toward creating charters has gained momentum over the past several years. Most new charters began serving ninth-grade students only or a combination of ninth and tenth graders. Consequently, the proportion of students served by charters is highest in lower grades. Approximately 34%[3] of ninth-grade students were affiliated with charters during the 1991–92 school year. The coverage rate among tenth- and eleventh-grade students was 36.2% and 34.7%, respectively. Among twelfth-grade students, fewer than a quarter (24.1%) were affiliated with charters.

Movement toward full school chartering has just begun in earnest. During the 1991–92 school year, seven schools enrolled half or more of all students

TABLE 4.2 Growth in charters by type, 1988–89 through 1991–92.

	School year	
Program	1988–89	1991–92
High school academies	12	23
Motivation	9	9
Other programs	9	50

within charter initiatives. Among these, three enrolled more than 70% of their total student population in charters. In contrast, three schools enrolled fewer than 15% of their students in charters during the year. Although there is some relationship between the size of the school and the percentage of students enrolled in charters—some of the smallest schools have enrolled the greatest proportion of students in charters, while the largest schools tend to have few charters and low student charter affiliation—this pattern is not uniform.

CHALLENGES TO THE DEVELOPMENT AND EXPANSION OF CHARTERS

Whether grandfathered in, expanded from a regular program, or newly launched, the process of becoming a charter within an already existing school building presents a number of challenges. For already established programs, the transition to charter can mean anything from minor changes to a complete rethinking of structure, curriculum, operations, and image. Newly created programs must develop a rationale, determine content and curriculum development, negotiate the location of the charter within the larger school, and attract and develop a full teacher complement. In these instances, charters have to find their place within the larger school as it is simultaneously restructured on other dimensions, such as mission and governance.

Therefore it is not surprising that the move to charters has raised a number of conceptual and organizational issues for comprehensive high schools. It was anticipated that charters would need to experiment with pedagogy and scheduling and to respond to students' needs; in fact, innovation in these areas is a desired end. However, several issues have proven to be especially pervasive and fundamental to the development of charters.

Ensuring Quality Instruction

A basic premise of charters is that the combination of interdisciplinary curricular themes, assignment of a core group of students to a core group of teachers across years, staff development, and related activities will lead to improvements in the quality of instruction. The notion is that these elements, taken together, remove some of the barriers to excellence in instruction and provide the conditions to reinvigorate and tap the potential of the faculty of comprehensive high schools.

Charters are designed to be protected places where new instruction can occur and *does occur*. The charter concept assumes that teachers are willing and able to think across disciplines, work in teams, take responsibility for student outcomes, and create a stimulating and effective instructional environment when treated as competent professionals. Moreover, the success of charters demands that these skills be manifest very broadly across staff. While one or two leaders can promote the development of a charter, it takes a full complement of effective staff to realize it. Obviously, then, a major issue in instructional quality is the capacity and willingness of faculty to accept these additional responsibilities. Hence the need for ongoing and sustained professional development.

Early evidence suggests that many teachers have risen to this challenge. Most teachers in charters have demonstrated a willingness to try new things, to participate in professional development, and to work closely with their colleagues. Some still may be unprepared or resistant. Teachers who appreciate the potential for improving outcomes are usually willing to work toward drawing other teachers in. These leaders (alternately referred to as "point persons" or "innovators") must convince their colleagues to explore and eventually embrace the charter concept. However, long-established mindsets about the nature of schools and schooling present formidable barriers to change. Tackling teacher resistance can be an especially difficult task in schools when many teachers are in midcareer and beyond and set in their ways, when some teachers simply have no interest in innovation, or when restructuring through charters is seen as just another in a series of district reform efforts. This process can be expedited somewhat if principals and/or other administrators are openly supportive of restructuring through charters.

Obtaining teacher investment beyond the initial idea for a charter has also proved to be difficult in some instances. Such a buy-in implies a change in past teaching style, expectations for students, program affiliation, and other teaching and classroom content. It is proving somewhat difficult to get a commitment to improved instructional quality from teachers whose discipline does not fit directly into the charter theme (e.g., in a communications theme, what is the role of math? in a science/technology theme, what is the role of English?).

Acceptance and Accommodation of Student Heterogeneity

One of the greatest challenges to the development of charters has been abandoning deeply held notions about the value of homogeneous ability grouping. Despite the abundance of evidence attesting to the deleterious effects of ability-group tracking, many teachers continue to question the concept of placing students possessing a wide range of abilities in the same classes. Understandably, this issue is exacerbated for charters that have evolved from preexisting programs targeted at well-performing students.

Early experience suggests several issues. First, the practice of placing high-achieving and low-achieving students into separate programs is simply difficult to change. Constituents of programs targeted to these groups—teachers, administrators, parents, and students—balk at the requirement that they have to become heterogeneous in order to receive the benefits of charter status.

Second, as charters operationalize the concept of heterogeneity, they are raising a number of questions. What does heterogeneity actually mean? What is the basis for assessing it? How wide a range is considered acceptable heterogeneity? Are special education students to be included? Do charters compete with magnet programs or are they to be heterogeneous within the traditional enrollment of the comprehensive high schools? Resolution of these issues is important in order to determine how real the commitment to heterogeneity is going to be within the charter concept.

Third, charters are facing issues having to do with recruitment. While it is certainly possible to be both heterogeneous and selective (for example, on the basis of interest in a charter theme), in practice this has seldom been a requirement of programs. Therefore charters are having to think about recruitment and develop strategies that could attract a wide range of students.

The initial experiences of charters suggests that the issue of charter selectivity represents a substantial challenge for schools and the Collaborative. Specifically, the Collaborative's vision of school restructuring and charter guidelines issued by the district require that schools develop charters that serve groups of students who are heterogeneous with respect to prior academic performance and ability.

Homogeneity within charters. Homogeneity within individual charters is a difficult issue. The greatest concern is that charters do not become thinly disguised tracks into which students are placed based on some arbitrary standard of performance or expectation. At the same time, if one believes that a substantial portion of students within comprehensive high schools are at risk, then the issue of heterogeneity might be an exercise in making subtle distinctions between essentially similar populations.

Data from the 1991–92 school year suggest that many individual charters enroll students who share similar academic profiles. That is, by some measures—age, special education status, and repeater status—students in a charter are generally alike. It appears that charters in the 1991–92 school year included a large number of programs that served better-prepared students.[4]

The fact that initial data suggest that students in charterlike initiatives tend to be better prepared academically than their peers not enrolled in such initiatives is not surprising. There are several factors that contributed to this situation in the 1991–92 school year. First, many of the largest programs that have been designated as charters—Motivation, several high school Academies, several academic magnet programs—have historically served the most academically prepared students within their schools. Consequently, the composition of students served in charters, when considered as a group, is highly skewed to the most able students in high schools.

Second, as schools have sought to develop new initiatives or charters, they have concentrated—as they were allowed to by the Collaborative—their efforts on first-time ninth graders.[5] However, simultaneously, the Collaborative has prodded schools to address variations in the ninth grade. They have learned that ninth grade includes a wide range of student experiences—students who have never repeated a grade and enter high school at age 14, others who enter high school at age 16 or older, and students who have remained in ninth grade for two or three years without earning sufficient credits to gain tenth-grade standing.

Third, because of apparent logistical and regulatory difficulties in combining nonmainstreamed special education students with regular education students, nonmainstreamed special education students are generally omitted from new initiatives.[6]

Representativeness of students served in all charters. As suggested above, the academic profiles of students enrolled in individual charter programs in 1991–92 indicate that charters serve students who are for the most part not special education students,[7] who are in ninth grade for the first time, and who are not substantially overaged for their grade.[8] The pattern is even more striking when comparing charters as a group. First-time ninth graders in these schools are four times more likely to be enrolled in charters and three times more likely to be enrolled in transitional efforts than are repeating ninth graders.

Schools, the Collaborative, and the district have not reached consensus about the integration of special education with charters *at the school level*. To some extent, the "placement" of special education students within a charter could be accomplished administratively without any substantial expectation that students in self-contained special education programs would be fully integrated into the life of the charter. But what would be the point? On the other hand, the precedent of excluding particular defined populations from charters may be problematic insofar as it is contrary to calls for mainstreaming of special education students, and it could prove to be a convenient strategy for excluding the most hard-to-serve students from charters.

Student stability within charters. The further unresolved issue affecting the schools' ability to extend charter coverage to all students concerns the stability of students *within* the charters during the school year itself and across multiple school years. In theory, charters are schools-within-schools units to which students are enrolled for the duration of their high school careers. However, maintaining such assignments is complicated. Experiences of students and charters during the 1990–91 and 1991–92 school years suggest that turnover within charter enrollments could be substantial. Cross-school migration is a major challenge for the district's public schools. As students' families move or as a result of disciplinary action, students may be transferred from one school to another.

In some instances, entering students who enroll during the academic year are assigned to those courses or, in some instances, programs where substantial attrition has reduced enrollment. While such an approach seems to preserve equity of burden on all teachers, in reality it constitutes placing students in situations where substantial student failure has already occurred. If one reasonably assumes that students who enter a school during the academic year are at some academic risk, it is apparent that such a practice places these students in a doubly disadvantaged situation.

The challenges involved in maintaining charter student stability *over* multiple years are largely unexplored. The examples that do exist—Academies, Motivation, and magnets—may be too specialized to provide much insight into the issue. However, if the benefits of charters are to be achieved, it will be necessary for schools and the district to develop safeguards on the integrity of student assignments within charters from year to year. New policies related to student mobility and assignments of students to charters and programs will need to be developed.

Making provision for uneven student progress. A related challenge for charters has to do with providing appropriate classes for students moving forward at different rates. The most obvious issue, and the one that charters are facing now, is how to serve students who fail. One argument made for large comprehensive high schools is that they are designed to accommodate diverse student needs, despite evidence to the contrary. In moving toward charters, each charter is finding it necessary to develop internal policies and procedures to handle grade promotion and retention. This is currently problematic since most charters are operationalized via grade-level-based block-rostering.

Solutions should most appropriately come from exploiting the unique potential of charters to fashion solutions that meet the individual needs of students. It would be interesting to see if charters can handle uneven student progress by, for example, abolishing grade distinctions (ninth, tenth, eleventh, twelfth) in favor of more individualized instructional sequences or competency-based assessments.

Maintaining the integrity of teacher teams. An assumption undergirding charters is that they will become communities of teachers and students whose activities are focused on a particular educational endeavor. At the heart of this notion is the formation of a group of teachers who can work collegially with one another and with students over time. As operationalized in early charters, this has meant that teachers from the four major subject areas, plus others, depending on a charter's theme, are assigned to work together with a group of students whose number is determined by the full-time equivalent (FTE) complement of teachers involved.

An additional issue concerns the assignment of teachers to more than one charter. In some schools, teachers teach across charters. While it is difficult to assure purity of teaching assignment in small and understaffed schools, charters in larger schools have not been immune to the problem. In one large school, up to 17 teachers have teaching responsibilities in a single charter, but only 1 taught within the charter exclusively. This situation obviously is counter to the charter premise. For students, a potpourri of teachers undermines program continuity and the ability to form relationships with teachers over time. It also creates problems in scheduling classes and in establishing common prep and planning time. A crucial district policy concerns teacher choice and stability.

Further, as leveling and staff shifting across schools occurred in accordance with district and contractual agreements, many charters have had teachers replaced in October and into November. Such changes represent a serious threat to charter stability. Because of the nature of the procedures that govern such transfers, charters that are heavily dependent upon staff who have less seniority are especially at risk of such changes.

Disruption of teacher teams is a serious concern for several reasons. First, loss of charter teachers means recruiting and training replacements. This can be a major task in a setting where team planning, curricula, scheduling, and instructional approaches have been tailored to the charter's theme and may be very different from the replacement teacher's prior experiences. It also means that other charter teachers must devote extra time and effort to the preparation of that teacher (an activity that the team may have thought it had moved beyond). Teacher movement in and out of charters also violates the principle of sustained adult contact.

Resolution of role conflicts. Another specific issue that arose early in the life of charters concerns the locus of instructional leadership. Most large high schools have separate department heads for most disciplines. Department heads serve as both instructional leaders and as quasi-administrators. In the traditional structure of the comprehensive high school, curriculum, scheduling, and instructional issues are all determined within a substantive department.

However, work in charters is interdisciplinary. Teacher teams make cross-discipline decisions about curriculum and scheduling. Teachers in a given subject may incorporate pedagogical approaches to accommodate other subjects that are not consistent with the preferred approach of a specific department. Further, as was noted earlier, teachers in charters are likely to want to deviate substantially from the pacing and content of the standardized curriculum.

Conflict seems inevitable given this type of matrix structure; and, in fact, concerns about instructional leadership roles are widespread. It would be easy to reduce these to "turf issues," but this belies the genuine concerns about standards and instructional quality that underlie some of the disputes. These issues will be difficult to resolve. Until department heads are not accountable for delivery of the standardized curriculum, they will continue to be in the unpleasant position of policing other teachers in their subject area. Further, as long as schools are not wholly broken into charters, it is reasonable to believe that there will continue to be a need for instructional leadership within subject areas. At the same time, a move to charters suggests that the emphasis ought to be on leadership that accommodates interdisciplinary needs and approaches to teaching. The question of shifting roles requires strong district leadership and decentralyzing of critical decision making to teachers.

CHALLENGES WHEN SCHOOLS ARE ENTIRELY COMPOSED OF CHARTERS

Engaging the Full Faculty

As long as charters remain one of several teaching options for faculty in the comprehensive high schools, the fact that not every teacher embraces the charter concept is an issue, but not an absolute barrier to success. However, one goal of restructuring is for the comprehensive high schools to be divided fully into charter communities. As this becomes more and more true, the need for all teachers to be engaged and supportive becomes more pressing.

Our sense is that charters have begun to emerge as a primary source of renewal within comprehensive high schools. Their initial success—including student performance as well as increased attention throughout the district— has allayed some of the concerns held by many teachers. At the same time, the promise of charters—including their structure, "differentness," and integrity —is integral to teacher support. When charters have not been fully realized either in structure or content, teachers have appropriately questioned whether charters are just another misadventure in school improvement, enjoying little support within the school or district administration. The challenge in ensuring continued and broad teacher support for charters and renewal will be in achieving the "promise" of charters.

Allocation of Resources

As schools become fully organized into charters, issues related to allocation of resources may emerge as a critical factor driving school operations and charter success. We perceive two areas of allocation that will likely need to be addressed—access and control over common school resources and equity in distribution of allocatable resources to charters.

As schools coalesce around charter organizations, how is access to facilities, services, and courses offerings apportioned among existing charters? For example, does a business charter receive primary access to computer science facilities and course offerings? Do students in a vocationally linked charter receive preference in courses in vocational education? If an arts-focused charter emerges, does this mean that all music and arts teachers are assigned to it and that the charter has direct control over music and arts facilities? Issues concerning access, control, and use of common school resources are just now beginning to surface in schools. The devolution of common school resources to charters might represent a substantial challenge to schools that will need to examine assumptions and presumed prerogatives over these resources.

The second issue related to school resources concerns the distribution of allocatable resources—budgets, staff, renewable supplies, and equipment—among charters. As schools are currently configured, the allocation of resources theoretically occurs equitably since all students have relatively equal access to such resources. However, under a charter configuration, it is unclear how such resources would be distributed. For example, a science-based charter may require substantial investments of resources in both renewable supplies and specialized equipment on a relatively continual basis. In contrast, a humanities charter may require substantially fewer supplies and relatively little specialized equipment. Recognizing that schools will continue to face tight budgets, what will be the process for providing costly equipment that might be fundamental to a science charter balanced against equally compelling needs of health-, humanities-, or arts-focused charters? Simply deciding that each charter deserves an equal proportion of resources based on enrollments probably belies the genuine differences in needs across charters. Similarly, efforts to prioritize allocations on the basis of "contribution to the school or students" would likely introduce even greater discord within the school.

Governance

The emergence of charters within high schools immediately challenges traditional responsibilities concerning oversight, monitoring, and evaluation. For example, in those schools in which assistant principals had been assigned responsibility over specific academic departments, such assignments may become superfluous. Similarly, as noted above, issues related to evaluation of classroom practice become very cloudy in schools that retain department heads and charter coordinators.

As governance issues are advanced under the district's movement toward shared decision making/school-based management, what will be the role of these different positions in that structure? Will the governance council reflect charters or departments or both? How will this be accomplished? Will governance councils have limited or absolute control over matters within charters? What will be the principal's responsibility over charter affairs?

Governance also emerges as a key issue *within* charters. At present, charter coordinators are technically *appointed*. In some instances, an incumbent is placed in the position on the basis of consensus by other teachers assigned to the charter. In other instances, the principal selects the coordinator. The scope of charter coordinator responsibilities varies substantially across charters. In some charters, coordinators are the primary administrator for that charter; in others, coordinators have assumed primary educational leadership for the charter as well. Some charters are organized hierarchically; others make decisions consensually.

CONCLUSION

Charters have emerged as a school-based, institutionalized approach to restructuring comprehensive high schools. They offer both students and teachers a degree of affiliation that had become virtually impossible to develop and sustain in large urban secondary schools while simultaneously preserving some of the broad range of opportunities afforded through large educational settings. As charters have developed, they have provided an occasion for rethinking curricula, and instructional approaches as well as alternative ways of delivering a full range of services to students. Many charters have emerged as laboratories for educational renewal and reform. They have given both students and teachers the "space" to explore different approaches to learning and teaching. Charters offer a compelling approach to restructuring. They consciously build on the strengths of individual teachers, and they permit these "front-line" educational practitioners to have substantial control over how education is delivered to students. Finally, as more of their instructional potential is realized, charters can provide students with a transformed educational experience that offers strong instruction, academic and social support, and a setting that focuses on the individual needs of each student.

NOTES

1. Including three that were off-site, essentially separate, schools.

2. It is important to note that designation as a charter does not necessarily mean that all criteria have been achieved. For example, many new charters that began in September 1991 comprised only 60 students (i.e., two classes of ninth graders) but were anticipated to quadruple the number of students served as the program evolves into a four-year, vertical house.

3. The level reported for ninth graders is somewhat misleading. In at least two schools, more than 25% of all ninth graders are assigned to programs that are classified as transitional programs from which ninth-grade students will move into bona fide charters in the subsequent grade.

4. It should be noted that several charter and transitional programs were specifically designed to serve at-risk students, including repeating and overaged ninth graders. However, there were relatively few of these programs and the number of students they served is quite small in comparison with the size of charters that serve the most academically able. It is important to recognize, though, that charters targeted at repeaters and overaged students also create homogeneous student bodies.

5. To some extent, this may be a function of school and staff perceptions of recruitment for new programs. In general, in developing a new initiative and then soliciting students to enroll in it, charter and program coordinators have relied heavily upon recruiting students within feeder schools. Consequently, the bulk of students entering these programs are first-time ninth graders and often drawn from students who are not classified as special education or who have not been retained in grades in elementary or middle schools.

6. Data available about students enrolled in the more than 80 separate charters during the 1991–92 school year reveal that some progress is being made in some charters to include more potentially hard-to-serve students within charters. For example, more than one-half of all the charters enrolled 10 or more repeating ninth graders. On the other hand, special education students were rarely enrolled in charters. Only six charters enrolled more than 10 special education students. In our analyses we have used a slightly more restrictive definition of special education than is normally used within the district. Specifically, we have excluded from the special education student classification those students who are labeled as itinerant special education students whose roster assigns them for the majority of time to regular education courses. Itinerant special education students are counted as regular education students in our analyses. However, it is important to note that relatively few students are classified as itinerant special education students. For example, in the 1990–91 school year, only 697 of the more than 38,000 students across all grades in comprehensive high schools were classified as itinerant special education students. We conclude that counting these students as regular education students results in no detectable differences in findings and interpretations.

7. As noted above, we count as special education students all students identified by the district as special education students *with the exception of 697 special education itinerant students* who take the large majority of their academic program in regular education classes.

8. This latter characteristic is used as an indicator of previous failure or retention in grade at the elementary or middle school levels.

REFERENCES

Bennett, S. (1987). *New dimensions in research on class size and academic achievement.* Madison, WI: National Center on Effective Secondary Schools.

Brown, D. J. (1991). *Decentralization: The administrator's guidebook to school district change*. Newbury Park: Corwin Press.

Carroll, J. M. (1989). *The Copernican Plan: Restructuring the American high school*. Andover, MA: The Regional Laboratory.

Education Commission of the States' Task Force on Education and Economic Growth. (1983). *Action for excellence*. Denver, CO: Education Commission of the States.

Fine, M. (1986). Why urban adolescents drop into and out of public high school. *Teachers College Record, 87*, 393–409.

Goodlad, J. I. (1983). *A place called school: Prospects for the future*. New York: McGraw-Hill.

Hamilton, S. (1986). Raising standards and reducing dropout rates. *Teachers College Record, 87*, 410–420.

Hess, G. A., & Lauber, D. (1985). *Dropouts from the Chicago public schools: An analysis of the classes of 1982, 1983 and 1984*. Chicago: Chicago Panel on Public School Finances.

Marburger, C. (1990). The school site level: Involving parents in reform. In S. B. Bacharach (Ed.), *Education reform: Making sense of it all*, pp. 82–91. Boston: Allyn & Bacon.

McMullan, B., Leiderman, S., & Wolf, W. (1988). *Reclaiming the future: A framework for improving student success and reducing dropout rates in Philadelphia*. Bala Cynwyd, PA: Center for Assessment and Policy Development.

Oakes, J. (1985). *Keeping track: How schools structure inequality*. New Haven: Yale University Press.

Passow, A. H. (1990). How it happened, wave by wave: Whither (or wither?) school reform? In S. B. Bacharach (Ed.), *Education reform: Making sense of it all*, pp. 10–19. Boston: Allyn & Bacon.

Powell, A. G., Farrar, E., & Cohen, D. K. (1985). *The shopping mall high school*. Boston: Houghton Mifflin.

Sizer, T. (1984). *Horace's compromise: The dilemma of the American high school*. Boston: Houghton Mifflin.

Wehlage, G. (1983). *Effective programs for the marginal high school student*. Bloomington: Phi Delta Kappan Educational Foundation.

Wehlage, G., & Rutter, R. (1986). Dropping out: How much do schools contribute to the problem? *Teachers College Record, 87*, 374–392.

PART II

Silencing, Inquiry, and Reflection in Public School Bureaucracies

Michelle Fine

1984—*Silencing by Exiling.* Eight years ago, I was studying a cohort of high school dropouts and "stay ins" in a South Bronx alternative school, only to "discover" that dropouts were significantly *less depressed, more politically* aware, more *concerned with racial and class injustice,* and *less conforming.* I finished that work worried about dropouts who carry powerful social and educational critiques as they flee and are exiled from their schools. I was equally worried about students who stay in schools growing depressed, self-blaming for social problems, unconcerned with racial and class injustices, and highly conforming.

In 1984 I started writing about dropouts as critics, about the silencing and the purging of social critique that characterize public schools. Little did I know the depths of public schools' commitment to shutting down critical conversations about students' experiences lived through race, ethnicity, class, gender, and sexuality.

1985—*Silencing Through a Pedagogy of Control.* I spent a year in a public urban high school, in Manhattan, trying to understand how only 20% of the typical ninth-grade cohort ever graduated; why dropping out was more typical than graduation. I observed classes, interviewed graduates and dropouts, analyzed the written texts of ninth and twelfth graders, and watched conversations such as the following get shut down:

TEACHER: Who knows what EOE stands for?
BLACK MALE STUDENT: Equal overtime.

TEACHER: No. Anyone else?
STUDENT: Equal opportunity.
TEACHER: Right. Now, what does that mean?
(*No answer.*)
TEACHER: Well, it means that no one can be discriminated against in employment if the store says EOE.
BLACK MALE STUDENT: But I know stores where they just hire white people.
TEACHER: Not if it says EOE. Then they can't discriminate on the basis of race, gender, or marital status.

Changed subject.

When I asked this teacher why she did not pursue this conversation about discrimination and racism, she explained that it would "demoralize the students." It was then that I started writing about silencing as a pedagogical form of control by which educators evict the lived cultures and experiences of students from the very classrooms in which they are supposed to be educated. Soon thereafter I came to see how thoroughly educators, too, have been silenced in public schools.

> 1989—*Silencing Through Race and Class Flight: Residential Redlining and Lawsuits for "Choice."* I served as an expert witness in a New Jersey racial deintegration case. The white elite parents of students were suing in the name of "choice" to switch from an integrated suburban high school to an exclusively white and elite suburban high school in a neighboring community. When I interviewed students in the [white] segregated school to which the plaintiffs would be transferred, one student indicated: "I hope they [white transfer students] do come here. My father pays taxes. So I deserve to go to the best school possible. Everyone has choices. Those students should be free to come to this school, and not have to go to school with kids who wear torn clothing."

In 1989 I started writing about such calls for "parental choice," covers for race- and class-based flight, as a form of silencing, a legitimation of injustice. Privileging those historically privileged and disadvantaging those historically disadvantaged, New Jersey's residential and academic segregation reinforced, in the minds of many, what appear to be "natural" distinctions among classes and races.

Across four year I had accumulated lots of evidence of the strategies by which students' voices, cultures, and passions were silenced inside public schools—through strategies of suspension and alienation, through pedagogies of control, and through the "free choice" of white middle-class and middle-class parents of color, to flee integration and engage in redlining.

Now: 1988 through present—*Silencing as Bureaucracy*. Now I work with this major urban restructuring effort. By dismantling large anonymous bureaucratic structures of high school, educators and parents are inventing educator-designed, parent-involved, and student-empowered communities of learning called charters. Through my work with these high school educators, parents, and students and work with Chicago, New York, and Baltimore reform, I have come to see how thoroughly *silencing* defines life inside public education bureaucracies. The risks attached to speaking aloud, raising critique, voicing possibility, questioning traditional practices, and challenging social injustices are felt to be enormous. In many major cities, educators echo horror stories about what happens if you are not "loyal." The adverse consequences can be devastating.

I now understand that the African American and Latino dropouts in the South Bronx, the ones who voiced critique and were purged, should serve simply as a metaphor for the suffocation and exiling of critical voices throughout public education bureaucracies. I now understand what a risk it is for educators, students, or parents to speak aloud of social and educational injustices, to try to construct classes that engage these topics, to reinvent the work of schools and classrooms to create democratic, critical conversations about race, ethnicity, class, gender, and sexuality. Further, I have come to see that public schools in the late twentieth century have the awesome job of containing a major contradiction of public education. On the one hand public schools are supposed to be *the* site in which hard work reaps benefits that will allow young people to hop social classes, to escape the scars of racism and classism, to collect the skills that will "free them" from the overdeterminism of their upbringing. On the other hand, schools end up reproducing the very class, race, and gender inequities we want to believe they can erase.

Schools have become tense, contradiction-filled, and contradiction-containing sites in which educators, even those with the best of intentions, confront a paradox. Do they open the spaces for young people to explore the pains and possibilities of life inside an unjust society, or do they "paper" over the inequities and anesthetize the pains? As a deeply disempowered group themselves, educators often opt for the latter strategy. Without a sense of power to control their own work lives, much less to influence the life courses of their students growing up in poverty, many educators lean, as I might, toward avoiding the difficult topics, which may inadvertently give students a sense that they are not supposed to voice the pains, worry about the tensions, or even imagine the possibilities.

THE COSTS OF SILENCING

The costs of silencing remain relatively undocumented and are visible only in a most distorted form. Silenced students look passive and unmotivated and seem to have a "bad attitude." Silenced teachers look burned out and callous. Silenced parents look like they are apathetic, as if they just do not care about education. Once we blame *them*—students, teachers, and parents—we need look no further at the systemic causes, or consequences, of silencing. And yet . . .

All those teachers who fled the system, for the same reasons that the dropouts did—because they were depressed, concerned about social injustice and carrying powerful critique about bureaucracy—were muted and banished. The loss of these teachers is an enormous cost. Educators have shared with me their belief that some of the most creative teachers leave within the first few years of teaching, like those South Bronx dropouts. Others say they quietly shut their doors to keep the bureaucracy from invading the creative possibilities of their classrooms. In the name of "autonomy," they privatize public education and diminish their own investment in a public democratic community called school. Among those who go and among those who stay, there is a serious cost to the spirit, empowerment, and sense of community; they are diminished inside schools that feel "like prisons" to the teachers and students who attend, or those who do not.

The costs to students excluded, marginalized, and ultimately lost are enormous. Those students who are kept out of "good" public schools, because of geography, class, and/or race, lose out on what is considered a "quality education," while those in schools that are segregated, that is, all white and elite, are deprived of a diverse social education necessary for critical democratic citizenship. Those few tokens who are "allowed" into "good schools" usually pay a price of suppressing their biographies, voices, pains, passions, and sense of history. They pay dearly. As one African American young woman explained about her almost exclusively white school, "They like me as long as I don't remind them that I am black. So I can't act too black."

In many urban neighborhood high schools, only 20% to 40% of ninth graders ever graduate. When most leave prior to graduation, it is assumed somehow "natural." If we assume that they have been silenced, discouraged, and expelled—and made to look as if it was *their* doing—then the injustice is stunning. Ultimately the costs to a democratic and pluralistic society are enormous. If we cannot figure out how to invent participatory, democratic learning communities inside public schools, rich with respected differences, then I worry that the prospects for inventing such communities anywhere are dismal.

THE POSSIBILITIES OF INQUIRY

The chapters in this section reveal how tensions about silencing and inquiry have waxed and waned within this district's school reform movement. Over the past four years, undoing silencing and provoking reflection have been central to transforming "what is" into "what could be." Toward this end, educators, students, consultants, and parents have been engaged in two very different forms of speaking aloud—reflecting critically on institutional conditions as they have been, and imagining schools as they could be. Our work has been designed to provoke a sense of possibility with educators who have labored long and hard within institutions left behind by "select high schools," educators who have learned to *not* reflect publicly on student outcomes, educators who have learned not to dream, who have been suffocated for an average of 20 years in federal, state, and local bureaucracies. In the beginning, these adults addressed neither school-based inequities nor school-based possibilities.

Inquiry and reflection, more than any one of us knew, proved to be delicious and dangerous territory. Many felt they could not invite students into inquiry because reflection felt so unsafe to them, individually and collectively. Piercing the air of fear and vulnerability that hovered over our first two years, conversations about race, class, culture, or gender, as well as intellectual inquiry, were nearly impossible to ignite among colleagues, within schools, or in coalition with parents.

The chapters that follow trace the biographies of these silences and anxieties as well as the conversations that were finally pried open within charters. Inquiry has developed into a powerful, sometimes exhilarating, thread in our reform movement. The five chapters in this section speak to the crustiness of silencing that has saturated public schools, and they give witness to the dramatic transformations in relationships, pedagogies, curriculum, and assessment provoked once messy forms of inquiry are engaged in. In Chapter 5, Virginia Vanderslice and Shirley Farmer write about a group of faculty, parents, students, and community members who pursued an activist research study of their school–community relations aimed at transforming school culture through broad and critical analysis of life inside and outside the building. In Chapter 6, Jody Cohen writes about the intellectual and political delights and minefields that constitute life inside a vibrant charter that has positioned inquiry at its heart. Linda Powell's Chapter 7 takes us into family group, where educators ask students and each other to pry open "personal" and "social" stories to blend with and transform "academic life." Nancie Zane, in Chapter 8, examines the critical unraveling of "discipline" within traditional schools and then charters. Finally, Pat Macpherson commits the ultimate narrative trick in Chapter 9, as she turns inquiry back onto a group of ethnographers who thought we were simply inquiring about "them"—a set of educators in charters. At the whim of Macpherson's pen, "we" became the object of ethnographic inquiry.

Together these chapters tell a story of the deep and essential connections between silencing and bureaucracy, and between inquiry and reform. While these chapters reveal the treacherous aspects of life in public bureaucracies that keep inquiry and reflection remote, they also expose the delights and surprises that critical conversations can produce inside democratic, public educational communities. Reading these chapters, you will hear why inquiry is so important to reform and how rupturing it can be to the traditions of silence that constitute public schooling.

5

Transforming Ourselves: Becoming an Inquiring Community

VIRGINIA VANDERSLICE
SHIRLEY FARMER

Following the true intent of action research (Argyris & Schön, 1978; Lewin, 1948; Lippitt, 1965), data can be collected and generated, analyzed and utilized to continually inform and transform the vision of restructuring toward which individual schools are working. In this chapter, we take as an example one school currently in the midst of a full restructuring effort to describe the variety of ways in which the staff has come to seek out and use data to inform the process of organizational change, to become a community of critical inquiry.

As part of the Philadelphia Schools Collaborative effort to support the restructuring of comprehensive high schools, Muñoz Marin High School (MHS), a relatively small neighborhood high school, became a school committed to fully rethinking the educational and organizational structure of their school. As part of this process, a core of MHS staff evolved into a "community of inquiry" as they embarked upon, and continue to work through, the ongoing process of change.

As the restructuring process has developed at MHS, subgroups of the MHS staff and community learned to systematically gather and examine data about the school community, students and parents, teachers, and themselves. The context within which this has occurred has been one in which, prior to restructuring, quantitative data had been collected and used at the district level to identify schools that were not performing according to district standards. Individual schools had no input into which data were collected, nor were they asked how accurately the data reflected the specific situation in their schools or how they would interpret them. Thus schools had little if any experience that would lead them to view research as a vehicle for creatively gathering information that could be used productively in problem solving and decision making.

The restructuring process at MHS has been informed by a variety of types of data. Quantitative data about the demographics, attendance, and achievement of MHS students represented the most traditional form of data used by the group. For the first time in their history, teachers could examine these data and generate their own interpretations as "planners" of a more effective high school. This use of data diverged dramatically from previous encounters with district-generated data. In the past, educators had been presented with predetermined statistics and interpretations. These moments were always experienced as "pointing the finger of blame" at teachers for poor student performance. They had never been asked which data or analyses they would like, never been asked to engage in interpretation, and never been invited to use data for generating future institutional images.

Second, qualitative data were generated by the MHS staff and parents in a deliberate attempt to better understand the working-class community in which Muñoz Marin High School was located. This included general staff observations about the student population as well as structured interviews of current students and their parents, entering students and their parents, students who had dropped out and their parents and community members.

A third form of data was generated by the Restructuring Council at MHS through self-reflective research. In some cases the Council attempted to learn the attitudes of the broader staff and then use that information in problem solving or decision making. This kind of data often involved making *implicit* assumptions *explicit* (e.g., that only a small number of staff were enthusiastic about creating significant change) or giving voice to multiple perspectives that then allowed for the creative generation of solutions (e.g., determining the varieties of reasons that staff were not committed to implementing particular programs, such as family groups). In other cases, the Restructuring Council used interviews and questionnaires to assess their own perspectives and experiences as Council members. This process allowed members to voice opinions they felt were potentially too explosive or divisive to express individually (e.g., issues about dissatisfaction with the lack of participation of some Council members, frustration with decision-making processes, and concerns that racism was a factor in Council decisions).

The fourth type of data collected involved information about possibilities for urban secondary school reform. These data were generated from investigating what other schools were doing and what was "working" in other districts from reading the relevant literature, inviting principals and teachers from other schools to talk to staff at MHS about their programs, and visiting schools outside the district. These data served to stimulate people's visions about what could be as well as motivate them to move toward those visions. Basically, these data helped unfreeze, for school staff, notions of structure, instruction, and assessment (e.g., the 48-minute period was not sacred, school did not have to begin in September and end in June, affective needs could become part of the curriculum, serious learning could take place in settings outside the classroom, disciplines did not have to be taught separately and in sequence, and the school day did not have to be limited to six hours).

The convergence of these divergent data, over time, has continued to shape and reshape the direction and motivation for change within the school. In the next section of this chapter, we detail four pivotal and descriptive moments that provided the settings in which research became an integral part of our efforts at school change. Those moments were (1) the Phoenix Project; (2) the internal school struggle about whether and how to implement family groups; (3) Restructuring Council planning retreats; and (4) responding to new information about student attendance and achievement. First, we present some background information on Muñoz Marin High School to establish the context in which this change effort is taking place.

AN INTRODUCTION TO MUÑOZ MARIN HIGH SCHOOL

Muñoz Marin High School serves nearly 1,000 students in an urban community that was once entirely white working class. Today it is 41% Hispanic, 15% African American, 7% Asian American, and only 37% Caucasian. As the restructuring process was getting underway, in 1988–89, this high school had extremely low student attendance rates (average daily attendance for the previous year was just over 60%) and extremely high dropout rates (out of 380 entering ninth graders, 73 graduated in 1990).

MHS was staffed by 60 teachers who, consistent with the pattern throughout the district, had been at the school for an average of 14 years. Many felt demoralized by poor student attendance and low achievement. The focus of conversations about what needed to happen to improve the school was either to "find a way to force students to attend" or to "create programs to attract better students" ("the kind of students we used to have"). A small number of teachers believed that different kinds of educational programs needed to be developed to better speak to the variety of learning styles of the students who did come to MHS. In addition, MHS teachers had worked under the same principal for 17 years. He was characterized as obstructing the entire concept of school-based change.

The restructuring process began at MHS as a response to the districtwide initiative for every high school to rethink and plan programs for the ninth grade. Existing data made it clear that this was the critical year in which large numbers of students dropped out. At MHS the first glimmer of turning teachers into researchers occurred as one teacher collected available data weekly and monthly from students' attendance sheets, roll books, and report cards, recorded it graphically, and disseminated it to the full staff. At that time, the Renewal Council (a 10-member planning group made up of six teachers, a department head, a vice principal, the principal, and the building representative) reviewed the data but found they were not detailed enough to provide much guidance in program development. As one Council member said, "We see these circles indicating student absences in our roll books and yet we don't know the stories behind them."

THE PHOENIX PROJECT

In the 1989–90 school year, MHS was still showing no progress in reaching students who were poor attenders and/or were dropping out. However, before that school year began, the principal resigned and was replaced by a woman who had been a vice principal under him. She was both energetic and deeply committed to providing students with a successful educational experience. With her support, the Council concluded that the school needed broad and deep restructuring if students were to be reached and the school was to survive. The Philadelphia Schools Collaborative agreed that the student performance to date indicated that the school's entire educational process needed to be rethought. With that in mind, the Collaborative agreed to fund a summer institute for rethinking this high school, for as many staff members as were interested. They engaged in 50 hours of thinking about and planning a new vision for education at MHS. This project became known as the Phoenix Project and took place with the participation of 42 staff members, parents, and community members during the summer of 1990.

The planning for Phoenix was designed by a subcommittee of four teachers representing different perspectives in the school, the principal, and an organizational change consultant. Shirley Farmer was one of the teachers on the planning subcommittee and Virginia Vanderslice was the consultant. The process was loosely based on a problem-solving model that self-consciously transformed participants into researchers, using a variety of data sources to inform their planning efforts.

Prior to the beginning of the program, each participant was given a notebook of readings selected and compiled by the planning subcommittee. All participants were given time before the first session to complete the readings, which included conceptual and applied articles covering organizational change and school-restructuring efforts from across the country. As one planning team member put it, "Participants need a common language and this is one way to give it to them." Teachers on the planning committee designed this "reader" so that participants would consider innovative educational strategies. They believed that the readings would also challenge teachers' beliefs in the inevitability of a 48-minute class, seven- or eight-period days, teaching only one subject at a time, and grading only by standardized tests. They were right. Learning about and examining a variety of educational plans allowed Phoenix teachers to cull elements they believed they could use to better respond to their students. It also legitimized the process of replacing assumptions about how schools had to be structured; it freed and inspired them to imagine a dramatically different school.

The second type of research that took place during the Phoenix project took the form of inviting principals and teachers from four schools in other cities, with somewhat similar student populations, to describe their programs to Phoenix participants. Their presentations cultivated images from which Phoenix participants drew ideas about possibilities, provoking participants to generate creative ideas for improving the educational experience for students and teachers. The idea of charters as smaller learning communities was a notion that many staff found compelling. As one member put it:

> [In a charter] you get to know more about kids—everything including their blood type. When you thought about it, there we were with kids from 7:47 to 2:46—all those hours, four years, and *nothing*. It had to be wrong. Knowing a smaller group of students intimately has to change our relationship with them. The charter structure was a place in which we could change and accept our share of the responsibility for student achievement and failure.

These presentations were the source, for example, of the idea of family groups that was adopted later by the Phoenix Project as a key piece of their new educational plan. Family groups are a small group of students (8–15) who meet with one adult (teacher or staff member) two to five times a week to discuss academic, affective, and personal issues. Family groups can be structured in a variety of ways, but the intent is usually to provide students with one adult who knows and cares about them, as well as to create a grouping of students who care about and help one another. Often family groups include students across all grade levels, and students stay in same family group for their entire high school life. The family group concept captured the MHS staff suggestion that students would benefit from more intensive and regular contact with at least one adult, and that that adult would be in a good position to learn what kinds of assistance individual students needed and to access appropriate resources.

The next process for transforming these educators, parents, and community members into applied data-collecting researchers was one of the most powerful moments in the Phoenix Project.[1] We realized that in order to do effective planning, Phoenix participants needed data about students who stayed in and dropped out of school as well as about the community that MHS served. This was critical because very few MHS staff members lived in the community, and many lived outside of the city limits. Teachers on the Phoenix planning team strongly believed that turning participants into researchers would be a powerful strategy for getting staff to understand the community in which their students lived. The team developed a plan in which all participants were assigned to 3- to 4-person groups. Each group contacted and interviewed—by phone or in person—students and parents from a list of current and incoming ninth graders that included regular and irregular attenders as well as dropouts. Staff were given a basic interview format they could alter. Interviewing do's and don'ts, presented by community members, called attention to cultural differences in Hispanic and Asian homes. This was particularly important since, with only two Hispanic staff members, most teachers were unaware of subtle cultural dynamics. Community members and parents told staff what to expect and how to best present themselves if they visited people in their homes. For example, one community worker told the teachers, "If you go into an Hispanic home and both the mother and father are present, direct your questions to the father out of respect for his position in the family or he will be insulted."

To maximize community awareness, groups that interviewed exclusively by phone were asked to spend at least one hour in the community as participant–observers of community life.

This moment in our collaborative work proved to be a major turning point for Phoenix participants. Through their roles as researchers, staff gathered data that changed their thinking about students, the community, and one another. Staff who had initially feared, and therefore resisted, going into the community were convinced by conversations with parents and community members that it was safe to make home and community visits. They returned with both wonderful and depressing stories about their experiences and the data they had collected. They also came back eager to share and compare feelings, experiences, observations, and information.

The process of doing these interviews allowed educators who had worked together for an average of 15 years to construct a unified yet complex picture of the many dimensions of the school's community and students' lives. They developed a new sense of the potential for connecting school and community. As researchers, staff began to believe not only that the school could be different but also that they were not alone in their desire to make it so. They had previously presumed they were working against the community and that parents did not care. Through the interviewing process, they found out how wrong they were. Interested community members were eager to be of assistance and parents were willing to be involved if only someone would tell them how. The interviewing experience forced them to confront individually the narrowness of their own attitudes and beliefs about students, their families, and the community and to concretize, collectively, the concerns and needs their school would have to address with community resources. For example, one teacher noted his surprise in learning that some parents, rather than being uninterested in their child, felt out of control and unable to influence their child's behavior. Similarly another teacher told us, "One parent I interviewed wanted me to find a residential program for her daughter where someone else might be able to get her to change her behavior. She told me her daughter just watches television all day and she can't stop her." Other teachers learned that parents were frustrated with the "thin communication lines" between school and home. As a direct result of this interviewing experience, many of the participants voiced the strong opinion that all teachers should be required to do interviews in the community at least once a year.

The team interviewing process and entering the community together changed the relationships among staff participating in the retreat. One teacher commented:

> Participation on these interview teams has changed teachers' attitudes about each other. Their previous shared experiences had almost all taken place inside the school building and, even then, were limited to discussions of curriculum and complaints about the earlier administration. This process allowed us to experience each other in new ways.

Following this experience, the tone of the group changed. Staff members who had previously kept an uneasy distance from one another began joking with one another. One staff member said, "Before this summer, I never thought Mark and I had anything to say to each other." Another staff member, who was generally viewed as antagonistic in his relationship with the renewal leadership group, publicly announced appreciation for another member's leadership role in the group by standing up and asking the group to give a round of applause for this person's leadership. Staff who had expressed negative attitudes about the school began to find constructive channels for their energy. A teacher who began the Phoenix Project with a strongly negative comment, became one of the leaders in suggesting deep, creative, positive changes.

The effect of Phoenix spread beyond the direct participants during the fall. We began the school year with a meeting in which members of the Phoenix Project addressed the full staff to update them on the summer's work. The Phoenix group stood together in the front of the auditorium, wearing T-shirts created to commemorate their summer planning, and presented their vision for the future, inviting other staff to join the effort. A staff member who had not attended Phoenix commented:

> That was the moment that I knew things were going to be different. I felt the energy of the group in the front of the auditorium and I knew that I wanted to be part of it. For me, this was a major turning point. I

had been completely shut down for the past 10 years, and I never would have believed that I'd ever feel that there was any hope of things really changing around here. I was prepared to simply wait it out until retirement.

SELF-REFLECTION AS RESEARCH

At the end of its first year of operation, the MHS Council again used research to facilitate its work. This time, the Council was the focus of its own research. In an effort to identify areas where it had been successful and areas where improvement was needed, Council members customized a survey originally developed by Philadelphia Schools Collaborative consultants, and then each member filled one out individually. Included were questions about such issues as how well parents had been integrated as Council members, how successful the Council had been at communicating with the larger staff in the school, how much support Council members thought they were getting from the school administration, how successful they believed they had been in planning and following through, and generally how well they perceived the Council was functioning as a working group.

The Council's consultant tabulated and summarized the answers. The Council then scheduled a planning retreat at which the summarized data were presented. The data provided the focal point for the Council to understand what they had done well (in terms both of process and outcomes) and what they had not done well. The Council discussion of these data became the basis for planning for the fall. A major problem that was identified, for example, was that we had not yet discovered effective ways to involve parents in the decision-making process or the planning of Council agendas. One difficulty in utilizing parental input was the shifts in their work schedules and employment situations, which prevented consistent attendance at Council meetings. The survey data helped us to verbalize this problem. An hour-long discussion followed during which we decided to schedule our meetings to maximize the opportunities for parent involvement. During the discussion we learned, for example, that our tendency to call meetings without much advance notice and routinely to change the day and time of meetings according to when staff could be available made it difficult, if not impossible, for parents with set schedules to attend.

Another issue indicated by the data from the self-assessment survey was the need for improved communication strategies with the whole staff. Our collective opinion about our lack of success led us to examine what communication strategies we felt had and had not worked. Out of this examination came several new ideas for getting information to the staff and input from the staff. Ideas ranged from having regular, short, whole-staff updates, to the creation of a Council newsletter, to increasing our efforts to include staff participation on Council task groups. These ideas have guided our efforts this year to keep staff included and informed.

FAMILY GROUP PROBLEM SOLVING AS RESEARCH

One of the significant agreements to come out of the Phoenix summer was to institute family groups on a schoolwide basis. This would have meant every student would be connected to a staff member by participating in a small (10- to 15-member) family group. Staff members from principal to custodian would be responsible for a family of students across grade levels. We were invested in this idea because it addressed our concern that many students were just "floating" in and out of school without the sense that someone really knew them, noticed whether they were there or not, or cared. We believed family groups would address students' emotional as well as academic lives.

Before any more decisions could be made about family groups, we needed to understand all the problems and issues that were the basis for negative feelings about family group in the staff. Our first effort in data collection was to gather and organize the information that each of us already had. Our goal was to create a common understanding of the issues and concerns surrounding family group implementation. In order to do this, we participated in a structured problem-solving process. First, we defined the goal: to have each student connected to one adult in the school in a meaningful and ongoing relationship. Then we defined the problem: Some staff did not want to participate in a family group. Next, we undertook a force-field analysis in which we listed the factors that were keeping us from reaching our goal and the forces that would help us reach our goal. The list of blocking forces was an accounting of all the reasons staff had given for not wanting to participate.

We offered an evening family group training session open to all staff with the purpose of providing a clearer idea of how family groups worked and what kinds of issues could be discussed in that forum. The turnout was very high, much greater than expected.

After the training, the Council realized that even if we could solve the problems we had identified, we did not know how many staff members were seriously interested in working with family groups. We heard some people complaining, but we had no idea how many. More research was needed. At that point, the Council developed a questionnaire and distributed it to the staff. We found, to our surprise, that well over half the staff were interested in being involved in family group. We were thus disabused of our notion that only minimal support existed for this program. We believed the information and training sessions that we planned had changed some people from negative to positive. We learned how to use research to get "unstuck."

FOCUS ON ATTENDANCE

Substantial amounts of quantitative data about attendance and achievement of our high school students were collected at the end of the 1990–91 school year. Unfortunately, the data showed clearly that on both attendance and achievement measures, MHS had had a pattern of continuous decline over the last three years. Even in programs that were specifically created to improve attendance and achievement for a defined student population, neither attendance nor achievement improved, compared to similar student populations in focused programs in other comprehensive high schools. The data were distressing. The first thing that we did, once these data were brought to the attention of the Council, was to appoint a subcommittee to pursue attendance issues. This group was to be expanded to include representatives from each charter and transitional program in the school. Its task was to track the data to determine which programs were successfully improving attendance. Then the subcommittee was to decide how to expand and support those efforts in charters or programs that were not experiencing as much success.

First the subcommittee requested that the data coordinator create a weekly summary of attendance data by grade level within program. One dynamic that was clear from the data for the first month of the 1991–92 year, for example, was that students in charters and transitional programs had an attendance rate that was about 14 percentage points higher than that of noncharter students. We saw immediate charter expansion as a way to include more staff in charters at a time when staff members who were eager to get involved could not see a way in.

Next, we wanted to identify initiatives being made within charters and programs to improve attendance and to learn what seemed to be working. We asked charter coordinators to describe their efforts, and in the process we all learned much that we might not otherwise have discovered—or at least we would not have discovered so quickly or in such a systematic way. The coordinator of the Business Academy (which was in its second year) told us, for example, that last year they had taken attendance during advisory (second period) and then called students' homes later in the day. They found this strategy yielded an immediate, but only short-term, effect on attendance. The students they called showed up the next day, but did not continue to come. So this year, the charter staff modified their plan. Now they take attendance at the beginning of the first-period class and one teacher who is not teaching that period calls homes immediately. Another suggested using some of the charter's grant money to hire a parent for an hour a day to make morning calls to homes.

Another charter decided to tie participation in trips to attendance. For the week prior to a program trip, students had to attend all classes. To track attendance, each student was given a trip ticket to be signed by each charter teacher in classes the week before the trip.

Each charter had other interesting attendance strategies that they were devising and revising. Coordinators found this initial meeting so stimulating that we decided to catalogue all the strategies being used, noting what different programs had learned about what was working and how to improve it. Then we would publish the catalogue for all teachers to stimulate their thinking about how to improve attendance. This would also be a method for giving recognition to staff who came up with new ideas.

At the moment, we are still following the attendance data each month and developing or expanding strategies that will have a long-term effect. We are also in the initial stages of creating a system within each charter for tracking the effect of such programs as calling homes or having charter staff teams interview students to see whether these techniques are changing students' behaviors.

IN CLOSING AND CONTINUING . . .

We write this at a time when we are immersed in the process of change, and we have learned much. There are many ways in which the school staff as a community has evolved over the last three years, and we are still struggling to make many other changes.

Transforming ourselves into a community of researchers—asking questions, collecting relevant data, and then planning actions based upon that data —has not been a process that has grown easily out of our experience. It still seems more automatic for us to hear or see that there is a problem and then to craft quick responses. When we make plans for a specific change, for example, and two or three staff voice strong opposition (regardless of how well informed they are), our first response is still to say, "OK, we can't do this because people don't like it." Or often we leap to an analysis of the negative implications and remain bogged down there. We find we have to be very self-conscious about asking people *what* it is that they do not like and *why*, and then finding out the extent of the opinion or concern. Or we see that our student attendance is not improving and know that we need to address the problem quickly. So we immediately develop five ideas to heighten student awareness about attendance without carefully researching the reasons for poor attendance (we often still do not think to ask the students themselves). Or, on the other hand, when something positive happens—for example, last year 78% of the students in our senior class were accepted into college—we do not automatically think to do the research to find out why. If we did, in the future we would know how to support whatever efforts yielded us the desirable result.

But we are learning. This year as a Council we have become much better at asking research questions and collecting data so that we can plan programs and track success. The presence of a data coordinator in our school, giving us regular attendance and achievement statistics and putting data in a form that is useful to us, has helped to keep the idea of research in the forefront. Also, as we become more adept at systematic problem solving, our ability to think clearly about research as a tool to help us define and solve those problems has improved.

Another thing we are learning slowly is to keep our planning process focused on our research findings. For example, we collected much data from the community and from students and their parents through our community research effort during the Phoenix summer. In retrospect, we find that the *process* of research was, at that time, more important than any specific results. The educational plan crafted during the Phoenix summer contained many ideas generated as a result of hearing from other schools as well as many of our own ideas that developed as we became less restricted in our thinking about what was possible. But the connection between our plans and any specific findings from our research was more by accident than by design.

As we think about the reasons it is so difficult for us to maintain a "research" approach to our restructuring work, several factors come to mind. The obvious one is that this is not the way we are accustomed to doing things. But, then, by definition, restructuring has little to do with any of things we are used to doing. We as teachers and staff sit inside a system in which we have mostly experienced research and data collection as a process of telling us how we are not measuring up. That has not made research very appealing. So we have had to learn how to use it as a basis of positive and creative action.

We are also used to doing things quickly and somewhat randomly. Research requires a slower process of clearly defining what you want to know and why you want to know it, then figuring out what information you need, and then determining the best way to get it. Once you have got the data, you need to make sense of them and then plan in relation to them. Our history in the school has been to seize any opportunity for a program that comes up and might have some benefit for our students. If you do not, it might be gone. Research and planning require thinking broadly and systematically when most of us are used to thinking more narrowly about our own classes or disciplines. Changing paradigms takes time, practice, and experience.

Despite our inability to consistently behave as researchers and to plan on the basis of our data, we have learned much about the ways in which the process and outcomes of research can help us as planners for our school. We have learned, for example, that research can be a means of melting resistance. That is, when research is designed to get underneath people's opposition to change in order to identify their real concerns and is followed by a plan that addresses those concerns, it both gives a hearing to multiple voices in the school and opens the way for creative ideas that encompass a composite of perspectives. This process of research and change wins people's support because they feel included. Revised plans, which account for the concerns of people who have appeared resistant, can dispel their opposition.

As introspective researchers, we have learned to use the research process to clarify and focus on issues we need to address. The research process has evolved into a vehicle for both taking the time to step back and look at underlying issues and to put them on the agenda for discussion. Perhaps becoming an inquiring community as a staff and as a Governance Council is a process parallel to creating an inquiring educational environment for our students. Both take time; both require new ways of acting and responding; both require constant reflection; both are uncomfortable; and both can be deeply satisfying.

NOTE

1. Portions of the description of this part of the Phoenix Project have been presented in M. Fine & V. Vanderslice (1992). Qualitative activist research: Reflections on methods and politics. In E. Posavac (Ed.), *Methodological issues in social psychology* (pp. 199–218). New York: Plenum.

REFERENCES

Argyris, C., & Schön, D. (1978). *Organizational learning: A theory in perspective.* Reading, MA: Addison-Wesley.

Lewin, K. (1948). *Resolving social conflicts: Selected papers on group dynamics.* New York: Harper.

Lippitt, R. (1965). The process of utilization of social research to improve social practice. *American Journal of Orthopsychiatry, 25,* 663–669.

6

"Now Everybody Want to Dance"

Making Change in an Urban Charter[1]

JODY COHEN

"One knows the world by seeking to change it"
(Sartre, quoted in Hess, 1992)

Caught in a crossfire of expectation and critique, many public schools today are living the contradictions of change, as they host both reenacted routines and a passionate revisioning by staff, students, and parents. The tension
that critical educators have located between "structural determinants" and
"the consciousness of individuals" seeking to implement change (Weiler,
1988, p. 147) might be better described in the case of current school reform
as an ongoing tension between and within many seeking to change a system in
which they have also invested: autocratic and compassionate administrators,
teachers with building seniority, students who "know the ropes" but fail to
comply. This chapter will take us inside a reform movement where the
Inquiry charter opens up the challenge of real educational change. In the
company of students and teachers we will encounter the risks, pleasures, and
contradictions of interrupting structural silences—a microcosm of schools in
the midst of structural and instructional reform. We will hear the reverberations of students and teachers pressing change at the site of practice in a system still driven by centralized and constraining policies.

AT INQUIRY CHARTER

Students in Inquiry Charter describe their education in terms of personal
and collective, academic and programmatic change:

> If I were asked in tenth grade if I were going to college, I would have
> given a straight "no." I was never one who tried to do or accomplish
> anything. I now know I have abilities . . . [Inquiry] has changed me; I

feel as though if I study criminal justice, I can probably make a change. (Chans, senior)

I know a lot of students don't want to do the work, 'cause like on Friday you know you gotta do the work 'cause you gotta act in Monday's class. The first year nobody didn't want to act, now everybody into it, everybody want to act, everybody want to dance. (James, junior)

The comprehensive high school that houses Inquiry enrolls close to 2,000 students, almost 90% of whose families receive Aid to Families with Dependent Children. In recent years student attendance has averaged 65%, the dropout rate has approached 25%, and mean SAT scores have fallen 300 points below the national mean. Described by Inquiry teacher Bob Fecho (1992) as the "bottom of a hierarchy that siphons students off the top," Ali High is now undergoing the "charterization" of its faculty and student body as well as decision making on site-based management.

Founded by three teachers at the invitation of the Collaborative to invent a program, the charter is home to 260 students who represent a mix of ninth through twelfth graders, 8 core subject teachers who teach solely in the charter, and 15 elective subject teachers who teach across charters. Most classes are in a wing across an indoor bridge from the main building. The charter describes itself as a teacher-driven, writing-intensive, academically rigorous, project-oriented program committed to active, cooperative learning and a heterogeneous student body. The group belongs to the Coalition of Essential Schools, a university–schools partnership based on a belief in "the constructive confrontation of able teachers and willing pupils" (Coalition, p. 1). Participants believe in "personalized" teaching and learning to "[help] adolescents learn to use their minds well," the "governing metaphor [of] student-as-worker" and the curricular maxim "less is more" (p. 2). A student explains how this philosophy shapes charter life: "[Teachers] here want to know *why* you got one plus one is two, *how* you did it, and they'll probably get you up there and put you as a one and then another person, they'll want you to act it out!"

An opportunity for students and teachers to co-construct community, the charter has achieved a partial freedom, rare in the district, to fashion its own structure, subject to limitations of time and the isolation of breaking away from the shared system (Glickman, 1990). While initially core classes experimented with double "lab" periods weekly, now these classes meet every other day for 90 minutes, supporting more substantive and collaborative work. Rostering is accomplished within the charter to accommodate both this alternative organization of time and the assignment of *all* students to intellectually challenging courses such as algebra and physics.

The charter is described by staff and students as academically rigorous, setting high expectations for students to pose and solve problems and to meet responsibilities. The curriculum is demanding: Students read such works as *Hamlet* and *The Autobiography of Malcolm X* and write in genres from journal and lyrics to textual analysis; in algebra and elementary functions they utilize texts to create problems, which they collaboratively solve; chemistry students grapple with implications of nuclear regulations and policies. Data evidence impressive student outcomes, including better attendance, more credits earned, a higher percentage of major subject courses passed, and minimal student turnover. The charter is also designing performance-based assessments to reflect student outcomes. A pilot project required seniors to critically examine a common text and defend their thesis before panels of educators, parents, and peers.

As Coalition members, staff annually construct an interdisciplinary "essential question" rich enough to encompass a range of curricular requirements and engender provocative, substantive inquiry. Math teacher and union representative Ann Bourgeois reports to a student researcher:

> [Staff] argued about it for hours. I don't know whose idea it was, I don't
> remember now, but over the summer we spent many days meeting in
> each other's houses and discussing what our question would be. . . . You
> pick a question that is an *important* question; it's not going to be a waste
> of anybody's time to deal with it; it unites all the subjects.

Such a process, collaborative rather than individualistic, complex and conflicted rather than unidirectional, resembles the work of the real world more than the traditional school search for "right answers"; it provides a model for students to engage in the "substantive conversation" central to authentic intellectual endeavor (Newmann, 1990).

A Note on Methodology

Having entered during Inquiry's first year to do research with students on the charter and participant observation in an English class, I reentered the next year as an ethnographer working with students and teachers to collect data and feed back snapshots and initial analyses of charter life. To these ends, negotiating with staff, I documented classes and meetings. I conducted interviews with students, talked informally with students and staff, and worked with a group of students as both "informants" and co-researchers. I also facilitated a group for young women.

Alfred Hess (1992), an anthropologist engaged in school reform issues, poses this challenge to researchers of education:

Are we there merely to catalogue what is going on . . . [or] to also seek to have a profound impact on how schooling is done in our societies? Do we simply catalogue? Or do we also critique? And if we critique, is that critique detached and dispassionate? Or is it engaged and active? (p. 178)

My intent is to offer engaged, critical reflection *for* rather than simply *of* the charter in the interests of collective efforts to change how we accomplish schooling. In its second year, classes revolved around the unifying, interdisciplinary theme of change as elaborated in the question, "How do people, events, and conditions influence change?" Below I document the evolution of Inquiry Charter as a learning community, drawing on data to tell a story about the charter as a community of faculty and students who rally and regroup around change.

STORY #1: HOW DO PEOPLE INFLUENCE CHANGE?

When I met with student researchers in early February, students were talking excitedly about that morning's events:

KURT: It was the history classes that were having the walk-out, we was supporting them. Not complete black history, we were asking for all history together, connect it, and if the demand wasn't met, they was gonna walk out of class and knock on the other doors to let us know they needed our support.

DAFINA: Not everybody was aware we had a meeting with Mr. Fecho this morning and then we had another [staff] meeting. That's why Mr. Fecho's class didn't walk, we knew about the meeting and we was like, why leave now. Give Mr. Fecho that respect to see what the outcome of the meeting was gonna be.

Next period Dafina and I took field notes as student representatives articulated "demands" to the staff:

KURT: We want more black studies in social science and history classes, this month especially. We don't want a complete makeover of the curriculum, we want how blacks tie into what's already being taught. . . . We realize this takes time, we don't expect drastic change immediately.

RASHID: If we don't know that history, like if we didn't know about slavery, it could happen again. We need to know more about blacks as a whole. Like with Martin Luther King, the history books focus on the "I Have a

Dream" speech, but not how Kennedy and them used him. If we know history as a whole students in Inquiry and even in the city and the whole country could unite. We need to look at black leaders' philosophies. Learning about the great things blacks have done builds black self-esteem, like if he did that I could do a little better. We want linkages, not straight black history.

(Bell rings, and meeting continues into lunchtime.)

LEE WEINSTOCK (TEACHER): I'm disappointed that you didn't see this with American government.

RASHID: But we only read the bad things; I'm sure blacks did good things.

LEE WEINSTOCK: It was not about individuals. I tried to show how the government works and how it doesn't. For Caucasians, African Americans, and others. . . . Also, we have three required years of social science/history. We could add a fourth year in African American history, or an elective.

BOB FECHO (TEACHER): Also linkages between what's taught and what it means for the African American community will be spread throughout the curriculum and help focus the course.

For many of us, the story unraveled backwards, so that the opening lines were not revealed until well into the event:

JODY: What happened with the substitute?

JAMES: What happened was he put on the tape, students were listening to Farrakhan which is, some people can take it in different ways, they feel like it's a negative attitude. The head of the social science department came in and cut off the TV, that made the students kind of mad, you know, and they then were asking why, if they had it on Kennedy or somebody, maybe he wouldn't've took it off. You know, they took it in a bad way and they wanted to have walk-outs and everything.

If, as Deborah Meier (1992) suggests, the task of schools today is to help "young citizens . . . have wonderful ideas, invent theories, analyze evidence and make their personal mark on this most complex world" (p. 271), then this story offers a window on the process, as students and teachers grapple with theories of history and relationships between institutions and individuals, knowledge and change.

The story begins with a confrontation between a (African American) substitute who had altered the lesson and a (white) department head whose lines of authority in this reforming school were already felt to be hazy. Wedged between two liminal characters claiming authority over their learning, students begin to shape their own educational imperatives. That students themselves hold multiple, shifting views becomes evident in their words and sometimes contradictory actions for change: While several express no interest in black studies, many more sign petitions, negotiate in classrooms, and plan meetings with staff and a walk-out in which 11 students sit in the marble stairwell before heading home. Students claim and gain collective voice by demonstrating commitment to change and acting within the system to articulate their concerns to staff. For some students, the academic content of social science offers a site for analysis of change.

By inviting students to their meeting and responding to their concerns, the staff demonstrates a flexible stance in relation to student interests. (African American) science teacher Phil Hand applauds their activism: "When I went to school blacks weren't in those books. . . . So we have this problem. We're proud you see it and come forth. Just let it be your own." Inviting students to co-construct a pluralistic curriculum, he draws boundaries that exclude the substitute from this community. By the time of the meeting, (white) social science teacher Lee Weinstock has begun to rework her curriculum, taking on the challenge of negotiating knowledge with students within the strictures of state and departmental imperatives. She advises students as active learners to help create the "linkages" they seek. (White) charter co-coordinator Bob Fecho suggests that the group also reconsider next year's courses.

Whereas in many schools ringleaders would have been suspended and collaborators silenced, here representatives are invited to negotiate with staff, and student activism, while causing unease for some, is welcomed as a sign of critical democracy. The status quo survives as the forces of change percolate. While students voice a range of opinions about the revised course of study, curriculum control has shifted from the exclusive domain of the (state, department, and) teacher to the shared, negotiated domain of teachers and students. A black studies course in the works for the coming school year indicates that this shift goes beyond the classroom to the charter. A new homeostasis was formed with students as active participants in formulating intellectual content.

Regarding pedagogy and decorum, teachers express the need for continued conversation. Lee Weinstock designs lessons to promote "orderly discussion." Students concur that although the materials have changed, teaching methods have not. (White) science teacher Natalie Hiller voices her discomfort with "not knowing where all this [student] negativity was coming from." Several teachers voice disapproval of the walk-out. There emerges a collective desire to fortify the charter as an orderly and secure learning environment, which may run counter to the drive to pry open with students' basic issues about how teachers should teach, students learn, and human beings behave in school settings. Teachers are socializing students into an ethos with which they continue to struggle, in which community is built not by suppressing but by acknowledging difference without continually referencing hierarchy. The charter rallies and regroups, neither totally retaining a hierarchy of decision making nor abdicating all control to students but establishing a new, workable, and always fragile balance of shared authority.

STORY #2: HOW DO EVENTS INFLUENCE CHANGE?

In late March I joined Bob Fecho's English class in the library as they began to research the Harlem Renaissance. Investigation of this understudied era would require students to use secondary sources to locate and interpret primary documents, such as journalism and literature of the period, pictorial representations, and musical lyrics: The task is to re-create a day during the Harlem Renaissance. Students are to select one of several possible locations to re-create sites of important activity, such as the church and the meeting hall. Then they are to draw on a range of resources to research their area for a performance. Groups will prepare reports, create scenarios, and perform on Harlem Renaissance Day.

> **Field notes:** Students have selected groups: nightclub, meeting house, library, church, *Crisis Magazine*, and media. Bob stresses that this research is oriented toward performance, so that pictures, for example, are important for re-creating scenes. Groups will draft reports, confer with him to locate gaps, then work toward performance. Students are having trouble locating resources: This era is rarely indexed, so how to find material on their topics? How to divide the work? The *Crisis* kids begin to find key figures; the nightclub group has nothing, then finds a pictorial history and pores over hairstyles. Bob ends class by applauding students' "great start" and reminding students of "the fine art of browsing" and the creativity of research. Several in the church group complain: "This project is *too* hard."

The next week I talk with students about the project:

JAMES: Mr. Fecho, instead of just tell us, well this is the Harlem Renaissance, he'd say, well you have to act it out. So we have it in our minds, so when we get like 30 years old we could look back and say, I know what the Harlem Renaissance was and know what it *felt* like. . . . Sometimes you remember what you *do* better than what you been *told.*

ALICIA: I like it. We still on the research part; it's going to be decent. We looking up black ministers and churches, we gotta find out how the church looks and stuff like that.

JAMES: I'm doing meeting hall. . . . We trying to have a march, you know with a band, and then a meeting, set it up as they had it. I think I'm gonna be Marcus Garvey . . . because in his mind he was like saying, you know, this wasn't the place for us and we gonna have to go back to Africa. There's more to it, and that's why I wanna keep looking into it, to find out what he was really trying to say. . . . I'm not sure if it was for us literally to go back but I really think that he was trying to say for us in America, remember where we came from and be strong so everybody could be united.

Field notes: Students from all four of Bob's classes are seated at long tables in the cafeteria. He quiets them to review their upcoming double periods here and hands out worksheets to structure their performance plans. As they move from the research to the planning phase, some students lose concentration, talk to neighbors, wander from their groups. Leaders emerge, not always the ones I would've guessed, and carry along others who begin the worksheets. In the church group three young men dominate while the young women sit quietly, then express mounting frustration. The meeting house group, too, coalesces slowly, with young men taking lead roles and young women volunteering to question these public speakers.

A week later: Again all four classes in the cafeteria, and chaos mingling with productivity. The nightclub group is collecting tapes and negotiating roles. In the church group Ron and Derrick write out their sermons, and the young women design the action and set. The media group lines up interviews with key players. *Crisis* awaits Gail's return from the computer. Several sit unoccupied: One tells me he's been absent; Danielle disparages the project.

Two days before the Harlem Renaissance Fair: Energy runs high. Danielle is conflicted over whether to buy a dress and pumps for Friday. Bob takes the nightclub kids to Room 250, where they decorate, practice, have a blow-up fight, then *really* practice. Rashim returns after a week's absence, and I hook him up with Laketa to relate his Langston Hughes to her Jessie Faucet speech. Would they be exhorting whites or blacks, and what difference would it make to their speeches? Students creating a church in Bob's classroom position the "pulpit" to reflect the preacher's position in relation to the Lord.

The Day: Many of us, performers and audience, dress for Harlem Renaissance Fair Day, though Danielle wears jeans and sneaks. One young woman wears her grandmother's sequined gown; Derrick has borrowed preacher's robes; Natalie Hiller displays gloves and feathers. The young woman who lip-synchs Billie Holliday doesn't talk in class.

Church is hot with fans going and the audience joining in song. Students praise it as "decent" and "realistic." Keisha adds that meeting hall and library are "decent too, that's where you learn what people were thinking about back then. You learn the substance." Some parents attend. Another charter teacher's students request "a project like this." In L.A., rioting continues. Does this event constitute a response?

The Harlem Renaissance project as an *event* of collaborative research, planning, and practice took place over six weeks. The performance took place over six hours. In the life of the charter the event is significant: Time and space are restructured to involve students as collaborators and audience; the subject matter is responsive to students' black studies initiative; and the scope, depth, and creativity of the project flesh out the curricular maxim "less is more." Teacher and students reconfigure themselves as critical actors: The teacher forgoes more predictable methods for the risks and imperatives of collaboration and performance. Cut loose from standard questions and answers, students must seek questions and enact answers, negotiating new roles with teachers and peers.

While history classes study the era and dance class works on the nightclub, this project represents the vision of Bob Fecho from start to finish. As such, it displays the autonomy of the teacher in a microsystem that reflects ambivalence as it seeks to value both autonomy and the development of community. In the context of the larger bureaucratic system that has undermined teachers' autonomy over a median of 22 years, compelling them to "close their classroom doors" to gain autonomy, images of teachers engaged in mutual influence and communally shaped staff development have been scarce. In the smaller community of the charter, autonomy can promote change through the creativity and risk taking of individual teachers. Situated in this dialectic, the Harlem Renaissance project is an expression of teacher autonomy that may promote community by infusing into the system approaches that support valued pedagogical objectives such as collaborative, inquiry-based learning and by experimenting with a system of communication among charter teachers and students.

If we read this story in terms of the tension between a teacher's autonomy and the charter's coherence as a teaching and learning community, Inquiry's challenge might be how to let this event influence practice across the system without subverting the autonomy of individual teachers as happens once standardized curricula and teaching "packages" are adopted. Charter teachers need contexts to share efforts and generate approaches that resonate with their questions and passions. Given fertile conditions where autonomy is respected and community supported, such tension can nourish growth.

STORY #3: HOW DO CONDITIONS INFLUENCE CHANGE?

Both students and teachers, male and female, talked about classes where males did most of the talking. In Marsha Pincus's English class, where students grappled with gender and violence in *Othello, Antigone,* and *Beloved,* a comparison of African American male and female autobiographies opened the door to talk about gender, voice, and authority in this classroom:

KEVIN: Women's autobiographies turn me off. You be reading and then you get interested, it could be breakfast in 1942, then it 1992, it mess my head up.

DAVID: I like it, it's decent and funny to me.

MARSHA: I want to hear from the ladies.

KEVIN: This is a male-dominated class.

LATOYA: Women write to express themself because they don't think men is gonna listen— (*Several males interrupt*)

MARSHA: You proved her point.

LAWRENCE: We know the truth but don't act it. How many men think women are equal?

MARSHA: We still don't hear from the women here. When Latoya spoke three men jumped on her.

KURT: I don't feel men dominate this classroom, sometimes people just don't feel like talking.

MARSHA: Ladies, how many of you are quiet now and were not quiet in the first or second grade? (*Of seven females in the class, five hands go up.*)

KEISHA: [The males] got a whole rooting section over there!

Several of the young men continued to struggle with the issue: Student researchers Kevin and Kurt asked in a student survey, "Are males or females more outspoken in Inquiry, or is there no difference by gender?" While a majority saw "no difference," a significant minority circled "males." A senior, Lawrence, describes how his essay on change was inspired by English class and a play he saw over the weekend:

I haven't truly *showed* any changes yet, but I feel the changes inside of me. I never thought I disrespected the ladies but after the play it seems that I was disrespecting them by expressing some of the major thoughts that I had against them in class . . . like they can't do this or that. The women in the class, they weren't really, they weren't expressing themselves as much as I expressed myself. . . . But now I'm gonna try to stop saying things like that. I'm gonna try and stop *thinking* like that.

Across several levels of the organization, females raised the need for young women to talk together. When conflicts erupted among girls, Nina suggested "group talks":

PAM: Like "Young Black Men"? They should have it for girls. I asked about that and I was told "no" because there was not a woman interested.
KIMBERLEY: I think that would help people.
JODY: What would you want to do in that kind of group?
VOICES: Talk! Talk about what's on our mind!

When female students and staff discussed issues young women were confronting, they, too, considered a "girls group," and a student suggested my name as facilitator. For 10 weeks a group of us shared lunch and talk about pregnancy, abortion, child rearing, relationships with men and women, abuse, school, the future. Our talk spilled over into relationships in and beyond school.

Back in the classroom, volatile issues of gender intersecting with race and violence were again addressed through reading an article about an alleged rape committed by fighter Mike Tyson:

NINA: I feel as though [the teacher] shouldn't have talked about Mike Tyson's case because that happened out in the street and if you bring it into school there's gonna be a lot of conflict 'cause everybody got different opinions, and when we was in advisory everybody was arguing—
PAM: I think she wants us to think about it, be interested—
KIMBERLEY: She likes us to argue though.
PAM: She don't like us to argue, she like us to learn how to say what we wanna say *without* arguing. . . . She was just asking, "Ya'll read the article, how do y'all feel about the article?" And the way we did it, she would ask me and if you had a rebuttal you raised your hand.
KIMBERLEY: It's OK to talk about it but not to get into it *too* much. You know, it could start something big, 'cause we was talking about it in class and it was Lisa, that teacher threw her out 'cause she started getting into a discussion with everybody. Everybody just arguing, everybody not worried about the math work. (*Laughter.*)

How does the "condition of difference"—most evident here in terms of gender—influence change? This series of encounters with difference illuminates a dialectic around the exclusion and inclusion of voices. In typical educational settings, nonmainstream voices tend to be silenced or marginalized. Reflecting on female silence in their classrooms, teachers describe young women as quiet because they are "intimidated" by what others might think, anxious to be perceived as "good students," and concerned that males would not listen. In group work females often organized, while males wanted their ideas heard.

In this third story, students address gender differences as they affect and are affected by the curriculum. The teacher provokes students to analyze patterns of participation, and several males pursue the issue of gender difference in the charter. The issue is also pursued by females seeking spaces with "no boys [where] we can *really* say what's on our minds." The charter invents two strategies to create more "speaking roles" for young women: Safe (segregated) spaces are created for females to talk with one another, and key figures exercise power to help launch and navigate a sometimes treacherous discourse of differences in the coed classroom.

Data support the need for young women to have a space to develop their voices by exploring commonalities and differences (Bell, 1991). Again, students convey the need for change, and staff attend. While the structure is partial and temporary, it provides one image of how difference can be engaged among and between (shifting) identities of students. If the charter's imperative is the full participation of young men and women in the construction of knowledge, work in integrated classrooms remains crucial. Teachers' exercise of power to engage female voices may involve acknowledging obstacles to taking on difference in the classroom. Macpherson and Fine (in press) describe a differences discourse as marked by "destabilization of knowledge," the compensating "power of questioning," and the coexistence of multiple and competing discourses (in press). For young women in Inquiry, addressing the Tyson case destabilizes dominant knowledge about male aggression and female victimization, unleashing competing perspectives that are dangerous and stimulating. The classroom "event" reverberates throughout the system, as students struggle to deal with difference without resorting to aggressive postures.

STEPPING OUTSIDE: CHANGING THE SYSTEM

How teachers and students in this charter reconfigure authority, community, and difference provokes a set of questions relevant within Inquiry and reverberates to other parts of an educational system in the midst of change. When accustomed hierarchies are challenged by newly empowered voices, how might change protect stability while nurturing growth? How can teachers be supported in their (collective) development of practice-based inquiry (see Chapter 10)? How can tensions between constituencies with intersecting interests (e.g., department heads and charters) be negotiated without camouflaging important differences? How much autonomy does a charter need from the rest of a school?

Two seniors frustrated with decisions made for their senior class talk about making change at their school:

NINA: [Change] is not a one-man thing. I think everybody should come together, speak up just like we spoke up about history, we wanted to know more about black people. That's what people need to do is talk and tell them what you want.

PAM: Because [charter] want us to make ourselves heard.

When schooling is about building participatory communities, students learn to make themselves heard—to occupy speaking and acting roles in their educations, to co-construct with teachers what knowledge, whose knowledge, and how knowledge is produced in school. Just as the charter's philosophy encourages students' critical thinking and action, the charter itself entertains conflicting forces and goals, forging temporary syntheses that enable the closely linked reflection and action that Clark (Chapter 2) calls "reflaction." How can the charter as central unit of change in this restructuring movement be supported, provoke ripples in its school, and incite radical change in the larger bureaucracy?

Still marginal to the mainstream of American public education, charters as a locus of reform must seek a delicate balance between attending to their own developing identities and engaging with the broader educational communities they need in order to flourish. Charters must have resources to address among themselves shared worries, goals, and conflicts, to develop their visions of curriculum, instruction, and assessment. At the same time, charters must interact productively with others seeking change—to co-construct public knowledge about accountability, to address differences across and within schools, to confront vested interests and power asymmetries that dictate the contours and limits of public education.

Charters must continue to move at once inward and outward, seeking self-definition in relation to dynamic boundaries and values. So, too, the educational reform movement must develop itself in the very process of transforming the mainstream, attending at once to the contradictions endemic to its work and to the immediate, dire need for public education that addresses the capabilities, desires, and needs of students. Marsha Pincus reflects with a student researcher on the evolution of Inquiry's essential questions:

We started out having kids make connections between learning and themselves. And we said, once you make those connections you can bring about change. It makes sense for next year's question to be about power: What is power, who's got it, how do you get it?

NOTE

1. Many thanks for the help of Inquiry staff and students and of David Dan and Michelle Fine in preparing this chapter.

REFERENCES

Bell, L. (1991). Changing our ideas about ourselves: Group consciousness raising with elementary school girls as a means to empowerment. In C. Sleeter (Ed.), *Empowerment through multicultural education* (pp. 229–250). Albany: State University of New York Press.

Coalition of Essential Schools. (1989). *Prospectus*. Providence, RI: Brown University.

Fecho, R. (1992). *Rings of context*. Handout from presentation at Ethnography in Education Conference, Philadelphia, PA.

Glickman, C. (1990). Pushing school reform to a new edge: The seven ironies of school empowerment. *Phi Delta Kappan, 72*, 68–75.

Hess, A. (1992). Anthropology and school reform: To catalogue or critique? *Anthropology & Education Quarterly, 23*(3), 175–184.

Macpherson, P., & Fine, M. (in press). Hungry for an us: Adolescent women narrating sex and politics. In J. Irvine (Ed.), *Adolescent sexuality: Cultures, communities, and the construction of identities*. Philadelphia: Temple University Press.

McLaren, P. (1989). *Life in schools*. New York: Longman.

Meier, D. (1992, September 21). Get the story straight: Myths, lies and public schools. *The Nation*, pp. 271–272.

Newmann, F. (1990, April). *Linking restructuring to authentic student achievement*. Paper presented at the Indiana University Annual Education Conference, Bloomington, IN.

Sleeter, C., & Grant, C. (1991). Mapping terrains of power: Student cultural knowledge versus classroom knowledge. In C. Sleeter (Ed.), *Empowerment through multicultural education* (pp. 49–68). Albany: State University of New York Press.

Weiler, K. (1988). *Women teaching for change: Class, gender, and power*. New York: Bergin & Garvey.

7

Interpreting Social Defenses: Family Group in an Urban Setting

LINDA POWELL

Scene 1: After her exposure to ideas about urban high school students' feelings of anonymity, an experienced teacher reports in a training session that she has tried something "radical" in her classroom and is shocked at the positive impact it seems to have had: On the first day of school she asked her students to introduce themselves and say a little about their hopes for the year.

Scene 2: Two teachers who have worked together for almost 20 years are serving on the schoolwide renewal team. The first mentions proudly that her daughter's college graduation is upcoming. Her co-worker responds incredulously, "Oh, you have kids?"

When we truly listen, students and teachers in urban comprehensive high schools tell us how much they value stability, continuity, and mutual respect. As they cherish these values, they may be describing what is most absent from their daily school lives. For far too many people, feeling known in ongoing relationships is a rare commodity in large urban high schools.

The realities of the anonymity and deindividuation in urban comprehensive high schools are well documented (Fine, 1990). The student experience is one of disruption, instability, and irrational change. Teachers also fare badly, with discontinuity and punishment as regular experiences in their professional lives.

This is not simply the isolated experience of students and teachers in urban high schools. Anonymity and feelings of alienation are increasingly common experiences in American life. The identities of human beings are formed in groups. Schools, churches, and workplaces help shape our deepest hopes, fears, and longings. Increasingly these groups, beginning with but not limited to families, are not "working" in a profound sense.

As this transformation takes place, a primary task of schools—training young humans for the survival of the species—becomes increasingly political, complex, and fraught with difficulty. Newman (1974) notes:

To establish schools, adults have had to form groups to portion out and administer their accumulated lore and learning so as to make possible the communication of increasingly complex sets of learning to increasingly large groups of children and young people in increasingly bewildering sets of interrelated societies.

Perhaps for the first time in human history, adults are being asked to train young people in skills we may not possess or have not consciously developed, such as community building, peace making, and finding strength through diversity.

This chapter presents one story of the process and results of a two-year "experiment" that has included hundreds of people—students, school staff, parents, and consultants. This experiment has been an attempt to develop an idea—not a "program" or "project" or "research effort." It has been a stumbling, halting, genuine exploration of a specific question: What would happen in urban high schools if *relationships* were developed and valued as a crucial vehicle for *learning*? I will describe my experience at two levels. Closest to the surface, in the realm of dates, places, and behaviors, it is one woman's chronological description of the implementation of family group in this school district: who, what, when, and how. At a deeper level, in the realm of hopes, dreams, and impulses, this chapter is an attempt to transform disjointed, isolated, and sometimes depressing facts into a coherent whole.

I will use the notion of *social defense* as a heuristic for understanding family group's positive impact on school culture.

WHAT IS FAMILY GROUP?

During July 1990, I served as co-convener of a summer institute designed to develop curricular, instructional, and social notions around education innovation.

The institute was composed of teams of teachers working with young people identified as "overaged ninth graders." These students arrived late in ninth grade or had been unsuccessful at their first attempt. For eight days, we read, evaluated, and debated a variety of strategies tried around the United States to address the special needs of these students.

Group meetings were marked by strange undercurrents that were not completely accounted for by our large size. There was much about race, equity, and custom that was left unsaid in the large group, but later passionately recounted on an individual basis to the conveners. There was much talk about the "population" of overaged ninth graders, but little mention of individual students. Teachers found the readings for the institute "too academic" and uninteresting, but brought great passion to debates about parking, the site, and snacks. The afternoons seemed like years to conveners and participants alike. There was a free-floating hostility about the work that expressed itself in unclear debates and personal attacks. In curious ways, the behavior of this group of teachers paralleled their descriptions of their classes of students!

Anonymity—the sense of being unknown and unimportant—was the invisible thread weaving these dynamics together. Not only did these teachers not know many of their students in meaningful ways; they did not know one another! Many of them attended the institute in "teams" with members whom they had never met or had not been "told" that they were, in fact, on teams.

After nearly two years of working with teachers and students, and seeing what happens in schools that even partially introduce family group for a specific group of students, I better understand experiences of students and teachers by using the notion of *social defense*. In the area of psychoanalytic theory, writers such as Newman and Menzies suggest that organizations, like individuals, have "personalities," including characteristic patterns and tendencies. Individuals who join these organizations do not have to agree or "approve" of these tendencies, but they participate in these defenses at some level or they must leave the institution. Following extended conversation with teachers and students, I began to ask different questions, starting not with "Why do teachers do this" or "Why do students do that" but with "What must it feel like to be in a certain place or do a certain thing?" or "What is *not* being talked about this moment?" I began to wonder if alienation and anonymity might not be symptoms of bad organizational design or the outcomes of outdated policies or even personality conflicts. What if these features of school life were ways in which institutions were "coping" with complex feelings? I began to wonder what those complex feelings might be and how family group as an innovation might affect them.

Menzies's (1975) classic study of a hospital offers us a model for pursuing those kinds of questions. She was invited as a consultant to help the hospital solve a number of problems in training nurses. They were most concerned about their ability to provide high-quality patient care while also training professional nurses. By the time the consultant was called, the hospital had tried many strategies to no avail; the system was stumped and close to crisis.

After talking with many people throughout the hospital, Menzies did not make predictable suggestions about schedules and personnel. What she hypothesized was that the hospital was "organized" in such a way as to manage the strong feelings, anxiety, and difficulties that nurses, student nurses, doctors, patients, and their families felt. Various strategies, which seemed counter to the expressed mission of the hospital, were employed at all levels throughout the hospital to help people cope with unspoken difficulties. Menzies labeled these strategies "social defense" and noted that they included tendencies and policies such as splitting up the relationships between nurses and individual patients, routinizing tasks, underutilizing talented staff, denying the significance of individuals, and avoiding change.

While these social defenses were not altogether successful in containing anxiety, they made it possible for the hospital to superficially function, albeit poorly. Menzies recommended redesigning the organization so that understanding and mastering these difficult feelings became part of the work of the hospital, not something to be hidden or avoided.

How does this idea of social defense help in understanding the importance of family group and its impact on charters and schools? First, it changes our questions and directs our attention to the ways in which distance and anonymity protect young people and adults in schools and perhaps the larger society. Second, it compels us to discover *what* the difficult feelings, concepts, and relationships are that we may be avoiding. Finally, the notion of social defense reminds us that avoiding change is symptomatic of an ongoing process, not a static fact. With great concerted effort on the part of groups or individuals, these social defenses can be modified. School-restructuring efforts are more likely to succeed when they adequately acknowledge the impact of the social defense system and provide alternative coping mechanisms for teachers, parents, and students.

By the close of the summer institute, having sorted through many options, teachers chose to explore a concept imported from an alternative high school in New York. During the summer institute, their staff described the impact of a simply executed but amazingly effective program that had been instituted five years earlier. Every adult in the school, including the principal, office staff, maintenance staff, aides, and teaching faculty, was assigned to meet on a regular basis with a specific group of students. This group was maintained over the period of each student's high school career. A primary source of a student's school identity was his or her membership in a specific family group, placing him or her in a specific set of relationships with others. This connectedness revitalized and grounded the relationships between and among students and teachers.

Although desperate to generate creative approaches to working with their students, many teachers were not immediately sold on the idea. They noted that alternative high school educators would have greater latitude for creativity and innovation as well as smaller class size than they would. They were concerned about their ability as teachers, not social workers or trained therapists, to handle complex emotional questions. They were certain, for example, that suicide and abortion were certain to come up in open discussion and that they would be completely incapable of managing these topics. They were afraid of being overwhelmed by their students' lives and needs. They expressed worry about their ability to facilitate a group as opposed to teach a class.

Another way of understanding the difficulty of opting in was understanding what was truly at stake: We were asking teachers to make a direct intervention against distancing, anonymity, and the splitting of relationships—key elements of the social defense system. Family group was not simply a new classroom technique but a promise of knowing students and colleagues better, of sustaining an ongoing conversation with others about the nature of teaching and learning. What many teachers intuitively recognized is that family group represents a radical restructuring of relationships in urban schools—between student and teacher, teacher and colleagues, and among students themselves.

Begrudgingly—and with much teacher concern that family group would not work for "their" kids—intensive training for a small group of leaders and tentative implementation in some charters began.

What Happens When Family Group Is Implemented?

In the widest scheme of things, family group has very ambitious goals:

- To help young people learn to think and feel at the same time, to become self-reflective, to take greater responsibility for their own learning
- To build community, to encourage all participants to apply their minds to the issues that are most immediate and crucial to their lives
- To help students and family group leaders appreciate this kind of activity as a legitimate part of intellectual inquiry

Because family group may represent a frontal assault on the social defenses of urban high schools, it can provoke unusually strong reactions from people who know nothing about it! For this reason, it has been important to clarify what family group is *not*. Family group is not a "replacement" for families, although it is designed to be a reference group or "home base" or "school family" for students in otherwise large institutions that make students feel anonymous. It is a replication of the cohort-group approach that is used to support achievement in many private K-12 schools as well as professional graduate schools. Important relationships—including those with parents and family—can be discussed and worked on during the group itself. Family group may actually bring parents into the school in an altogether new way to co-lead groups with school staff or provide other kinds of support to ongoing groups.

Family group is not for "bad kids" or "dummy classes." It is not a behavior-modification technique to "improve" them. It is a space where student voices are valued and encouraged. One effect seems to be that family group improves dialogues within schools, making their climates more conducive to learning, as students are empowered to better negotiate with administrators, teachers, and one another.

Finally, family group is not group therapy, although at its best it uses an inherent power of groups for good, nor is it the sole domain of social workers or psychologists. Family group was conceived and developed by education professionals and is designed to be led by school staff and community participants.

The contrast between the imaginings of uninvolved teachers and students and actual experience of family group participants may tell us something about the content of school social defenses. What actually happens in family group is that students become more expressive and discover their ability and desire to learn. They feel more confident of their ability to speak clearly, which may often lead to more assertiveness and a greater tendency to think critically about their actual experience. Teachers routinely remark that while conducting family group, they come to like their students better and to feel more competent as teachers in the process. They shift from describing their students solely by their deficits to including descriptions of their gifts. What actually happens is that students and teachers are able to bring more of themselves to the classroom, their serious problems as well as their hopes, goals, dreams, worries, and delights. All of these become grist for the mill for inquiry.

Leaders report that family group provides remarkable results in increasing self-awareness and stimulating motivation and commitment in their students. In a recent survey, teachers defined family group in these ways:

Family group is about the business of teaching and learning.

A group of students, totally integrated, who meet in an effort to improve school performance by means of improving their self-image and identifying with and learning to trust the other students in the group.

A place where students and faculty come together to talk and experience the sharing of ideas, cultures, and information while providing a place for each to be heard.

Students' descriptions are more affectionate:

You get to see other points of view of people, instead of just your own. (*Interviewer: Why is that important?*) Because everybody's opinion is not the same as everybody else's. You can't just go around arguing. You don't have to agree, but you can see that there are other points of view than your own. (*Interviewer: Why is that important?*) Less arguing!

It's not just only all classwork. It's getting to hang out with the teachers, with each other, expressing yourself more. We get to know each other and learn more, 'cause your *minds* are together.

Perhaps the most important aspect of family group in the school district has been the focus on training teachers to work with specific, sometimes controversial, content. Since 1990, more than 200 family group leaders have been trained by an interdisciplinary team of teachers, social workers, and psychologists. If family group was to be truly oriented toward student interests and student space, teachers had to be prepared to responsibly facilitate discussions on a wide variety of topics. Early training focused on the nuts and bolts of group facilitation and providing an opportunity for family group leaders to build their own community of shared goals and strategies.

After months of experimentation with charters, family group leaders identified the topics that young people routinely raise. They requested specific materials to help them develop these discussions in their classrooms, since many of them fall within the "evaded curriculum": that terrain of power normally silenced in public high schools. To the extent that there is a "core curriculum" for family group leaders, it focuses on the following eight themes:

1. *Group building/group development*: Creating reliable environments for learning, peer support, and conflict resolution
2. *School achievement/school-charter life*: How to successfully negotiate (and even change) school culture, avoiding suspensions, detention, and so forth
3. *Relationships*: in-school, family, community
4. *Gender questions/women's issues*: Questions about masculinity and femininity, sexuality, sexual harassment, and power issues between men and women
5. *Health issues*: Sex and sexual activity, including teenage pregnancy, drug and alcohol abuse and prevention, hygiene, general health questions, and sexually transmitted diseases, especially AIDS
6. *Violence/death and dying*: Questions about loss, grief, and death provoked by news items and community events as well as death of students
7. *Homelessness and poverty/class questions*: Issues provoked by both the social issue of homelessness, presence of students who reside in shelters in a given charter/school, issues of consumerism and societal division
8. *Race/racial identity/racism*: School and community

Confronting race and racism is a good example of how this approach has worked. During training sessions, many teachers subtly accused their colleagues of self-fulfilling, low expectations for minority children and of preparing them only for minimum-wage jobs and unfulfilling lives. Others indicted their colleagues for inadequate knowledge of and empathy for the issues confronting poor, urban students of color. Still other teachers refused to think about these questions because of their own discomfort about ethnicity and multiculturalism. At times, lightning-swift confrontations erupted across predictable racial boundaries, but not always. Sometimes teachers of color discovered their deeply entrenched differences. These complicated tensions blocked teachers' work within their schools and often proved to be a thorny obstacle to effective teamwork within charters. The difficulty of unbraiding color, inequity, institutional racism, and poverty afflicted the institute with strange, vague silence or rageful, passionate conflict. Honest, "straight" talk among teachers about these questions was rare at the beginning. Family group training attacked this issue straightforwardly by scheduling an overnight retreat for leaders to confront and problem-solve how best to work with students around the issue of racial identity.

During the training, teachers were especially surprised to discover the enduring impact of their own schooling on the values that they carry into their classrooms. When asked to identify individual teachers who had had an impact on them (for better or worse) or the issues of race and class that shaped their adolescence or their personal discovery of intellectual aliveness, teachers rediscovered excitement and curiosity about their chosen profession.

In charters where family group is conducted, consultants have also offered on-site training for teams of teachers. These sessions often provide the first time and space for teachers to explore their own values about the nature of education, their goals as individual practitioners, and their feelings about the family-school split. These are risky conversations for sometimes fragile collegial relationships.

SOCIAL DEFENSES RECONSIDERED

In October 1991, five students from a family group that had been meeting for over a year agreed to do a demonstration for interested teachers from across the school district. Two young women and three young men allowed us to eavesdrop on their discussion about the impact of family group on their lives. They explored their relationships with the adults in the group and the qualities of honesty and emotional availability that they valued in them. The group reflected on the loss of the social work interns from the previous year and cheerfully "warned" the new interns of an inevitable testing period until the group could trust them! The students responded with comments about belonging to a reliable unit that mattered to them; they identified practical support that had been offered in the group, such as help with child-care problems or tutoring for an especially demanding biology class. They described a feeling of mastery over succeeding in school, a feeling of competence and hopefulness. Family group experience helped them with situations and relationships outside the charter and outside school.

These young people were living proof of the efficacy of family group. Some onlookers had a predictable response: They assumed that these were "middle-class kids." They certainly were not. But what these onlookers labeled as a "class question" was the unique outcome of human and organizational variables that had been creatively leveraged.

During the last two years, family group has had a major impact on students, teachers, and school cultures. We know that it makes schools more hospitable and manageable for everyone in them. Students feel known in a deeper way and are less likely to disappear because they feel unnoticed. They can admit their needs and seek help with them with less shame and exposure. Imagined gaps between teachers and students narrow; teachers remark "I never would have thought that about *my* students . . ." Students and teachers find themselves more tolerant of one another, more understanding of the constraints of their roles, and more hopeful about learning from one another.

Family group has done for students what family group training has done for teachers: provided a safe space for expressing and exploring difficult feelings, mastering them in adaptive ways, and reducing the need for social defenses. The best support for this analysis is in the public talk of conflict. Social defenses operate to stifle and redirect legitimate anxiety. Now family group leaders hotly debate various topics, including their role as educators, their ambivalence toward greater involvement in their students' lives, the nature of learning, and the parameters of quality preparation for life and citizenship in the twenty-first century. From the outside, this probably looks like "resistance" to a "program." From the inside, however, this debate is exciting and important: Teachers are passionately exploring questions they did not even *ask* two years ago. *These are the profoundly uncomfortable questions that social defenses are designed to obscure.* These kinds of questions can only be profitably taken up in groups of people prepared and committed to exploring them.

Teachers and students are risking being known in dramatic new ways. They are relinquishing their anonymity and telling the truth about their own values and their own commitments. What we must hope is that large high schools and centralized school districts have the will to introduce the structural changes that nourish the seeds of this kind of community of teachers and learners. If not, the downward spiral of social defenses will replace the real work of educating young people. What we hope is that this experiment will continue, in larger and riskier ways, for the sake of the students whose school experience can be dramatically altered.

REFERENCES

Fine, M. (1990). *Framing dropouts: Notes on the politics of an urban high school.*
Albany: State University of New York Press.

Menzies, I. E. P. (1975). A case-study in the functioning of social systems as a defense
against anxiety. In D. Colman & W. Harold Braxton (Eds.), *Group relations reader.*
Sausalito, CA: Grex.

Newman, R. (1974). *Groups in schools.* New York: Simon & Schuster.

8

When "Discipline Problems" Recede: Democracy and Intimacy in Urban Charters

NANCIE ZANE

In an era when assaults on and by students are reported frequently in urban schools and the use of metal detectors and armed security is being viewed as a necessary precaution, there is little question about the severity of the disciplinary problems confronting big-city schools or the negative impact that disruptive, threatening, or violent behavior has on the overall educational process.[1] It is therefore worth asking whether the current movement toward educational reform and school renewal has anything to offer to educational institutions that see themselves in danger of losing the battle for disciplinary control.

My role as an organizational consultant with the Philadelphia Schools Collaborative (PSC)[2] has enabled me to work closely with a number of the comprehensive high schools engaged at differing levels with the district's restructuring process. After three and a half years of involvement, I have become convinced that the process of restructuring schools makes possible a radically different understanding of, and response to, the issue of disciplinary practice.

This chapter argues that a significant shift in the conversations about discipline occurs when educational reforms are accompanied by democratic participation of all stakeholders in previously large, impersonal school bureaucracies. In the early stages of the school restructuring process, disciplinary issues occupy the *foreground* of discussions among teachers and administrators. A sense of despair over the lack of consistent, effective responses to students' disruptive behavior dominates conversation, while the restoration of institutional control surfaces as the critical goal of reform.

As restructuring matures, the issue of discipline recedes to the *background* of school talk. When the traditional structure of large high schools, divided by departments and dependent on distant hierarchical relationships, is reorganized into charters or smaller "schools within schools," administrators, teachers, students, and parents can begin to build smaller learning communities. By replacing anonymous bureaucracies with communities founded on shared educational visions and intimate connections, a new organizational culture is produced. Isolation is replaced by affiliation, antagonism by cooperation and interdependence, and impotence by risk taking. Not only does students' behavior change, but teachers' and administrators' perceptions and experiences of what constitute disciplinary problems and appropriate institutional responses shift.

For the purpose of this chapter, I draw on my experience with four of the high schools involved in the district's restructuring efforts.[3] Although my work in these various schools hinged on some aspect of educational renewal, the unexpected theme that linked my experiences across the schools related to student discipline and disciplinary practice.

In the scenarios below, I have tried to capture the ways in which the fetish with disciplinary concerns diminishes as schools (and the administrators, teachers, and students inside them) become more relationally oriented and more democratic. I end the chapter by re-viewing this perspective through a set of collaborative lenses—the eyes of several teachers and administrators, some whose experiences helped build the theoretical framework for this chapter, others who have been intimately involved in the restructuring efforts in their schools. By inviting their critique, I hoped to hear the questions and issues concerning disciplinary issues that were most relevant for them as well as discover the rough edges and loose ends that I may have smoothed over—perhaps in an (unconscious) effort to have a happy ending to this educational chapter.

IN THE BEGINNING: DISCIPLINE AS CONTROL OF INDIVIDUAL STUDENTS

Let's be brutally frank about this and not be indirect, the major issue here is one of student discipline.

—Teacher

The school seems built around teachers, administrators, and then parents. Students fit in where they can.

—Student

As I reflect on the conversations I held in 1989 with teachers and administrators at Ida B. Wells and Rosa Parks High Schools, I remember the vehemence with which some teachers discussed the problem of student discipline. They seemed to be engaged in a battle with students for control of the school. "Before any changes take place in this school, we need to take control back from the students!" "They have become a rather unrestrained student body." The teachers represented themselves as passive victims of the students' disruptive behavior, blaming individual students for the problem. "Some of the students are good kids, but there are a lot of bad apples that we have to deal with out there." There were few recognized relationships.

Many of the teachers believed that disciplinary problems operated on a group level as well. For some it reflected the "breed of students" currently populating the public school system. "Students today are not like we were when we went to school. They have little self-control and place little value on education." Additionally, "these students" had few role models within their families and/or communities to guide them. Teachers also observed that many students were in a bind—familial demands often conflicted with their academic requirements, contributing to high absenteeism and poor grades.

Viewed through a "we–they" lens tainted with race and class, teachers felt, regardless of the reason, that students were not behaving appropriately. Consequently, they had lowered their expectations of students over time, and had grown, by their own admission, preoccupied with discipline. A "good" class had less to do with the enthusiasm that students demonstrated toward the curriculum and more to do with the small number of "problem students" in the room.

. Early on I asked these teachers what "taking control back" might look like to them. The most frequent response was establishing "disciplinary codes [for students] so that everyone's clear what behavior's expected." Teachers and administrators felt obliged to develop a wide-ranging list of explicit rules and regulations and apply them consistently in order to hold students "accountable."

While teachers and administrators voiced legitimate concerns about the disruptive potential of certain "problem students," they failed to see the impact of *school organizational structure* on students' *individual and collective behavior*.[4] This perspective, however, parallels both the conservative and liberal educational literatures, which abound with books and articles about the problem of *individual* students who challenge or disobey the tacit or written rules. The causes for such negative student behavior fall into a variety of categories: students' lack of self-esteem and self-control (Bybee & Gee, 1982; Rutter, Maughan, Mortimer, Ouston, & Smith, 1979); alienation and isolation related to oversized classes and lack of decision-making power (Bybee & Gee, 1982; Carnoy & Levin, 1985; Iani, 1989); poor and/or nonexistent relationships with other adults (Alshuler, 1980; Metz, 1978); and unfair and inconsistent application of the school rules (Bybee & Gee, 1982; Curwin & Mendler, 1988; Rutter et al., 1979).

Despite the fact that many theorists understand students' behavior[5] to be rooted at the intersection of individual, relational, and structural problems, the prescription for the problem rarely transcends the focus on controlling and changing individual students' behavior. The most often cited solution is the establishment of clear, systemwide standards and rules, fairly and consistently applied by classroom teachers and administrators (Bybee & Gee, 1982; Curwin & Mendler, 1988; Rutter et al., 1979). Recently, an enormous proliferation of methods such as "assertive discipline" have been generated to enable teachers to go beyond merely *controlling* student behavior by creating a means for students to internalize school norms (Brophy, 1987).[6] Ironically, the individualistic understandings of discipline exemplified in the responses of those interviewed and mirrored in the traditional literature may hamper the long-term goal of educational reform if they enable people to *avoid* wrestling with the difficult intersections of student behaviors and school structures/instruction.

IN THE MIDDLE: DISCIPLINE AS RELATIONAL

In the past nobody wanted to teach ninth grade—teaching any ninth-grade course was considered the booby prize and people would try to negotiate out of it. Now, with the opportunity to work collegially, to have control over our resources and our lives, many of us see working with ninth graders as special and an important challenge.

—Teacher, Parks High

Upon my return to Wells High 18 months later, I reinterviewed several administrators and staff and heard three interesting shifts in teachers' and administrators' perspectives on the educational change process and the role discipline played in defining their work. First, while discipline problems were still defined as individual transgressions of the rules, teachers were beginning to see connections among student behavior, organizational structure, and teacher–student relationships. Second, as teachers and administrators struggled with shared governance, they began to work more collaboratively around the development and implementation of a few key but critical disciplinary rules. Although they had no "hard data," teachers believed that the "number of disciplinary problems was down" and the climate was more amenable as a consequence of their more coordinated, consistent approach. Third, in reflecting on their own process, the "leaders" of the restructuring process believed that student discipline had diminished as a priority and as a problem.

What had happened to alter the nature and tone of the conversations taking place in these schools? A number of events had occurred simultaneously, and their convergence seemed to have had an important impact on the framing of discipline within the schools. Conversations with the PSC nudged schools to shift focus from behavior to the life of the student mind. Although the PSC encouraged governance councils to tailor their restructuring plans to the cultures of individual schools, it nonetheless authorized a posture of educational reform in which educational transformation of student outcomes, not discipline, was the central concern. Additionally, as teachers became engaged in democratic decision making, a number of the more "controversial" teachers—many of whom shared the PSC's view of progressive education—were empowered to move from the shadows of their schools into more visible leadership roles. Further, by utilizing a participatory process to design their school's restructuring plan and implementing small, student-centered programs, teachers were establishing closer relationships with one another and with their students. In light of these factors, the dialogue for change broadened beyond the deficits and transgressions of individual students.

At Parks, the summer institute of 1989—a program established by the Governance council to discuss the needs of incoming ninth-grade students— serves as a metaphor for these three dynamics. The conversation opened with a sense of futility—because "no matter what you do, ninth-grade students are immature and simply out of control." Several of the teachers pressed the idea, however, that the school itself, with its multitude of disjointed programs, was out of control. They then began wondering out loud about the efficacy of more "special programs." They started to discuss the problems of categorizing and labeling students, as well as the effect on those leftover students tossed into the "general" school population. Faculty began to critically analyze their fragmented system.

The summer institute was designed to nurture a sense of community among the diverse incoming students and teachers. Reflecting on the institute, teachers commented on the meaningful bonds created with students. One said, "I had gotten close to kids, but never had gotten involved in their personal lives. My work this summer gave me a different perspective. I feel more relaxed with kids and want to be more involved." One administrator noted that the students' response to him transformed his role in the school as disciplinarian.

> Kids usually see me as a hard-ass, someone to avoid. The kids in the summer institute saw me as a nurturer, a father figure. They sought me out, and I felt something special for them too. I feel more caring, and I've tried to relate in a more interpersonal way.

In addition, teachers and administrators felt closer. One teacher, who described herself as aloof and disconnected from her peers, said she now saw herself as "part of a team."

A number of the teachers also commented that the relationships built with students reduced the number of disciplinary problems. One woman connected the reduction in students' sense of anonymity and isolation with a lessening of acting out. Another added wryly, "Students know that being visible and known means that teachers will be able to put the finger on them right away."

The students, too, commented on the loss of anonymity. One observed: "The program was great. When school started, I had to show my friends and my cousins around because they were lost. They told me to stop bragging because I knew my way around, knew some of the teachers, and they didn't." Creating more intimate spaces within the school enabled students, teachers, and administrators to connect, and such connections mediated discipline problems.

Wells High School provided another example of a school where changes related to restructuring and school-based management had an impact on discipline—both enacted and perceived. The principal observed that as teachers and students connected, "teachers started realizing what students needed and began to advocate for them rather than focus on disciplining them." The coordinator for the ninth-grade institute had another way of understanding the reduction in disciplinary problems. She believed that having teachers and administrators work more collaboratively together—around disciplinary issues as well as other educational change efforts—helped create a more positive work environment. "I used to teach and go home. There was no way to share ideas, no way to discuss issues that really mattered. I was definitely experiencing intellectual stagnation. Now, there's so much to talk about. . . . The sky's the limit." She speculated that the focus on discipline was based partly on "reality"—students were disruptive and were not as respectful of the rules and teachers' authority as they "should" be—but that the issue also served as a convenient dumping ground for other problems among teachers and between teachers and administrators. It was "like a black hole, a proxy for negative feelings in general."

Relationships alone, however, while necessary, are insufficient for establishing durable educational change. Relationships must be enjoyed not only by caring individuals, but secured inside structured learning communities. Academic cultures need to be negotiated in serious, ongoing conversations among educators, students, and parents. Only in the context of such communities can questions about power, control, and discipline be safely visited.[7]

Thus the development of charters—small, educationally rich thematic clusters in which a team of 8 to 12 teachers and 200 to 400 students are located — represents an attempt to build, indeed, to institutionalize, such safe places within the schools. The establishment of these communities shifted the primary responsibility of discipline from the school as a whole to smaller units within the school.

IN THE NOW: DISCIPLINE AS EMBEDDED IN CONTEXT

If we think about our work as a team, no one of us had accomplished alone what we are now doing together.
                                        —Teacher from the Inquiry Charter

In Ali High School, the teachers who had been working in Inquiry—the first charter to be developed in the school[8]—believed that the move to charters had radically transformed the issue of disciplinary concerns between and among students and teachers. The teachers felt that the charter's organizational structure—smaller, more intimate units of academic and relational continuity over a four-year period—was key to setting a context in which change from a focus on discipline to a focus on student outcomes could happen.

As the charter entered its second year, teachers were quick to note how few disciplinary infractions had transpired in the first three months. Those problems that did occur appeared benign—students talking in class rather than verbally or physically fighting among themselves or with the teachers. Teachers attributed the positive changes in students' individual and collective behavior to a number of pedagogical beliefs embedded in the charter's core.

High Expectations of Students

Some of the teachers understood the decrease in disciplinary problems in individualistic terms—as a result of students' enhanced sense of self-esteem. They credited this change in self-concept to the high expectations that teachers in the charter held concerning students' capabilities. These assumptions, in combination with the knowledge that support was available if needed, purportedly stimulated in students a sense of "I can do it [the work]."

The heterogeneous design of the charter also communicated the message to both students and teachers that "there were no dumb classes here, no A B C" —in other words, no core groups of students who were having trouble, being treated differentially, or feeling labeled as a member of the "dummy group." Students did not experience the frustration, humiliation, and/or boredom that often accompanies life in more traditional school settings.[9] Students rarely acted out as a response to feeling academically incompetent or generally mistreated. In fact, quite the opposite occurred. Many of the students began to have high expectations of one another. The group norms slowly evolved from a situation in which it had been unacceptable to "show your smarts" or "be a brain" to a point at which working hard and striving for individual and collective "success" was valued. As one student commented, "You get noticed for good work . . . it's not cool to be dumb here." Thus the normative question around negative behavior became, "Why would you want to behave like that?"

Close Student–Teacher Relationships

At a citywide conference on charters sponsored by the PSC, one of the students from Inquiry stood up and characterized the nature of the student–teacher relationship in the charter:

> At Inquiry everybody is like a family. We feel like teachers are on our side, not against us. They're challenging our minds. . . . We don't think about them as teachers, we think about them as friends.

Thus, after 15 months of working together, students feel connected to adults who care about them and want to see them grow. One teacher explained that developing positive adult–teenager relationships meant nurturing open communications and respecting students' voices.

> Students know we will sit and listen. They can get angry and disagree, and we'll help them work through it. If teachers ask them a question, students know that teachers legitimately care about their response. The teachers take time to explain why they're asking certain questions . . . and if they are wrong about something they will apologize. . . . Students now trust talking rather than fighting.

The fact that teachers no longer make the assumption that a "disciplinary problem" is necessarily located just in the student helps reinforce the notion of students and teachers in educational partnerships. Teachers are quick to look at how they or their colleagues may be contributing to the problem. "We don't assume teachers are right and students are wrong. . . . It's not us against them. In fact, if a kid is having a hard time with a teacher, he can go to another teacher for help." At the same time, however, since students are discussed at great length among the faculty, "it is unusual for students to be able to avoid the scrutiny or make legitimate claims about being picked on."[10]

Shared Teaching/Learning Environment

One of the developments within the charter that has been surprising to the teachers is the way in which students "keep each other in check." One teacher explained, "It matters to them that the program doesn't get destroyed." Another thought that the relationships built between students and teachers no longer focuses on "controlling students, keeping them quiet, and feeding them information." A third teacher, building on this explanation, said that students viewed themselves as part of a community working toward common goals: "Kids get the message that it's selfish to act disruptively, because it keeps others from learning."

One teacher was quick to note, however, that being respectful did not imply student passivity. He explained that in a previous school where he had taught, maintaining orderly classrooms was the hallmark of being a good teacher. Consequently, keeping students quiet was critical, and their disobedience had implications for teachers and students both, whereas "the expectation here is to have students noisy with enthusiasm" as they focus on their work. Such an emphasis reflects the charter's pedagogical commitment to students' active engagement in learning.

Education is not about the teacher. Teachers are not the be-all and end-all. It's not that we're loose here . . . students know the rules and can function even with substitutes . . . it's that we're interested in letting students see that if they listen to one another, they can help each other.

Teachers used attendance in class as an indicator of students' commitment to their own success as well as the success of the group. Attendance in Inquiry has been phenomenal this year, with only the rare student missing class. "My classes are packed" said one of the teachers in the program. "I was doing the overall attendance in my classes . . . where you're supposed to record absences. I was shocked at the number of students who haven't missed a day of classes . . . one or two was a lot." Even more impressive to some teachers is that "students not only show up, but they come prepared—they no longer leave their textbooks at home." To teachers' great surprise and pleasure, students seem to have "bought in."

FINAL NOTES

The notion of the "metamorphosis" of discipline in the context of school restructuring emerged out of my empirical observations and discussions with teachers, administrators, and students. However, in an effort to move from a more traditional social science approach into a more collaborative process of inquiry, I asked a number of teachers[11] to reflect/question/theorize with me about discipline. My request was met with enthusiasm, given the district's most recent attempt to tighten security within the schools, such as random metal-detector checks by plainclothes police.[12] The topic of school discipline had moved, again, to the foreground for all.

Each teacher affirmed, from his or her own experience, the transformational nature of charters and the links between tightly knit, curricularly rich educational environments and the displacement of discipline as the central concern within charter life. In fact, most felt confident in saying that the reported outbreaks of violence as well as the noted deterioration of certain school climates[13] tended to involve unaffiliated, rather than chartered, students—further reflecting the positive impact of charters. However, new tensions are emerging.

Disciplinary Policies: Tension Between Charters and Schools

There has been little dialogue across charters, or between the charters and their schools, about how to realign assumptions underlying disciplinary policies and practices. Several teachers pinpointed the need to change schoolwide disciplinary policies from "policing and monitoring" to "individual and collective accountability and growth."

One teacher, for example, described the difference in the meaning attached to "lateness" in her charter versus her school. While her charter does not condone lateness, teachers prefer to keep students in school, rather than remove them. "We have a student who went from being 20 minutes late to class to 5 . . . we see that as improvement. The school still insists on suspending him." Charter teachers experience the school administration as enforcing disciplinary policies that undermine their work with students.

Teachers also point to a linked, but contrasting, side of this issue. In some schools, teachers report that administrators have abdicated responsibility for maintaining any sort of schoolwide disciplinary standards. With much concern, one teacher described the "chaos in the halls . . . in the school . . . where there are no agreed-upon controls by anybody." Since most charters are not physically segregated from one another or from the rest of the school, students and teachers (who may not be responsible for instigating the tumult) are still confronted by it. "We need a vision that comes out of a whole-school conversation . . . everyone needs to participate, we can't afford any weak links."

The Erosion of the Charters' Defining Features—Smallness, Boundedness

Smallness. A number of teachers commented that as the charters have continued to expand (from 200 to 400 students), "the seams of the charters feel too tightly stretched." Some worry that they will soon grow beyond the capacity of their teacher teams to stay on top of the details of charter life or, even more importantly, that the relationships within and between student and teacher groups will begin to suffer. Undergirding these concerns is the anxiety that the interpersonal and collective forces that have influenced student behavior and charter climate will be compromised.

The problem of the student–teacher ratio is linked to a number of complex political and logistical issues. However, two factors concerning continuity and stability that teachers focused on included teacher attrition and student transfers. Many charters have lost at least one, sometimes two teachers each year who have been "bumped."[14] With the teachers using a team approach to develop a thematically based curriculum and interdisciplinary coherence, the loss of a team member has significant reverberations for the charter as a whole. Consequently, charter members[15] have had to spend inordinate amounts of time and energy orienting and developing new teachers, while simultaneously supporting the growth and development of their students. All too often it has meant that other charter teachers have carried a heavier burden in an effort to compensate for "weak links" in their team. With a smaller number of students, teachers mused that charters might be better able to accommodate the fluctuations in the teaching staff.

Another critical variable that seemed to place the charter resources under stress was the way in which internal and external transfer students who entered the school during the year were handled. Regardless of the reason for their transfer—some were transferred from other schools because they had been labeled "behavior problems"; others moved due to the exigencies of family life —the charters were given little if any information about new students and their particular needs. While charter teachers purportedly had little resistance to the notion of incorporating new students—whoever they were—they wanted to have the extra time and energy it took to "find out about a kid" acknowledged, leverage the resources that the individual might need, and socialize him or her into the charter.

Boundedness. In some schools the roster office has been neither committed to, nor adept at, maintaining each charter's boundaries. In practical terms, students and teachers who have chosen to attach themselves to a particular charter have found themselves assigned to classes with either unaffiliated students or students in other charters. Such precarious placements were viewed by the roster office "as the only practical option," since their job was to balance the needs of all the individuals and groups in the school.

The teachers with whom I spoke believed that overlapping rosters had more to do with power, control, and technical incompetence, not concern for "what's best for the whole." Having taught themselves some of the basics involved in rostering, several teachers felt confident that whole-school charter rostering, although complex, might be resolved *if* school policies supported such an approach. Not surprisingly, teachers were worried that continuing to ignore charter boundaries would subvert the evolution of a community defined by a specific set of pedagogical beliefs and behaviors and reliant on immersion and continuity for promoting connection.

The Ambiguity of School-Based Management/Shared Decision Making

While the concept of a charter as a valid educational entity has broad support, the path to shared governance has been layered with ambivalence by the union, the district, and the high schools themselves. Whereas smaller "pockets" of democracy are being nurtured inside charter walls, the attempt to build and institutionalize democratic processes within schools is currently in question.

The sense that the district and union are moving away from the vision of democratic governance has significant implications for charters.[16] Since charters remain embedded in the larger school context, a shift back to top-down decision making threatens the evolving cultural norms of teamwork and problem solving within and across teacher, student, and administrative groups. Without a framework for maintaining democratic relations within a decentralized but explicitly aligned educational organization, individual obedience and institutional control once again become the primary goals of the school bureaucracy.

Thus I leave this chapter on a more circumspect note. The elements that I identified in the text as essential to creating more caring, less volatile learning environments (school-based management/shared decision making, well-defined charters, and consistent community rules) and that I suggested change the nature of disciplinary concerns, are being worn away by conflicting policies and practices at the school and district levels. Without creating an infrastructure that unambivalently supports charter values and directions, the charters will be unable to sustain the very purposes for which they were created and discipline problems will again prevail.

NOTES

1. Since 1969, "lack of discipline" among students has ranked as the number one concern 18 out of 19 times in the Gallup polls of "Public Attitudes Towards Education" (Gallup, 1969–88). In their book *Violence, Values, and Justice in the Schools,* Bybee and Gee (1982) reported that incidences of school-related violence and vandalism rose dramatically between 1950 and 1980 and had reached proportions "unprecedented in American education and perhaps in the history of education" (p. 89).

2. The renewal efforts have been spearheaded by the Philadelphia Schools Collaborative, a nonprofit organization created by the district to guide the work in the schools; to serve as a broker among the schools, the district, and the state; and to harness the resources of the larger community, including parents, industry, and academia.

3. I entered these schools for different reasons at different moments in their renewal process: Muñoz Marin, a racially mixed, working-class school, was in the very early stages of restructuring when I attempted to document the process by which their renewal team—a representative group of faculty, staff, and parents from within the school—took up the task of designing the school's initial renewal plan. At a school that contained both working- and middle-class African American students, I observed their first-year planning efforts and then revisited the school a year later to discuss with teachers and administrators the ways in which the school's renewal process had affected the school to date. As a way to document the change effort at Ford, a school filled with very poor African American students, I interviewed teachers, administrators, and students approximately two years after they had begun experimenting with new means of structuring educational programs. Ali, a school composed of poor and working-class African American students, was in its third year of renewal when I began consulting with teachers within individual charters who were seeking to build communities based on collaboration and intellectual inquiry. Ali was one of the more advanced schools in that teach-

ers, administrators, and parents had spent many years struggling with the complex issue of governance while simultaneously sanctioning the implementation of charters within the school.

4. It is important to note that while the majority of teachers and administrators shared an individualistic perspective about student disciplinary problems, small pockets of teachers—as well as administrators—made connections between individual student behaviors and the school environment. They assumed that in a large school with large classrooms, it was easy to feel lost and disconnected. Because teachers were expected to follow the standardized curriculum, little effort was made to create curriculum or instructional materials that were tailored to students' lives. Some teachers believed that the combination of being isolated and bored, as well as labeled, was a good spawning ground for alienation and, consequently, disruption.

5. Alschuler (1980) advocates for a more democratic approach to schooling in which students have some decision-making power over their educational life. Metz (1978) calls for both organizational and social change. Their positions are less common in the discipline literature.

6. "Assertive discipline" is one currently popular method used to set standards and "to provide the means for interacting with students in calm yet forceful ways that result in more compliant behavior." Another is exemplified by Jere Brophy (1987) in his article, "Classroom Management as Instruction: Socializing Self-Guidance in Students," in which "willing but ignorant" students are taught the skills of self-control.

7. Mary Metz (1978) notes that over the past 20 years there has been a shift in the way the student–teacher conflict has been traditionally played out—students have become less accepting of the power imbalance between teachers and students because they have become less trusting of their elders' intentions and beliefs. "They have become more skeptical . . . more openly challenging . . . [students have been] primed to ask pointed questions about justifications for commands given to them in relationship to authority" (p. 189).

8. At Ali High School, both the renewal team and the governance council, which succeeded it, pursued a multiyear plan: the establishment of the ninth-grade institute in the first year of the restructuring process; the creation of two charters, Connections and the Business Academy, in the second year; and the implementation of two additional charters and an academy in the third year. The strategy for the fourth year—dealing with those few students and teachers who are not chartered—has yet to be decided.

9. Bybee and Gee (1982) link disciplinary problems and self-esteem. They use Zimbardo's framework of "deindividuation" to suggest that students who have few experiences of academic or behavioral success go through an internal process whereby their self-perception is diminished. The lack of self-esteem purportedly erodes the internal psychological structures that inhibit disruptive behaviors. Consequently, students evolve into poorly behaved students.

10. A rarely exercised but important option for responding to student–teacher conflicts, which has become available as a consequence of the charter's structure and its interdisciplinary approach to curriculum, is having students switch teachers within the same discipline. Since each of the teachers is familiar with each of the students via team discussions, and most curricular plans are coordinated in an effort to create a coherent academic program, there are ways to reconfigure students' rosters so that they can be

exposed to new teachers without jeopardizing their scholastic program. As one teacher noted appreciatively, "If some teacher–student pairs just don't work, we can try switching classrooms because we now have some flexibility." Therefore, while the charter is a closed community, there is some internal flexibility that allows students and teachers to feel connected, but not necessarily stuck.

11. Two of the teachers with whom I spoke had already deeply informed the writing of this chapter. Their voices are already woven into the main body of the text. Two other teachers and an administrator (the school disciplinarian) were interviewed because they are deeply involved with restructuring.

12. As a response to a number of highly publicized violent clashes between students and teachers, the district had ordered the implementation of random security checks.

13. Some examples were students wandering the halls after the bell, more absenteeism, heated exchanges between teachers and groups of students, and so forth.

14. Teachers often begrudgingly leave charters due to the seniority policies concerning long-term substitutes. Teachers also request a transfer because of their negative feelings about charters, their team relationships, or their teaching evaluation by the administration.

15. This is particularly true for charter coordinators.

16. In a few instances, although the governance councils have been dissolved, the principal is committed to working as democratically as possible.

REFERENCES

Alschuler, A. (1980). *School discipline*. New York: McGraw Hill.

Brophy, J. (1987). Classroom management as instruction: Socializing self-guidance in students. In H. Clarizio, R. Craig, & W. Mehrens (Eds.), *Contemporary issues in educational psychology*. New York: Random House.

Bybee & Gee. (1982). *Violence, values, and justice in the schools*. Boston: Allyn & Bacon.

Carnoy, M., & Levin, H. (1985). *Schooling and work in the democratic state*. Stanford, CA: Stanford University Press.

Curwin, R., & Mendler, A. (1988). *Discipline with dignity*. Washington, DC: Association for Supervision and Curriculum Development.

Ianni, F. (1989). *The search for structure*. New York: The Free Press.

Metz, M. (1978). Organizational tensions and authority in public schools. In K. Dourgherty and F. Hammack (Eds.), *Education and society—A reader*. San Diego: Harcourt Brace Jovanovich.

Rutter, M., Maughan, B., Mortimer, P., Ouston, J., & Smith, A. (1979). *Fifteen thousand hours: Secondary schools and their effects on children*. Cambridge, MA: Harvard University Press.

9

Co-Making Ethnography: Moving into Collaboration

PAT MACPHERSON

My "double life" as an ethnographer began a year ago. I became ethnographer of a charter and of our ethnographers group. Writing this chapter about the ethnographers group has been quite an initiation into the tricks and traps, limits and possibilities of ethnography *for* (as well as *about*) change. This is for, as well as about, the teachers and ethnographers involved in reform. In writing this, I wanted readers to see reform in the midst and inquiry in the midst, to try to glimpse how change occurs at ground level. I purposely selected moments when issues felt unsettling, rough, and raggedy. During my first year of charter-based ethnography (which was also the charter's first year), I felt awkward, alien, naive, and ignorant. These are a teacher's most unacceptable feelings. Coherence, calm, and vast amounts of knowledgeability are what we wish to wear in school. I felt the same while writing this chapter. Yet I cling stubbornly to whatever remains of the rough edges of this piece, after much feedback from the "objects" of my inquiry and after much revision. I want us to look like we were making it up as we went along—just as the teachers are doing. We had to learn how to negotiate very different versions of "critical ethnographer" with one another, and we often got it wrong and collectively had to come up with a workable practice and narrative resolutions—always under deadline of meetings about to end and due dates overdue. In the end I discuss the reactions of the ethnographers to this chapter—some of which I have incorporated, burying my errors and earlier interpretations, and some of which I have marked as their version altering my own. My guiding principle is to present my interpretation of how change occurs—in teachers, students, schools, and, especially, in ethnographers as we try to document, reflect, feed back (so far, so good), and write about teachers struggling to transform their schools.

FORMING THE ETHNOGRAPHY GROUP

Our ethnography group formed in October 1991 when Michelle Fine invited five of us to research and write "biographies of charters" in their first year of life under the Philadelphia Schools Collaborative (PSC) restructuring project. Each of us was to pick a charter in a school, latch on to the teachers and students as a participant–observer of "charter life," and write a story of the charter for Pew Charitable Trusts—and for, even *with,* the teachers in the charter. In support of this work we would meet regularly together as an ethnographers group.

Michelle's idea was that we would discuss the problems and pathways we found as we entered into charter life and (even more intimidating) figure out how to write a public story of what were inevitably deeply personal teaching and learning stories. We would be *observing* how charters develop within the realities of each school, at the same time *participating* in the charter's development as change agents—first in order to *feed back* to charter teachers our interpretations and questions about their evolving charter and second to *research and write about* what we saw and did for an external audience. As ethnographers we would be making research activist *and* writing up activism (Fine & Vanderslice, 1992). Our interpretations and negotiations of all these tensions would be the subject matter of our ethnographers meetings (not to mention our waking worries and vibrant dreams).

As critical ethnographers, we all have multiple experiences teaching and working with teachers, whether as psychologist, consultant, or administrator. And we had each faced the difficulties of writing about education and change. Jolley Christman is a consultant who "works between groups" in education. She leads a journal workshop for principals, teaches an ethnography course at a local university to "train people to study what they do as they do it," and works in schools "to develop their capacity for self-study." She worked "downtown" and knows the school district bureaucracy. Linda Powell is an educational consultant who works with schools and Black churches. She starts with the premise that each group is its own "interpretive community" with the potential to "self-reflect, self-diagnose, self-correct." In particular, she works with teachers "to hold—not stifle—discussions on racism." She organized the family group program in this district, as she explains in Chapter 7. Jody Cohen was a high school teacher in New York and is now writing her doctoral dissertation about "the co-construction of knowledge" in one urban teacher's classroom. She works with graduate students and high school students and teachers on inquiry into their teaching and learning. She facilitated a girls group to discuss "life issues." Nancie Zane is an organizational consultant who supports teachers in new charters in developing into effective teams and reflective communities. Diane Masar (who joined the ethnography group in the spring) is a full-time high school teacher who works with Linda Powell on family group; she is interested in how to enable teachers to write about the different interactions that family group establishes among teachers and between teachers and students. Anne Okongwu, who teaches a multicultural education course to teachers at Queens College in New York, joined the group in the fall of 1992 to write about a parents group that was newly formed to discuss multicultural education. I was a high school teacher in a Quaker urban school; I now write about adolescent girls, teach seminars, and consult on curriculum with public school teachers. Michelle Fine is a social psychologist whose books on schools (Fine, 1991) and feminist research (Fine, 1992) inform her teaching (at the City University of New York) and her consulting for the Philadelphia Schools Collaborative.

MAKING PRIVATE STORIES PUBLIC

Our earliest and most frequent conclusion was that the best stories about charter life could never be told. They were always potentially damaging to someone. For me as a writer this was only incitement to find a sufficiently safe way to tell, as in this case, some behind-the-scenes stories about the ethnographers group. Other stories yet to be told are about the subtexts of class, race, and gender in schools, for instance, the gender inequities that result when male administrators have affairs with women teachers and the racial inequities that produce knowledge, loyalties, and conflicts that simmer unspoken but rarely boil into confrontation or resolution. These stories form schools. They are official secrets, gossiped about and informing power relations, but they are never publicly spoken. When and how is it safe for the group to name and confront its own secrets? We discovered as ethnographers that we could ask questions about these secrets that might bring them more publicly into view in meetings, in forms that sometimes made them discussable. But can ethnographers ever write about them? If we do, are we making "insiders" too vulnerable? If we do not, are we colluding in the silence? We are still wrestling with the task of writing about them for an audience that includes both the teachers themselves and an unknown public beyond the school's walls.

The collaborations necessary to co-make ethnography stretched far beyond our exciting discussions in Michelle's office downtown in the school district building where we women met. I would speculate where we had each just come from, guessing that Jolley's bright eyes and raised eyebrow meant she had a great story to tell, that Linda in her colorful jackets and scarves and with her excited demeanor had a full agenda of consulting before she would take the late train home to Washington, that Nancie in her black jacket and pants and with her briefcase had just come from meeting with her charter teachers, that Diane's face was thoughtful but her body tiredness meant she had spent the day teaching, that Jody in her sweater and stretchpants had arrived from newborn child care at home, that Michelle's combination of formal dress and drawn face meant she had just met with some seemingly immovable obstacle somewhere in the district, while I with my heavy bag of books and tape recorder and lunch looked schoolteacherish as always.

Into these meetings each of us carried stories from our school groups. At first we told stories about our developing relations at each school, sometimes comic, usually awkward in the way that newly invented forms of relationship are. "An ethnographer? What's *that*?" I had to laugh in bafflement myself, since we were all making it up as we negotiated our way into relationships. We found we had to find a function for ourselves beyond mere hanger-on, become enough of a player in the action to be effective in our group, which would then give people a real reason to tell us some of the stories cooking all around us. We had to enter into collaborations with teachers and students in the schools in order to see the stories as they developed. This enabled us to see the often alarmingly limited collaborative relations within the schools, whether between teachers and students of different racial or gender groups, or between teachers and students generally. Developing these new forms of collaboration across old (often unacknowledged) boundaries has become the focus of the restructuring effort of building charters and of our ethnographers' activism.

The activism we co-created used the following process:

1. The ethnographers intervened in charter dynamics through inquiry, by asking questions about the proceedings.
2. In the same way, within the ethnographers group we changed one another's interpretations of a charter situation by asking questions about the proceedings and the ethnographer's interpretations—modeling doubled inquiry that asks about an ethnographer's lense and frame as explicit parts of the analysis.
3. Out of this question asking and ensuing discussion, the group (whether charter teachers or ethnographers) saw new possibilities for action.
4. By addressing problems of audience and confidentiality for these issues, ethnographers pressed one another to find the forum to feed back our interpretations to teachers, and teachers were pressed to feed back their interpretations of the charter's problems to one another. Former secrets became the space of inquiry and the map for re-forming. But this remains treacherous territory.

Each charter's situation is of course particular in its history, dynamics, constituent parts, and context—and so is each ethnographer. So as each ethnographer negotiated her way into an existing yet changing dynamic, her role was shaped by—and in turn shaped—the charter dynamic. Six different aspects of "new authority" created by restructuring illuminate the six ethnographers' different negotiations with their different charters. (Anne worked with the citywide parent group our second year, and Michelle supervised overall charter development.) Jolley's problems "getting in" to her charter's action showed its search for its own internally defined authority and guiding ideology—a problem for charters across the district. Linda's group's concerns about the authority of students to speak and the authority of teachers to listen and facilitate made clear how radically the family group restructured the boundaries and interactions possible between students and teachers. Nancie, in always assuming teachers' new authority to plan a charter, helped them learn how to recognize and negotiate the complexities of democratic and diverse authority within a group. Diane, in seeing women's authority in the classroom, helped them learn from that experience while they developed new authority outside the classroom. Pat, in supporting and modeling women's new authority, helped address and challenge one pattern of sexist authority in the group. And Jody reflected and helped develop her charter's radical creation of students as authorities.

Access

Access was our first and most obvious shared concern, at first literally about getting into and around the school, then into classrooms and meetings (often understood as more private than public space), then into conversations—initially of the formal interview type, but gradually more private conversations based on shared confidences. Despite our wishes, there is no final "in." "You're in!" the coordinator of my charter told me in December after my third visit—but that meant only that I could hang around without teachers feeling too bothered; by July's charter meeting, which I facilitated, my being "in" meant getting wet in the backyard pool during lunchbreak. If I had not gone in I would have been thrown in, a teacher warned me as I arrived for our session that summer. Once in the pool, I heard story after story from a teacher who had never really spoken to me all year.

Access remains an ongoing negotiation for all six of us, but most of all for Jolley. Access often means going into spaces and toward questions that charter teachers have not dared investigate, finding the holes. What we might see as opportunity, teachers might see as deficit to be "repaired." Jolley's charter was in a search for program focus, the most fundamental and colossally difficult first step for all schools beginning to restructure themselves into charters. This is the step where most stall and get stuck. In describing this problem when Jolley began her work with her charter, I made such charter teachers into the "object" of restructuring and "the problem" that is districtwide. In my original text, for this chapter I objectified them, and Jolley's feedback caused me to revise by supplying more context and to question my own power to make objects out of teachers' toughest dilemmas.

Before Jolley's entry, her charter group had already incorporated an "outside expert" from a university who had written a grant proposal for them, and this "packaging" of them for an outside audience powerfully framed their identity and potential relations with Jolley, whose role was unclear, unnamed. How would *she* help build their legitimacy to the outside world? "The group has invented an identity outside themselves," Jolley said in the February 21 ethnographers meeting. "Official expertise—and charter legitimacy—lie outside the charter." This should come as no surprise to teachers long disempowered and marginal to policy work. Jolley later framed this into an inquiry question: "What do teachers who are forming a charter need to make themselves legitimate?" This question invites analysis of external and internal resources, group makeup and processes and goals, structures and supports. Then a second inquiry question: "Who is the audience for 'legitimacy'?" This question invites analysis of possibilities ranging from students to community to the teachers themselves to school staff or principal to parents to downtown school district officials to outside experts.

Jolley said her group had cohesion around concerns for kids but did not yet have a shared vision of their own intellectual agency in order to develop their knowledge of their program. We discussed the reasons for this common situation, which I related to some teachers' "fraud model" of themselves: Authority on curriculum has always been externally defined, so why should they now assume they have the resources necessary to generate a program? When they define such knowledge as external, then they collaborate around seeking outsiders to develop or legitimate the program—or resisting such outsiders. Jolley needed to help them to seek their previously unsought interior possibilities for intellectual work. We asked Jolley where in the charter she wanted to work.

> I'm most interested in community service, and students getting credit for their work with younger kids in recreation centers and elementary schools. The kids love it, and they're some of the most alienated students. . . . Family group is where they debrief. Students think the elementary students are off the wall. "Look at yourselves at that age," their teacher told them. He got them to do that. That's real teaching and learning going on in family group. That's why *charters* should look at family group to develop their program. But most teachers assume that action and jobs are *separate* from real learning, that family group and community service are *separate* from learning.

Access is difficult if school charters have no coherence; and in the public sector, teachers have only rarely had the opportunity to nurture a shared ideology or coherence.

The teachers in this charter have seen but have not developed the links between what they know students are learning in family group and community service and their teaching in their own academic program. Teachers' energy was going elsewhere, as historically it always has, Jolley said recently. "The context for this is that schools and bureaucracies spend so much time legitimating themselves to the outside world that there is *no model* there for teaching and learning as central. The charter's job is to invent the model *and* break the pattern"— while living in a traditional district.

Co-Creating Family Group

Linda's and Diane's work with a citywide collection of teacher leaders of family group had some interesting differences from the other ethnographers' work with charter teachers. Their creation of family group with teachers was "homegrown," in ways similar to charter creation, in their formative-vision stage of discussions about constituencies, necessary structures, possible procedures, and desired goals for students. (See Chapter 7.) But family group did not have an institutional history, had never had a place in any school's program or social relations or politics; in addition, the family group teachers came from different schools. As a notion imported from New York City, family group as an idea could grow and be locally nourished in some spaces "between schools." Ideology and coherence were no problem. But resituating family group within the boundaries of school was. Charters encounter their problems and find their solutions very much on-site, subject to their own history, program, social relations, and politics. Charter teachers struggle against and within these old authority structures to envision charters and create the new relations that are part of them. Teachers facilitating family group on-site create a new space for safe conversations about both the public rules and behaviors determining school life and the private life experiences that are the stuff of student identity and learning. Family group's provision of space and protection for each member to ask real questions of one another is one place for homegrowing new authorities in schools.

Linda's questions in our ethnographers meetings induced us to interpret each charter's group dynamics through a set of boundary themes: In the January 29 meeting she asked us to consider "how our negotiated relationships with our charter embody, reflect, and react to the charter's internal sense of its boundaries, loyalties, knowledge, and legitimacy." Linda's work with family group presented radical alternatives to some charter problems of self-limitation. For instance, knowledge itself is differently defined in family group, where the one-way (teacher-tells-student) model of teaching and learning is replaced by multiway asking-and-listening discussion. Once teachers have restructured boundaries with students in order to lead a family group, Linda's inquiry questions reveal the new possibilities opened up: "How are family group boundaries different from classroom boundaries? What is learned in family group and how is it learned? How does confidentiality operate in family group? What are the boundaries of secrets in the group? of secrets from one's family? of secrets of and with one's friends?"

Confidentiality and Feedback

This issue of secrets learned from and protected by our access to an intimately collaborative group is just as crucial to ethnography as to restructuring. Our access (to charters, teachers' lives, students' lives, ethnographers meetings, and developing friendships) grows from trust about boundaries and confidences observed—yet we are there in order to observe *and tell* what we see. The ethical response is *not*, as first assumed, *silence* as the measure of one's group loyalty, but rather *feedback*. Each member becomes accountable for listening and responding to the problems and views on the table. Yet feedback, conversation, and accountability are all threatened by the possibility of punishment in schools, which are not safe spaces.

Jolley, Jody, and I recently discussed the ethnographer's particular dilemma about confidentiality and feedback issues when each of us began to try to write about our charters for looming deadlines of conference, publication, and Pew. Our original deal with our charters was that we would share our writing about them with them first, and then negotiate its final form. Jolley (from her paper in progress) framed the agony succinctly: "I'm not yet writing about my charter because *writing will interrupt inquiry*." While she is still working with her group this second school year (as am I), her oral feedback is constructive as part of their ongoing discussion of ongoing problems. Writing about the charter must be accompanied by conversation—but even so, writing inevitably alters relations, making the ethnographer's power manifest. When we write for our charters do we lose the enabling illusion of freedom, of stories still privately plotted and told to (but not by) the ethnographer in the group, which is still in the risk-taking stage of the formative vision?

Timing, Jolley decided, is crucial to *telling* different audiences about charter problems and solutions. We decided that only after a charter has moved on from its particular set of issues and relationships can its members best collaborate on a fit forum for exposure to a more public audience. And the ethnographers group, like charter teachers groups, first needed confidentiality for problem solving. Only in such privacy would members feel free enough to air their trickiest, ugliest, angriest, most vulnerable, most humiliating, or silliest dilemmas, and receive the feedback, challenge, support, audience, and motivation to continue. Silence about problems, particularly the stalled situations, tended to delay us as well, whether as teachers, consultants, or writing ethnographers.

Ethnographer as Activist

At the same time as ethnographers must be active members of the group, we must avoid being the sole central authority, mediator of all responses, and final interpreter of and for the group. Linda's and Diane's family group ethnography is currently planned as a collection of teacher writing about their family group work. Diane said in the September 4 meeting, "Critical ethnography has no central authority," and cited Don Dippo's work with "multivoiced texts. He records. Others in the group will do the analysis." Michelle asked: "But does this just hide the central authority? Does self-effacement render you gone or just invisible?" And Nancie asked: "When is it OK to take on your authority role?" Michelle, as usual, would press even further: "As theorists and activists, don't we have a responsibility to interpret, risk, and revise?"

The work of restructuring and collaboration creates space for new authorities within schools: teachers, students, women, even ethnographers. This is where our research activism found much room for interpretation and intervention—and nervous retreat.

Teachers as Authorities

Nancie's work with her charter explored many of the difficulties teachers have in becoming authorities on program and accountable for their own collaborative process. In our September 4 meeting Nancie said, "Charters change authority structures in schools; they create space for people to manage authority between them." I had skeptically asked why the average teacher would buy in to charters when they demanded so much initiative and follow-through, and Diane had pointed to the silencing and isolation of teachers in most buildings: "Where in school does a teacher get to *say*?" Teachers learning how to say the previously private, officially secret, openly critical, or otherwise unspeakable was one feature of Nancie's work with teams—establishing methods and manners for communication. Why and how could one critique a colleague for poor teaching? for poor participation with colleagues? Weren't administrators the authorities responsible for evaluating and reprimanding other teachers? What kinds of authority get recognized in a group of teachers? For instance, what kind of authority is attached to one's gender? one's race? one's class? one's subject taught (math versus English versus counseling versus special education versus physical education versus auto shop versus art versus "consultant")? one's investment and work in charter creation? Recognizing authority as it plays out in the group's dynamic was the first step of inquiry that Nancie made explicit in her feedback to charters, in this way modeling an inquiry mode for the charter as its own "interpretive community."

Diane in our September 4 meeting on how and what we were writing about our charters asked questions about teachers as authorities in family group. Diane said she did not want to speak for other teachers. What would Diane write as a teacher herself and as facilitator of the teachers' family group? And the teachers in the group: "Are they data—or authors?" How would the group's feedback on Diane's writing then change her final draft? This is when Nancie asked, "When is it OK to take on your authority role?" Against Diane's possible self-silencing to allow the group to speak, Nancie was arguing for some authority for a single group member's interpretation of a group.

Earlier Nancie had described "my internal struggles about stepping into my authority"—her judgment about when and how to assert her authority and when to respect the teachers' boundaries around their work and her input. We all nodded knowingly at Nancie's example, because we all found it difficult. This recognition enabled us then to empathize with (not just recognize) teachers' problems with authority. We discussed the difference between a sense of "internal authority" that assumes one's agency and influence in a group, and a sense of "external authority" that assumes power is external and the self had better mind the rules or be shot down.

Diane provided an example of the struggle with authority from her other job—not the PSC, she later emphasized. She was working with a group of women high school teachers planning a strategy to deal with a problem that a male administrator had asked them to address—and then the group was dismissed out of hand by him after they delivered their proposal to the faculty. "Women's power has been in the classroom," Diane said. "When you move outside, your work is dismissed—or worse." Power *is* largely external and structural, Diane was arguing. Women are right not to feel confident in taking action: "Why feel secure when everything can change at any minute?"

In our discussion we moved from individual to structural power and authority—and how it is changed and negotiated. We, like charter teachers, had to struggle as a group to take the focus off personalities as problems—one version of what Michelle called "getting stuck in the local"—in order to bring into focus the ways the system disabled or enabled members to fulfill responsibilities to the group. Michelle called these "transformative issues." As Diane's example showed, teachers' growing authority depended on new kinds of professional accountability that had to be systematically created and supported, not individually assigned and then brutally canceled. Our local ethnographies could direct inquiry toward the most vulnerable teachers to find them needed support (in any form, from co-teachers to computer access to curriculum planning), but resulted in exposing or isolating them as "the problem."

The issue of women as new authorities and men as old authorities remains one of my charter's most visible yet unspoken dynamics. A year ago my outsider's eyes widened at familiar gender types in play. Men were either presumed leaders, or boys (playful jokesters or temperamental bullies), or discounted wimps. Women were either mothers who would fix all family problems (most powerful), wife-workhorses (middle management), or sexual objects or partners, commented on or self-announced, always in the form of jokes. Male–female relations almost always seemed to start with double entendres, ostensibly to establish social ease. But my ill-concealed unease and nonparticipation began to raise the unasked question: Whose authority is enabled and whose authority is silenced or disabled by such joking? If the women have assumed that "going along" makes them members of the boys' club or the sexually powerful, my "difference" has begun to turn that assumption into a question. But it is a question I have not found a way to ask publicly. Yet here I am writing about it.

In collaboration with my charter's female coordinator, and based on many private conversations with teachers interpreting the sexual politics of the group, we have facilitated in meetings a "new" model of female leadership that asks questions for the group to answer, guides discussion toward resolution, and clarifies accountability and follow-through. Old authority is less democratic, more concerned with enforcing policy and settling boundary disputes. Such changes are dependent on each charter member's interpretation of the group dynamic, including what gender "means." After several different women's confrontations with boys-will-be-boys behavior in charter meetings and other events, a new plot has developed, with women publicly addressing "jokes" that are unacceptable to them and then carrying on with the business at hand in a spirit of humor and inclusion. I support, even instigate such changes; as an ethnographer, I have to find ways to talk and write about them.

Students as Authorities

In the ethnographers group, only Jody's vision and work made students central to revising programs and relationships within schools. Jody listened to students in and out of class, chatting informally and audiotaping interviews. In the process she enabled students to become authorities on their experiences in school, on classroom dynamics, on teachers' different methods and effects, and on their own lives and the roles and results of learning for their futures. (See Chapter 6.) In the process she became an audience for students' knowledge and invited teachers to become an audience for students' interpretations of how school works. Jody's charter had begun with a vision of student learning at the center. To gain access, to participate as a player, and to address and develop the charter's theory and practice, Jody generated multivoiced feedback on both vision and the ground-level reality of charter life.

Significantly, in the ethnographers group Jody was the most self-effacing and least heard. I noticed this only after one meeting in June when I had rudely invaded her sense of confidential knowledge and loyalty, mistakenly assuming she felt my own sense of "privacy" of ethnographers group for all confidential matters. Why had her different view of boundaries (and knowledge and loyalties and legitimacy—all Linda's themes) not been clear to me? Had Jody been unheard or devalued because she was the students' advocate and their views were still marginal—both to restructuring and to our definition of ethnography?

When she only recently read my analysis of her and her charter, Jody said she thought I had underrepresented the charter's essence and success: student-centered learning. But everyone seems to find a way to downplay their success. One of the "star" charters is enormously resisted by colleagues. Why? Jody worries that her charter's success as a student-centered teaching-and-learning community may be its biggest problem in relation to other charters—and even to itself, as it pulls in new teachers and students. Her charter had an earlier start (at least one year ahead) and several extraordinary teachers with already impressive student achievements to their credit. Their success became a distant target for others: an unreachable ideal, an unreproducible exception, an envied elite, or an unfair head start. Most of Jody's issues for the ethnographers group were different from the issues we were struggling with, and so she often remained silent rather than daunt or demoralize us with successes and failures of a type we were not sure we would ever get to. Our sense of possibility was in this way diminished by the marginalizing of "the success story." We have yet to analyze thoroughly the differences that her charter makes in the restructuring effort.

Building Audiences for Ethnography

The treacherous territory of audience for the ethnographies came up most dramatically in our April 13 meeting with Dick Clark, consultant–evaluator–writer of the "master narrative" for the PSC report to Pew Charitable Trusts. His work and perspective are nationwide and include analyses of school district bureaucracies and their relationship to restructuring efforts. He assured us that "the district's messiness needs to be fed back to them" by such activist research as his and our own. We agreed; we marveled at the difficulty of engaging in self-reflection in a bureaucracy that may well be structurally opposed or even openly hostile to change.

When the subtext turned to Dick Clark's "use of what ethnographers are learning" for a different audience than the teachers and ethnographers themselves, we all began to imagine the "bad audiences" possible. Jolley, who has worked in the district, asked: "What response and what use would the school district have as audience for our ethnographies? Wouldn't teachers and their principals quickly be punished for the messiness of their experimentation—for not having 'things under control'?"

We were back to Michelle's question from our first ethnographers meeting: "What's the relationship between a school district that sits relatively still, school charters in the midst of radical restructuring, and our inquiry about the contradictions?" Only now we were in the middle of this tension, rather than observing it from the sidelines or theorizing about it at the conference table. Now we all had at least six months of relationships that we did not want treated as mere "data." We were now invested in protecting, nurturing, and furthering real people, partnerships, and projects, all held together by trust, risk, and optimism.

All along, Michelle had pressed us ethnographers "not to compromise the quality of the messiness that we—and charter teachers—are prepared to take on." She did not want "show pieces," but transformations in the midst. Although we all felt that we had more than met Michelle's challenge, we periodically sank with the weight of the cargo. What work would be compromised by showing such "messiness" to a wider audience? Yet if such messiness is the story, the stuff of change itself, how does one tell the story without detailing the messes? Was all work at the microlevel of teacher and student relations only possible with no public audience—when confidentiality protects everyone from the ravages of bureaucratic surveillance and enforcement—not to mention the already low opinion of inner-city schools held by the general public? What kinds of writing about charter struggles for what audiences can "interrupt inquiry," as Jolley began to ask—and how can the timing of ethnography serve teachers and students in the midst of change?

Negotiating Our Interpretations

This next set of questions for the ethnographers group was visited *on* the group by my writing this piece *about* the group. On November 2 "they" (suddenly no longer "we") reacted to "my" ethnography of them/us. Mainly they learned what it feels like to be objectified by a participant–observer who has been taking notes on their group process for a year. Mainly I learned what it feels like to be responsible for interpreting people and representing them, and then responsible for revising after their feedback. I love to analyze literary heroines in texts who do not talk back to my interpretation of them. Real people are harder to pin down and impossible to persuade. They keep talking! Does that mean I have to keep writing?

Our discussion on November 2 focused on how we negotiate and account for different interpretations (at least that is how I interpreted the discussion). As always, each ethnographer had her own interpretation of this dilemma, coming out of her own concerns. We came up with a collective sense of the nature of my authority, as well as a kind of permission for me to have my say. This was more than any fictional characters or deceased authors had ever granted me.

Michelle framed the context of our discussion as a "dress rehearsal" for discussing our ethnographies with our charters. "I think there are things to be learned from a set of folks asking questions aloud, before it's packaged." Michelle was, as always, initiating collaborative discussion, partly to promote my revision process, partly to get us to experience ethnography as the teachers would. "If we can't figure out a text where we can be public and slightly vulnerable, what are we asking teachers to do?" Anne Okongwu, new to the group and not represented in this chapter, said, "This helps ethnographers internalize what it means to be object." Then she laughed and said, "Of course I read it from relative safety." We discussed briefly how each ethnographer reacted to her own and her charter's representation, what had been selected, how she and her work came across. Appearances, for instance, counted. Jody did not like appearing in stretchpants, Michelle did not like her drawn face and implied defeat. Nancie thought she looked one-dimensional while Linda looked spiritual. And I had not described myself. (Linda and Diane were not there, being at work elsewhere; Diane phoned me later with their feedback.) Jolley thought I had protected myself and my charter while her charter came across as a big problem. In addition, she had not found a way to talk to them about her interpretation, and here was my interpretation about to be in print and not at all what she would have written. (I later revised both sections, about her charter and mine, after "thinking about this," as she urged me to do, and after a later long talk with her about specifics.)

Our discussion about the authority to interpret within a group took us from how we could reinvent this chapter to the nature of authority and participation in schools. I end with these selections from my tape of the November 2 meeting. In this way I wiggle away, while appearing to let each ethnographer and the group itself have the last words.

JODY: With this piece and the feedback, I'm wondering if the conversations get harder and less safe when it's around text.

NANCIE: Is that because it's not legitimate to have multiple realities? That somehow there's one that's more right than another?

JODY: I'm struggling with Pat having a version of this that's not what I would write.

PAT: We could write multiply not singly about the ethnography group. Abandon this particular narrative structure and divide it up in some way and have each write her own section.

ANNE: How do we include the input of people we're writing about? There has to be a place for their view. How do we include other alternative views but give some caveat about what is shaping the lense through which their view comes?

. . .

MICHELLE: That's what's getting interesting about collaborative work. Is it so coopted and negotiated that it's just safe?

. . .

ANNE: If alternative input doesn't mess with what we've written or how we have conceptualized it. . . . It's important to find a way to allow—with context— what an alternative interpretation is. [i.e.] I found something totally different from what I was expecting. That's what I love about ethnography.

People come up with something—*else*. But then you have to put a place for that.

. . .

JODY: You found a way of doing that after our late night conversation, Pat.

PAT: I wanted to add the element of time there. Having laid out my version you gave me a whole new angle in to think about it. It isn't for me about competing about which is right, but the way in which almost archaeologically things can be layered. And then the synthesis is gonna occur further down the line. And that's where the in-progressness of this piece is—

MICHELLE: —becomes important.

. . .

PAT: I think I want to make the case that there's something to be learned from describing shifts like that, for people who're trying to do this work.

. . .

MICHELLE: We have a lotta choices. One is, junk the piece, withhold it, it's too early. Another is to have many contradictory voices in the same text. . . . Or to create a narrative that has integrity through your [Pat's] analysis, but incorporates and begins to understand the vantage of other interpretations and demonstrates that, in a shift both in how you work with folks . . . and in how you construct a narration—

. . .

NANCIE: My reaction when we talked about [each] rewriting our own section was, What's the purpose? It feels like it would be trying to say my version so that I can get my reality in there—and also to protect my people. Also . . . that conversation we had with Diane about authority [in September 4 meeting] and what you just said, Michelle, about maintaining integrity but also providing a chronology that allows other voices. That's a way to acknowledge that in this instance you're maintaining your authority, which feels right to me, as opposed to everybody-equal-in-this. It acknowledges you as interpreter, although others are participating in interpretation. You're open enough to hear others. You're maintaining your authority but in a participative way.

PAT: Is this the ideal we've been under as ethnographers?

MICHELLE: And what education does is, it splits off authority and participation. If you do authority you're a [expletive deleted] autocrat who doesn't listen to anybody else. And if you do participation you're really off the hook and all you do is democracy. What people can't imagine is bringing those together so you can take a [expletive deleted] position and invite people into that process—but you're still accountable—whether you're Pat or the superintendent or any of us. I like the idea of bringing that together because it's a micro issue that's about ethnography and the charters but it's also about—transformation.

REFERENCES

Fine, M. (1991). *Framing dropouts: Notes on the politics of an urban public high school*. Albany: State University of New York Press.

Fine, M. (1992). *Disruptive voices: The possibilities of feminist research*. Ann Arbor: University of Michigan Press.

Fine, M., & Vanderslice, V. (1992). Qualitative activist research: Reflections on methods and politics. In Bryant et al. (Eds.), *Methodological issues in applied psychology*. New York: Plenum.

PART III

Teacher Inquiry as School Reform

Susan L. Lytle

In 1988 when the Philadelphia Schools Collaborative (PSC) was just beginning, secondary teachers from across the system came together to talk with the PSC leadership about the intellectual and social lives of students and teachers in the neighborhood high schools. Sketching images of failure and frustration, instability and apathy, these teachers nonetheless spoke passionately of what was and what could be, asserting their willingness to become planners, participants, leaders, and learners in a radical restructuring of the comprehensive high schools. Committed to altering the cultures of isolation in their own workplaces, they argued for the importance of conversations over time, within and across schools, that would deepen their understanding of their own practice and offer them space and support for change.

This image—of teacher collectives looking closely yet "publicly" at the nature of teaching and learning in their own classrooms—was nourished both by the experiences of local teachers who were already members of professional communities and by the growing national movement for teacher research. The Philadelphia Writing Project (PhilWP), established at the University of Pennsylvania in 1986 as a school–university partnership and an urban site of the National Writing Project, had already attracted a group of secondary teachers from comprehensive high schools whose extraordinary efforts on behalf of their students were essentially invisible to their colleagues or to the system as a whole. Through summer institutes, cross-visitations, and frequent meetings to discuss the interrelationships of literacy, language, and learning, these teachers with their elementary and middle school colleagues were trying to build an intellectual community *across* an immense bureaucratic system, in part to compensate for what was lacking within their own buildings.

Influenced by the efforts of action researchers such as Lawrence Sten-
house and his colleagues in the United Kingdom, builders of teacher networks
such as Dixie Goswami at Breadloaf, and school-based child study groups such
as Pat Carini and her colleagues at the Prospect School in North Bennington,
Vermont, project teachers and teacher educators working together at Penn in
the mid-1980s had begun to establish structures for the support of systematic
and intentional inquiry by teachers about their own school and classroom
work. These initiatives were intended not only to support the efforts of individual teachers but also to build district-based inquiry communities and to
strengthen the arguments for the institutionalization of inquiry as an integral
part of the professional lives of teachers. The local and national obstacles to
such a movement—the isolation of teachers, their occupational socialization as
self-sufficient and independent, and the technical model of professionalization
in which teachers are assumed to be consumers of outsider-expert knowledge—were all functioning to create school cultures that worked against raising questions and against taking the risks of interrogating assumptions and
common practices, essential components of the vision for reform taking shape
in the district.

The establishment of the Philadelphia Schools Collaborative, and the
invitation to secondary teachers to help shape its direction, came at a critical
moment for the emerging teacher leadership in the city and for envisioning
teacher inquiry as deeply embedded in and constitutive of meaningful reform. The PSC provided a context within which teachers could choose to
reconfigure their work to emphasize its fundamentally social and political
dimensions, reframe their classrooms and schools as sites of inquiry, and
begin to enact a vision of teacher research that was and is radical and passionate, deeply personal, and profoundly political—richly embedded in situations where the teacher's stance on his or her own practice and intellectual
life matters and where teachers' work lives, commitments, and relationships
are complex and entangled.

Having designated three schools as "intensive sites" for the initial phase
of reform, in the fall of 1989 the PSC and PhilWP worked together to establish the Seminar in Teaching and Learning, a teacher research community in
which teachers from across the disciplines began meeting biweekly at alter-
nating school sites to interrogate their own practices by reading, writing, and
conducting inquiries into day-to-day issues that emerged from their classrooms and charters, programs and schools.

As a teacher inquiry group focused explicitly on concerns about teaching and learning, the Seminar has become a vital intellectual community,
providing a rare context for co-laboring around issues and problems of common concern. Fundamentally different from a graduate seminar, such a researching community is not simply a place where individual teachers investi-

gate their own topics or issues, but rather a context for common inquiry in which questions take shape as the group becomes an interactive setting for looking beneath the surface of schools and classrooms and for opening up unsettling subjects for which there have been few if any other forums. In the Seminar in Teaching and Learning, many of these conversations have been about the failure of schools to educate culturally diverse populations and the profound disjunctions that exist between home and school, community and school system, teachers and students, as well as between teachers and their school- and university-based colleagues. To discuss these issues openly in diverse groups of teachers has meant investigating the meanings of difference in teachers' and students' ethnicities as well as confronting limitations in people's knowledge about values and cultures different from their own. In these conversations, teachers have typically posed rather than solved problems, elaborated rather than narrowed concerns, and often used systematic forms of oral inquiry to generate multiple perspectives for interpreting common experiences.

The chapters in this section explore teacher inquiry as a critical dimension of comprehensive high school restructuring. Chapter 10 provides an overview of the design of the Seminar in Teaching and Learning, showing how teachers work collectively to reframe their classrooms and schools as sites of inquiry. Written collaboratively by the leadership group of school- and university-based teachers, this piece draws on examples from the Seminar's first two years to show how the structures of a cross-school inquiring community can function to establish relationships that interrupt long-established practices and instigate school-based change. In Chapter 11, Bob Fecho writes about efforts to co-investigate issues of power and language with students, a project that is one of a series of studies Fecho has conducted on his own teaching practice over a number of years. A PhilWP teacher consultant, teacher leader of the Seminar since its inception, and one of the founders and coordinators of a charter, English teacher Fecho explores the theoretical bases of his practice and the linguistic and cultural resources of his students through the lenses of race, culture, and difference by making knowledge of language the subject as well as the medium of instruction. As a portrait of one teacher's critical pedagogy, the chapter weaves together Fecho's classroom experiences with collaborations with colleagues in the charter and Seminar contexts as well. In Chapter 12, Diane Waff, a participant in the Seminar for several years who became a Seminar leader and PhilWP teacher consultant, describes her work as a special education English and math teacher whose concern for what she calls "the peculiar burdens of being African American and Latina young women" led her to design a mentoring program in which students could bridge the disengaging oppositions of cultures in and out of school. In documenting the experiences of participants in a mentor-led "girl talk" group, Waff shows transformations that occurred as young women found a safe setting in which to voice passionately and in unfiltered language their deepest concerns and problems in school and as teachers learned from students' lives powerful ways to work with and advocate for them, both in and out of school.

Together, these three chapters suggest what happens when communities of teachers form relationships to interrupt the historic isolation of practitioners in schools, invent new ways of looking at the daily acts of teaching and learning, and demonstrate the power of generating new knowledge from a field-based perspective. Together teachers in these schools are taking on the hard social and political issues that inform instruction, bringing to the surface deep questions that involve increasing their vulnerability and disclosing the intimacies of their daily practice, and writing and publishing their work for national as well as local audiences. Efforts such as these suggest how teacher and student inquiries into critical issues of teaching and learning have become vital to the transformative agenda for social change inherent in the current reform movement.

10
Learning in the Afternoon: When Teacher Inquiry Meets School Reform

SUSAN L. LYTLE BOB FECHO
JOLLEY CHRISTMAN DINA PORTNOY
JODY COHEN FRAN SION
JOAN COUNTRYMAN

It is 3:15 on a chilly Monday afternoon in March. The corridors of
DuBois High School are silent, interrupted only by the occasional banging of
the custodial staff as they deal with the remnants of the day. In dimly lit Room
110, thirty-six teachers have moved from small journal groups of four or five to
form a large circle, ready to discuss an essay written by an English teacher
from another school. In the piece of teacher research about to be discussed,
the writer details how her own intellectual journey in feminist scholarship and
pedagogy transforms the male hegemony of her curriculum and classroom
over time.

The conversation begins with questions about the writer's use of Ursula
LeGuin's distinction between the father tongue—what she calls the language
of power, of expository and scientific discourse—and the mother tongue, the
language LeGuin calls another dialect, the language of stories, the language
spoken by all children and most women. As a preface to her essay, the teacher
has pointed out that the dialect of the mother tongue honors the personal and
the subjective—and then goes on to state her own intention to analyze and interpret her life as a teacher using only the mother tongue.

"Can men write in the mother-tongue?"

"There are lots of *I*'s in here—is this research?"

"Is it OK in research to say 'but I was baffled?'"

Teachers' questions come quickly and passionately. The essay seems to
have hit a nerve. One female chemistry teacher disassociates herself from the
mother tongue:

"Isn't this essentialized? Hey, women can write in father tongue. I write
like that."

Other teachers join the debate:

"Men can write in a personal way."

"Some people write in the third person, which makes it appear objective when it really isn't."

As it proceeds, the conversation coalesces around the writer's initial observation that five years ago, before she began exploring the implications of women's studies for her day-to-day practice, she was "keenly aware of a lack of fire in my classroom." Later in the essay, as she described her efforts to construct a more inclusive curriculum and a more culturally responsive pedagogy, the teacher claims, "I could feel the fire in the room."

"What's her evidence?" some teachers want to know.

"What made her know? What caused that feeling?" others ask.

"What exactly did she do?" another asks.

And eventually questions become:

"What counts as evidence here?"

"What does the researcher need to show the reader?"

"Who's the audience of this piece? Teachers? Others?"

Drawing examples from their own experiences, raising questions about the theory behind the practice and the practice behind the theory, the noisy debate continues as teachers formulate their positions, wonder aloud, refer back to the text, conduct sidebar conversations with neighbors as they stake out their arguments.

At 5:33 a member of the custodial staff sticks his head in the door. He tries several times without success to be heard above the din of heated discussion.

"It's time to close up now. Can you get out of the building, please? I have to close the building now."

At 5:45 the last teachers finish cleaning up and walk down the empty hallway, leaving the classroom as they found it.

SEMINAR IN TEACHING AND LEARNING

Conversations among teachers such as the one depicted in this vignette are not uncommon in the Seminar in Teaching and Learning, a researching community of about 35 teachers from comprehensive high schools in the school district. Participants in this particular session had recently attended the Ethnography and Education Forum, a local conference where teacher researchers from across the country shared findings from their classroom and school-based studies. The research under discussion (Brown, 1993) was being presented by a teacher who works at a secondary school in the district designed especially for pregnant and parenting teenagers. Several teachers in the Seminar had heard her at the conference and were anxious to read and discuss her paper with their colleagues.

At once speculative and certain, provocative and patient, freewheeling and yet focused, this kind of talk reflects teachers' individual and collective struggles to engage in a process of inquiry that supports their efforts to restructure their own classroom practices and their schools as workplaces. As they raised questions about Brown's purposes, they implicitly compared and examined their own. As they followed the evolution of her gender and literacy curriculum, they interrogated their own choices of materials and their design of particular activities to engage learners more actively in their subjects. And as they searched for and critiqued the evidence presented to warrant her claims, they prepared to collect and analyze data from their own classes in the months to come.

The talk of these Seminar participants is a form of oral inquiry into classroom and school experiences, a researching process that has enabled teachers from diverse ethnic and racial backgrounds, subjects, and schools to open up difficult topics, often deeply buried in the culture of isolation traditionally operating within their schools. As a form of inquiry, the talk has stemmed from or generated questions that reflect teachers' desires to make sense of their experiences, to adopt a learning stance of openness toward classroom and school life. Through these conversations and reading, writing, and talking together, they have formed a researching community to engage in collaborative analyses and interpretations of their work. And in doing so, they have not only enhanced student learning by improving their practice as professionals, but also generated knowledge about the daily work lives of teachers and students that may inform the efforts of others similarly committed to the transformation of schools.

Conceptual Frameworks

The impetus to form and sustain such a researching community has evolved from several interrelated strands of work, some programmatic and some conceptual. The establishment of the Philadelphia Writing Project (PhilWP) in 1986, an urban site of the National Writing Project, created a context in the city for K–12 teachers to explore teaching and learning through close study of writing and literacy across the grades and across the curriculum.[1] The teacher leaders of the Seminar are also PhilWP teacher consultants who have participated in a wide range of project-related activities linking professional development, collegial inquiry, and school reform. Conversations between the leadership of the Philadelphia Schools Collaborative (PSC) and PhilWP leadership and secondary teacher consultants led to the envisionment of an ongoing seminar for teachers from three of the comprehensive high schools initially identified as intensive sites of the Collaborative's work.

We based the concept and design of the Seminar on a set of assumptions or beliefs about teaching, inquiry, and reform that we have continued to explore and refine over the past several years:

- Teaching is primarily a deliberative, rather than a technical, activity and a critical form of inquiry. Together teachers and students co-construct knowledge and the curriculum (Zumwalt, 1982).
- Learning is a meaning-centered, social, language-based and human/personal process that occurs within classroom communities. These communities are constructed within multiple layers of context that structure ongoing activity (Lytle & Botel, 1988).
- Teacher research is systematic and intentional inquiry about teaching, learning, and schooling carried out by teachers in their own school and classroom settings. Research by teachers alters, not just adds to, the local and public knowledge base on teaching (Cochran-Smith & Lytle, 1993; Lytle & Cochran-Smith, 1992).
- Classrooms and schools are sites of research and sources of knowledge for school-based practitioners (Goswami & Stillman, 1987).
- Inquiry into practice is a way of learning from the processes of teaching across the professional lifespan. Teacher inquiries inform and stimulate inquiries by learners (Branscombe, Goswami, & Schwartz, 1992; Cochran-Smith & Lytle, 1993).
- Urban teachers need opportunities to explore critical issues related to race, class, and gender that inform their stance as professionals, their pedagogy, and their relationships to parents and communities (Cochran-Smith & Lytle, 1992b).
- Teacher inquiry communities foster collegial learning and professional development; they also provide strategic sites for knowledge generation for the field (Cochran-Smith & Lytle, 1992a). They provide rich sources of knowledge about the relationships among teacher inquiry, professional knowledge and practice, and school reform.[2]
- Change efforts should focus primarily on the complex interrelationships of teachers, students, and curricula at the microlevel of classrooms and schools rather than at the macrolevel of districts, states, and federal policies. The reform or restructuring of schools depends primarily on the reform or restructuring of the theories and practices of teaching and learning (McLaughlin, 1991).
- Rather than either global or discrete solutions, what is needed are opportunities for educators to construct their own questions and develop courses of action valid in local contexts and communities (Cochran-Smith & Lytle, 1993).

These assumptions reflect the embedded and recursive relationships of research and practice, relationships that call into question traditional connections between researchers and practitioners, researchers and the researched (Lather, 1991). They argue for a reexamination of the nature of research and the nature of practice, as well as the possibility of new roles in the generation of knowledge for school- and university-based teachers and for secondary school students. The Seminar thus represents a deliberate attempt to blur distinctions between research and action and to explore the empowering potential of research designed and implemented at several levels as processes of co-investigation.

In a recent call for stronger linkages between the teacher research movement and school reform, Dixie Goswami (1991) says:

> I am encouraged when I read about local, state, or national plans for school change, many of which emphasize teacher empowerment and include elaborate plans for including teachers in making decisions about curriculum, school management, and so on. But I am not aware of a plan or a program that takes seriously collective teacher research as a key tool for school reform, a program that provides support over a long period of time to develop research/reform communities and that is pledged to use the results for the purpose of restructuring schools to serve all children well. (p. 16)

In the remainder of this chapter, we show how the Seminar on Teaching and Learning functions as such a community for research/reform within the context of the high school restructuring efforts of the Philadelphia Schools Collaborative.

Design of the Seminar

Currently in its fourth year, the seminar involves teachers of music, social studies/history, English, science, mathematics, special education, health/physical education, humanities, computer science, home economics/human development, business, and TV/journalism.[3] As a credit-bearing graduate course, the Seminar meets biweekly on Mondays for 15 two-and-a-half hour sessions spread throughout the academic year. The location rotates each session among participating schools. In between sessions, teacher leaders meet informally with participants at their school and occasionally schedule extra school-site meetings.

Teachers keep biweekly teaching and learning journals, with observations from their classrooms and responses to readings, in the fall semester and project journals in the spring. In addition, they complete brief reaction sheets at the end of each session. Midyear, participants develop a portfolio of all their work during the fall semester. A bulk pack of about 25 readings is distributed in the fall, and additional readings are provided in the spring. During the second semester, teachers design and carry out an in-depth inquiry project based on issues and interests evolving from the fall's collaborative work. Some of these projects are conducted individually, while others are done collaboratively with members of the Seminar or other teachers in their schools.

The Seminar is facilitated by a leadership group, typically a combination of four school-based teacher leaders and three to four university-based teachers.

This group meets on alternate weeks to examine data from the Seminar and to plan strategies for facilitating upcoming sessions and activities. Small groups during Seminar sessions, however, are often led by participating teachers or are leaderless, as in the case of journal or project groups. Meeting time is typically divided into two or three segments, with a variety of small- and large-group structures and tasks. The group uses structured oral inquiry processes adapted from those developed by Pat Carini and colleagues at the Prospect School in North Bennington, Vermont. For the past two years, participants have attended and then discussed in a Seminar session the Teacher Research Day at the Ethnography and Education Forum,[4] and on occasion teachers from other schools have presented workshops on their own innovative approaches to interdisciplinary teaching and assessment.

Partial Perspectives

As participants in the Seminar and authors of this chapter, we write from our individual and collective experiences as part of a collaborative leadership team that has planned, facilitated, and documented the Seminar since its inception in the fall of 1989. Each of us has played a somewhat different role, both in the Seminar itself and in the process of writing about it.

These differences stem in part from our different professional perspectives. Three of us (Fecho, Portnoy, and Sion) are both school-based teachers and Seminar leaders, with special responsibilities for working on-site with the teacher participants from our own schools. Fecho is also enrolled in a graduate program. The other four of us are university-related, either as full-time faculty (Lytle), part-time faculty (Countryman and Christman), or graduate student (Cohen). In addition, one of us is an educational consultant/program evaluator (Christman), and another is academic dean at a local independent school (Countryman). We bring with us the frames and biases of our different worlds, and although we include excerpts from transcripts and teachers' written accounts of their inquiry projects in this chapter, the overall perspective on this community offered here is that of the leadership group rather than the participants.[5]

In this chapter we describe the work of the seminar as a researching community by examining some of its activities through three frames: teachers' talk, teachers' texts, and teachers' tasks.[6] We argue that teacher inquiry informs professional knowledge and practice by showing how inquiring teachers (1) restructure their classrooms to make their own and students' questions and knowledge central and (2) restructure their relationships with colleagues in order to transform their schools as workplaces. In these ways and others, teachers' inquiries are playing a critical role in the reform initiatives currently underway in the district's urban comprehensive high schools.

TEACHERS' TALK

In the Seminar, teachers talk constantly, even incessantly, about their work. While daily life in schools often demands that teachers solve problems posed by others, in the Seminar teachers pose and explore problems they regard as central to their practice. As teachers across different schools, programs, and disciplines describe to one another what they do in their classrooms, they begin to identify similar questions and theories and to reconsider the routines and possibilities of classroom life in the context of apparent "givens" of schooling. In this setting, then, teachers use talk to "go public" with their knowledge and their questions. Through this talk participants devise shared ways of reseeing practice. Over time, such talk creates and sustains an inquiring community, providing not only support but also a context for approaching hard or controversial topics.

Structured Oral Inquiries

We have used the structure of a reflective conversation (Carini, 1986) in the Seminar as one way to catalyze talk as intentional, systematic inquiry. Participants are asked to record impressions, definitions, metaphors, and other associations with a focus word or phrase. They then share these responses, letting them stand alone without comment. Designated members note and reflect back patterns and juxtapositions they heard from the group. Over the past several years, our focus words have included *teaching, tracking, diversity,* and *interdisciplinary teaching.*

In the first year, a group of African American and white urban high school teachers talked about tracking, inquiring into the ways students are typically grouped both within and across programs and classes. Together they raised questions about race, class, and gender, as well as about the impact of tracking on access to educational opportunities. Notes from the session convey some of the images participants shared as they explored their understandings:

> Tracks that leave a trace or mark, as do animal or needle tracks
> Tracking down those who could excel and making them mediocre
> Running on a track, around and around without a goal—just stuck there /
>   being able to ride only one track at a time
> The tracks on 69th Street and what it would take to switch tracks/the early
>   railroads, using cars on tracks to carry coal, everything had to be stan-
>   dardized to make it easier
> Tracks as having known destinations, placing limits on where you can go

Through this talk, teachers shared the pain and anger of their memories, as well as their outrage at the perceived connections between race and track in their own teaching and personal histories and in the lives of their students. The group's recollections stimulated discussion on their own expectations for students and how those expectations might reinforce rather than interrupt destructive patterns.

We use the structure of the reflective conversation for several reasons. First, teachers can adapt this structure to their own classrooms to help students unpack complex terms and to foster inquiry. Second, the reflective conversation can introduce an idea, such as diversity, that becomes an overarching theme; it illuminates people's prior knowledge, beliefs, and experiences as the starting place for generating new knowledge. Third, the reflective conversation helps unpack complex ideas, such as interdisciplinary teaching, to which participants bring a range of meanings and some unexamined assumptions. The reflective conversation focuses the group on concepts such as "tracking" that are both emotionally charged and central to the work of the group. Finally, when we (the leadership group) categorize and distribute data from these reflective conversations, we validate both the diversity of experiences and perspectives and the power of collective ways of knowing. We also challenge participants to incorporate this knowledge into daily decision making about practice.

Whole-Group Discussions

Sessions often close with less structured full-group talk about issues that emerged during the afternoon encounters. Occasionally, though, a particular experience or dilemma has necessitated a more prolonged full-group exchange, as in the session following our Saturday at the Ethnography and Education Forum. Participants had attended teacher-researcher and other sessions in an intense day. Our "debriefing" meeting began with the invitation to "write down a word that captures your feeling of the day." These words, read aloud around the circle, included *breadth, collegiality, jammed, intellectual, hectic, important, success, saturation, crowded, confusing, informative, innovative, surprising, rushed, packed, commitment, stimulating,* and *intense.*

Through talk, teachers questioned the knowledge base constructed by experts often situated outside of classrooms. They considered alternative sources and kinds of knowledge. Their talk also showed that inquiry into practice is not a bounded experience that leads to consensus, but rather a messy and sometimes almost incidental process that may lead to new ways of seeing what teachers encounter daily.

Small-Group Conversations

Other kinds of Seminar talk occur in smaller groups where teachers have the opportunity to share questions and concerns over time. The Seminar typically opens with journal-group meetings where participants discuss their written responses, often to topics connecting readings with practice and to questions that the facilitators design to invite description of particular classrooms and reflection on teachers' professional stance and philosophies, such as the following:

Describe the diversity in one of your classes.

What does it mean to teach and learn in your subject area?

Write about one student who comes to mind. Think about how some of the issues raised in the articles connect or do not connect with this student's experience in classroom/program/school. Draw on observations, schoolwork, what you know of family/home, conversations with others about student. You may want to interview the student to find out more.

What are some similarities and differences between inquiry in your own and the other subject area? What are the implications for interdisciplinary teaching and learning?

In their responses to these topics, written at home and shared in the group, teachers use key issues as lenses for re-viewing practice. At other times, small groups meet to discuss inquiry in a particular discipline, to analyze and interpret data from their work in progress, or to present research projects to one another. In each case, talk and text were woven together as teachers talk to compose and/ or critique the texts of others.

TEACHERS' TEXTS

Texts generated in the Seminar include teachers' journals and essays, field notes, transcripts, students' writing, and other writings in which teachers document and reflect on practice. Teachers' writing, which is often stimulated by dissonances they perceive in their classrooms, programs, and schools, serves to open lines of inquiry. On a regular basis teachers write journal entries before and reaction sheets after the sessions, using the Seminar talk and shared readings to explore disjunctures and questions arising from practice. Readers of these texts include the leadership group and small groups of colleagues. Midyear, participants reread and reflect on their own writings by putting together portfolios. In this process they use their own observations and reflections as data to identify patterns of concerns and questions. These analyses provide directions for their own inquiry as well as for the collective inquiry of the Seminar during the spring semester.

Portfolios

The examination of portfolios provides a moment when, after reflecting on the individual responses to the investigation we have done collaboratively, teachers raise those questions that seem most central to their particular situations. From these come more focused and formal inquiry projects. Over the years, the questions that emerge are increasingly about issues that have to do with collaborative work with other teachers and the impact of race and racism on classrooms and schools.

Throughout the Seminar, teachers found their perceptions of community changing, as the notion that teachers share ideas and conversations across classes, disciplines, grades, and schools became acceptable and even expected. The portfolios reveal many teachers' interest in deepening and extending their work with other teachers and ending classroom isolation. For those making such forays, however, the process is both hopeful and frustrating, and it also raises many questions.

A number of teachers use the portfolio to explore questions about how to work with colleagues in teaching and learning communities. In their questions about how to create and sustain communities with their colleagues, teachers ask not whether but how to forge and nurture connections among teachers. In her portfolio, one teacher described the nested contexts of collegial communities that characterized her teaching that year:

> The Seminar is an exercise in collaborating about what is important in teaching and learning. My whole life at school is wrapped up in collaboration. Decisions in the charter are made with everyone's input. My life on the governance council is geared toward opening up conversations on what a real learning community can be like. An exercise in futility most of the time, but an attempt nonetheless. Collaboration, for better or worse, has become my middle name.

Having begun to try out ways of working with one another within and across classrooms, disciplines, and schools, many teachers are unwilling to go back to the way it was.

In another setting, a teacher cited the loss of time and space crucial to building collaborative relationships. She voiced a critique of the system and a plea for help in responding to the perceived attack on community:

> I am concerned about the loss of empowerment by teachers at the school. Overcrowding of classes, noninstructional time spent with classes, and scheduling problems have placed serious obstacles in the way of teachers working together. I really want advice, help, suggestions on how not to be beaten by a system which seems to be stacked against teachers trying to take some initiative.

Still another teacher, working with ninth graders labeled "learning disabled" in a context more friendly to the forming of teacher communities, was joined by several of her team members in the Seminar that year. She reflected on how that "critical mass" of three was in turn enlisting the support of other members, creating community through a snowball effect:

> One of our teachers who is normally reluctant to participate in our outings volunteered to go on our trip to Bushfire Theatre Company. . . . She surprised us by her willingness to go and validated our belief that expectations are powerful. We expect 100% from the teachers as well as the students! We are beginning to erase the atmosphere of cynicism and hopelessness that used to cloud our conversations with this particular teacher.

In the portfolios, teachers raised questions about how in the process of forming communities teachers might revitalize one another as well as students, and about how inquiring communities of teachers and students might contribute to systemic change.

Over time, the Seminar has gradually become a community where participants can share such concerns. Teachers have posed questions to one another, such as what we should teach to promote respect for cultural diversity and who should decide; sometimes students have prodded teachers to ask questions. Different themes emerged from white and African American teachers. The portfolios show how many white teachers struggle to come to terms with the development of their beliefs about themselves as white teachers of African American students and with the dissonance they feel at times in their classrooms. One white teacher asked:

> Am I ready to do collaborative work with my peers so that I might better understand how I interact with kids from many different backgrounds? What's wrong with teaching kids "white middle-class" strategies if that's how their country is run?

While she framed some of her questions this way, at the same time she wrote about the way the process of reading and talking in the Seminar has affected her as a teacher:

> I hope that the accusations by teachers of color that white middle-class teachers are keeping their children in a powerless position are strengthened with a willingness to help me learn techniques that will teach my subject to all students.

Another teacher wrote:

> A student watching a . . . film commented on the fact that the students . . . were white! I had not noticed what color they were! Part of the knap-

168 *Teacher Inquiry as School Reform*

sack mentality. [A] student told me I must be black! When I asked him why, he said I could sense things very well even if I was not directly involved in the incident. My question is—is this a black attribute or a mother's antenna? Aren't children just children? Do we, by saying a child behaves a certain way because he/she is black, continue to isolate, stereotype, or stigmatize him/her? Aren't they all individuals with some qualities that are unique to them as people?

Many of the African American teachers raised questions about the impact of racism on their students and at the same time reached deeply into their own experiences and those of their families as African American students in both segregated and integrated educational institutions. They looked at racism in very personal and political ways, as members of families and communities, as both students and teachers.

One teacher discussed the historical educational experiences of her family, using this context to ask broader questions about the present conditions for minority students and teachers:

I come from a long line of teachers who were educated in segregated schools in the Deep South. These schools were run by Episcopalians and Methodists who had high expectations for the students they taught. . . . They were taught in a one-room school house with grades ranging from 1 to 12. [They] went to UNCF [United Negro College Fund] schools to become teachers, principals, doctors, and lawyers. Black students do not have to sit next to white children to learn, but they do need to have access to teachers who value them and their learning. How is the teacher of color different from that of the days before *Brown* v. *Board of Education*? Would desegregation solve the problems of urban education? Is desegregation the only way to insure adequate funding of inner-city schools? Are minority teachers more effective teachers of minority students?

Another African American teacher who had attended predominantly white schools wrote about her own educational experience as "littered with incidents of racism," saying that she had been denied opportunity by a white teacher who had discouraged her from pursuing an advanced degree because it "wasn't for her."

Teachers' questions about race and culture in classrooms often led to larger questions about systemic problems in changing schools. One African American math teacher connected issues of minority-student achievement with the institutional racism of the system:

> When I first started teaching . . . I thought I would and could make a difference. As a young African American woman who had no African American role models throughout most of my formal education experience, I felt that my sheer presence would make a definitive statement. . . . I know that I have reached some, perhaps many, but they are not nearly enough. . . . My issues and concerns evolve from this frustration. . . . It appears that a greater percentage of African American and Hispanic students are rostered to general math classes than any other group(s). I would like to research this. I suspect the reasons [this occurs] fall into these four categories: institutional racism, low teacher expectations, lack of proper counseling, and insufficient preliminary math preparation for the academic courses.

In their portfolios, teachers look critically at years of practice, at the structures of schooling in their workplace, as well as their own struggles to make meaningful changes in their classrooms and their schools—and from these reflections find directions for their own research.

Common Readings

Each year Seminar participants read teachers' texts as well as the work of other educators. Read critically with a practitioners' perspective, journal articles have helped teachers discover and shape their own questions as well as created another shared context for inquiry. Teacher researchers' work has provided important touchstones throughout. Eleanor Duckworth's (1986) research into the phases of the moon conducted with teachers in her class, for example, set up connections between inquiring teachers and inquiring students. Essays by secondary teachers (including several in the Seminar) traced dissonances that led to changes in their classrooms, addressing issues from conferencing with students about their writing to tracking and untracking advanced placement classes. Participants' repeated requests for more time to talk about the readings seemed to reflect the rarity of this kind of forum.

Discussions at the end of the first year about race and racism in schools helped to shape readings for the second year's Seminar, which began with texts exploring issues of difference and diversity in the form of both narratives, such as excerpts from Campbell's (1989) *Sweet Summer* and Kingston's (1975) *Woman Warrior*, and educational research, such as studies of Latino language-minority students and of African American students in a multiethnic context. Additionally, first-year inquiry projects stimulated second-year readings focused on classroom inquiry across disciplines and alternative assessment. Similarly, concerns and questions expressed in several forums at the close of the second year shaped reading selections for the third year. Participants' inquiry projects stimulated considerable interest in issues of educational access and opportunity, and participants also wanted to pursue connections between classroom practice and institutional change.

Readings for the third year explored these issues, beginning with interrogations of schooling practices such as Oakes's (1988) analysis of tracking as "a structural contribution to unequal schooling" and including analyses of race, class, and gender in relation to educational access. Texts also include programs and approaches that begin to "answer" these issues of access, such as Cone's (1990) inquiry into her own classroom in "Untracking Advanced Placement English" and Crichlow, Goodwin, Shakes, and Swartz's (1990) "Multicultural Ways of Knowing: Implications for Practice," in which researchers read the text of the classroom as teacher and students engage in intentionally multicultural ways of reading text. In the fourth year, readings made problematic the concept of "community" and were organized around the themes of classrooms, charters, and schools as learning communities, as literacy communities, as multicultural communities (focusing on race and racism and on diversity), and as collegial communities.

TEACHERS' TASKS

The Seminar's design reflects the assumption that the central purpose of teacher research as well as school reform is reinventing the tasks of teaching and learning. As teachers assume an inquiring stance toward their practice and thereby recast themselves as creators of knowledge about teaching, they also reconstruct their classrooms. In the preceding sections we have explored briefly how teachers in the Seminar use talk and texts to build a community that could support the tentativeness of inquiry and tolerate the dissonance of diverse perspectives and lack of consensus. In this section, we discuss how the teacher inquiry projects of the Seminar involve teachers not only in reseeing their classrooms but also in making changes in their practice that reflect and enact what they have come to know and value about what it means to participate in an inquiring community.

Midyear, teachers review their notes, journal entries, and reaction sheets in order to identify possible lines of research for their teacher inquiry projects; these become the focus of the second semester's work. The diverse research questions reflect the many ways in which the collective inquiry of the Seminar may intersect with individual teachers' classroom experience. Some of these questions include:

> How does the use of alternative assessment activities in a multidisciplinary unit influence the evolution of the curriculum and the interactions among the teachers involved?

What happens when a charter school explores a contemporary issue through writing across the curriculum?

What happens when a social worker and a teacher co-facilitate family group sessions?

What happens when students write about controversial and difficult topics in their journals?

How do students see manifestations of racism in the school? How can I help them think about this and consider and explore ways to handle these issues?

What happens when a music teacher invites a staff development coordinator to work with her humanities class?

Over the next several months, teachers met together in small research support groups determined by the focus of their inquiry in order to refine their questions, develop a research plan, share data, and lend differing perspectives to analysis and interpretation.

As teachers become involved in their inquiry projects, they often consider how to engage their students in posing questions and problems. They began to search for ways to invite students' knowledge and students' questions into their classrooms. In her initial proposal for her project, one teacher, Ruth Smitter contemplated the dissonance between what she was coming to know, her own practice, and the cycle teachers may inadvertently re-create in a tracked school system:

> I am concerned with the fact that in my general math class . . . I am just attempting to transmit information rather than engaging them in the learning process. . . . I am doing this because I am afraid of losing control of the class. . . . If I was willing to take a risk and try different things, such as group work, interdisciplinary lessons and projects, they would enjoy the class more and learn more. . . . I seem to spend too much time preparing for my academic classes and slighting the classes that probably need it the most.

Implicit here were questions about who holds authority over classroom learning. As Smitter's questions evolved, she shaped her research for the second semester. She had her students keep math journals and analyzed their responses as she implemented several important changes in her classroom, including small heterogeneous study groups. Smitter concluded her project with many questions:

> I still have many questions and many problems to resolve. How do I know if my students are learning more, and how can I evaluate this? Are

good results in the midterms an indication that my students are learning? Do I have the time and energy and creativity to pose problems to my students rather than just assign them seat work?. . . How much do I need to interact with my students?. . . Did the ESOL [English for Speakers of Other Languages] students in the classroom who felt comfortable doing math feel threatened by writing? Would they be able to work together in groups or would it cause a separation in the classroom?

Sam Karlin began his project paper with this satirical description of what his classroom looked like before the Seminar:

> But this is no ordinary teacher, and this is no ordinary class. This is the Department Head of Science, and this is the senior physics class. . . . The class stares in awe as this master sorcerer hurls flames of kinematics and charged bolts of scientific notation at those below from his "castle of physics." . . . Everything in the lands surrounding the "castle" is couched in numbers . . . but by far the most mechanical feature, the strongest statement of the power of numbers in this class, at least in the eyes of the students, is the computer printout that displays all their grades for every homework, lab activity, test, and class assignment.

Karlin reorganized his classroom so that students worked, either individually or in small groups, to explore their understanding of physics concepts by formulating problems. He described their efforts:

> Early attempts at writing to express concepts in physics were not very inventive and showed little understanding, but rather the students generally copied the problems that were presented in the book and substituted different objects for original objects and slightly altered numerical values for those values presented in the problem.

As students learned that their substitutions represented impossible conditions, they learned more about physics, and eventually they became more sophisticated problem posers. Karlin wrote:

> Students displayed an eagerness to have their problems included in upcoming tests. The problems were always accompanied by the author's name and some students felt as if having one of their problems included in the examinations was a "badge of honor."

Both Karlin and Smitter challenged traditional conceptions of who has knowledge, as they sought ways to share authority, to make their classrooms more student-centered, to evoke students' questions, and to learn from students.

Other teachers in the Seminar decided to explore how different ways of knowing illuminate concepts and issues. Margaret Klock and Pat Hansbury, English and history teachers respectively at Wells High School, focused on the connections that they and their students were forging between their two classrooms and subject areas.

> The question that Pat and I wanted to examine was whether students who actually had the experience of . . . joining their history class with their English class would benefit. Would they become more involved with both subjects? Would the joining increase understanding of the relationship between the subjects? Would it lead to the propensity to make connections between ideas elsewhere, not just in history and English class? Or would it merely confuse them? Faced with these questions, we determined early in the year to try to answer them in the spring, during what I now will always think of as the Season of the Revolution.

Klock and Hansbury documented the many ways in which they and their students connected the study of Orwell's *Animal Farm* (Orwell, 1954) with the study of the French Revolution. From their perspectives, theirs was a story of revolution—of how physical and intellectual barricades toppled in the face of a community of adult and student learners together creating knowledge.

> We joined the classes for an examination of the political spectrum. The idea for this lesson can actually be traced to a former student in my class and Pat's who is currently in the eleventh grade. Two years ago Pat was teaching her separate lesson on this topic. She had the class examine the whole political spectrum from radical to reactionary, using such issues as civil rights and women's rights. Suddenly this young man suggested that the class whose members had all read *Animal Farm* with me, try to place its characters on the political spectrum. From his inspiration, this year's lesson developed. (We must tell this young man that his idea sparked a kind of teaching revolution.)
>   One day after my class, the same young woman who was so perceptive about the Renaissance in her Julius Caesar test stopped to complain to me that George Orwell had been unfair to Napoleon Bonaparte when he used his name for his main character. Her point was that Bonaparte was a multifaceted person who along with his transgressions had done much that was good. When I reported this conversation to Pat, she soon used it in her history class to discuss historical point of view. Orwell, of course, was an Englishman, and the English tend to place Napoleon in the same league with Satan. The discussion came back to English class as we examined the "history" of the character Snowball as it was presented to the animals on the farm from the point of view of his enemy, Napoleon the pig.

Klock and Hansbury wanted their assessment of student learning not only to tap into the connections that students had already made during the course of study but also to provide additional opportunities for connection. Together they brainstormed a list of essay questions that would engage students in making new meaning of the texts that they explored in class. One of the questions was:

> Suppose that Napoleon Bonaparte had the chance to read George Orwell's *Animal Farm*. Would he be pleased or displeased? Writing in his voice, answer the question, giving three reasons for his pleasure or displeasure.

The teachers returned to their students' responses to this question in order to understand more deeply the kinds of connections pupils are able to make between history and English.

Teacher inquiry projects have become critical texts of the Seminar. At each year's closing session, for example, teachers choose a section from their projects to render aloud in a dramatic reading. Even these small selections make visible common themes and concerns, often bringing the voices of students into the Seminar circle. Making available published accounts of teachers' projects has linked teachers' inquiries within and across schools. Finally, teachers have begun to present their work to more public and distant audiences at local, regional, and national professional conferences and meetings. In the national conversations about educational reform, these texts foreground teachers' knowledge and provide important data about what matters to teachers.

INQUIRY AS REFORM

The teacher inquiry of the Seminar in Teaching and Learning happens within the restructuring efforts in comprehensive high schools. The formal nesting of the seminar within the activities of the Philadelphia Schools Collaborative has provided the opportunity for linking teachers' inquiry processes with structural changes underway in their schools. Building from their experience as inquirers in the seminar, teachers are re-creating their classrooms in ways that support student inquiry. Teacher research is thus providing "the grist for ongoing instructional revision and improvement" at the classroom level (Cochran-Smith & Lytle, 1993).

While we began with the assumption that teachers would look with a critical perspective at their own classrooms, we have come to see that teachers also use the critical frame of inquiry to examine and alter common assumptions and practices of schooling. In the concluding section of this chapter, we present some examples of how teachers have braided their individual and collective inquiry into their work as change agents in their schools. The examples we have selected reveal how they have reconceptualized their leadership roles to incorporate new understandings of how teachers learn, how they have infused inquiry into change processes by critically examining what they are doing as they do it, and how they have risked making problematic elements of the reform agenda to which they are most committed.

On-Site Staff Development as Collegial Inquiry

Many teachers in the Seminar serve in formal teacher leadership positions in their schools as charter and/or staff development coordinators and department heads, while others work informally to influence their colleagues. In a paper for a symposium about the Seminar in Teaching and Learning given at the Ethnography in Education Forum, Fran Sion (1991) described how her participation in the Seminar has influenced her re-forming of staff development at her school. Sion recalled her mode of preparation and her stance toward collegial learning when she assumed her role as staff development coordinator in 1975:

> I was considered to be the "expert". . . I read the latest journals . . . I talked with and observed teachers. I wrote . . .
> The memories are painful to this day. I was well prepared, as always, but my "listeners" were indifferent, totally uninvolved. There were no questions, no comments, certainly no sharing, absolutely no interest. I was delivering a monologue. Where had I failed? The formula worked so well with some departments, why not others? I had no answer. I truly believed that teachers learned best as we all had in college—by listening to well-prepared lectures and then interacting with the lecturer. Wasn't that the format I was structuring? (p. 3)

Through her participation in the Seminar, Sion reframed her questions about teacher learning and her role as an instructional leader: "How can I shape workshops to ensure that teachers would be participants rather than the audience? How do teachers working together learn best?" (p. 5). Sion sought data to address these questions by recording her observations and reflections in a journal as she changed staff development practices at Wells. In her journal, she wrote:

> About twenty-three of us . . . got together to share and discuss our experiences using cooperative learning strategies in our classrooms. I chaired the session and opened by *briefly* discussing some strategies. . . . I then turned the meeting over to my colleagues who had agreed to share their experiences and materials. We sat in a circle the whole time—no one assumed the physical stance as leader—including me! What a great expe-

rience this workshop was and the credit goes to my co-workers. They fielded questions from those who were considering the approach but were apprehensive. The time flew.

Sion's insights about on-site staff development were echoed in the experiences of others in the Seminar. At DuBois, for example, Dina Portnoy instituted a program of study groups in which small groups of teachers selected topics for collegial inquiry in lieu of attending sessions of mandated staff development organized by others. At Ali High School two of the Seminar participants instituted a Miniseminar in Teaching and Learning for interested colleagues as an alternative format for on-site staff development. Several teachers have begun to see collegial inquiry as a way of revitalizing their connections and redirecting their work with departmental colleagues and co-teachers in charter schools and other special programs.

In each case the teachers involved have begun to reinvent the collective work of charters, departments, and staff development sessions as forms of collegial inquiry and thus have essentially re-created the inquiring community of the Seminar in a variety of settings. In doing so, they are rearranging the organizational and structural features of schools to link inquiry with change processes, thus altering the culture of their workplace and the profession of teaching.

Teacher Collaboration as Collegial Inquiry

As we have discussed previously, teachers use the Seminar to make problematic many dimensions of teaching, learning, and schooling. Problematizing everyday interactions becomes a "habit of mind" that supports teachers as they risk sharing power with their students and colleagues and confront the consequences of involvement after entire careers of isolation and detachment. In her inquiry project, Meg Silli elected not only to collaborate with a colleague but also to conduct what she called an "anatomy" of this collaboration:

> Thinking that the most workable pair would be English and world history, I asked the history teacher, the long-term substitute, to do an interdisciplinary unit with me; he agreed. . . . I kept a journal, elicited written responses to questions from my partner, and got journals and test results from the students.
>
> These pieces of writing show me that the students benefited greatly from the synergy of the collaboration. They also show that our collaboration was unequal, that most of the problems that occurred were solved by one person, that the expectations both of each other and of the students varied, and that the perception of the need for structure was different for each teacher.

What Silli detailed in her report is a collaboration that succeeded in enhancing student learning but failed in providing a satisfying collaborative experience between teachers. What is important here is that Silli's inquiry involved her in a realistic and powerful assessment of the limits and possibilities of teacher-to-teacher work in this situation. It seems inevitable that teachers will confront disappointments when they attempt to restructure schools in order to build new partnerships. Inquiry provided Silli the opportunity to engage with and build her own knowledge about these problems rather than to blame, disengage, and/or simply become discouraged about working closely with others. Her teacher research project highlighted some of these issues:

> Problems with collaborating remain. The type and amount of planning needed must be negotiated at the beginning of any partnership. I feel that we were very far apart on this issue. In my next collaboration, at the beginning, I will insist that we negotiate how often we meet, who calls the meetings, and what we should get accomplished in each meeting.

Silli shared her paper with her partner, thereby making it possible for him to learn from the experience. She also included his response and thus his voice in her "anatomy" of their work together. In all of these ways, Silli is working through issues of power in pedagogy, teacher collaboration, and research and sharing what she is coming to know about the complexities and boundaries of collegial work.

CONCLUSION

The work of participants in the Seminar in Teaching and Learning exemplifies how teacher inquiry enacts the fundamental purposes of reform and constitutes a powerful alternative to more traditional forms of staff development. Posing problems and generating questions from experience are critical for the intellectual growth of students, teachers, and administrators. When teachers work together to research classroom and school practice, they position themselves individually and collectively as agents of change, committed to transforming organizational cultures in profound ways.

NOTES

1. The Philadelphia Writing Project is a school–university partnership linking the Graduate School of Education, University of Pennsylvania, and the school district. As an urban project, it focuses on professional development, collegial inquiry, and school

reform, with a major emphasis on teacher research into issues of writing/literacy and cultural and linguistic diversity, multicultural education, interdisciplinary curriculum, and performance-based assessment.

2. Research on the Seminar is part of a larger comparative study of three researching communities of urban educational practitioners with whom the first author (Lytle) is currently investigating relationships among inquiry, professional knowledge and practice, and school/program reform. In addition to the Seminar in Teaching and Learning (comprehensive high school teachers across the disciplines), the others are a researching community of K–12 teachers (part of a national network of urban sites of the National Writing Project) and another of adult literacy teachers and administrators (a project of the National Center for Adult Literacy). All three of these researching communities are connected to the Philadelphia Writing Project, a teacher collaborative for urban educators as writers, researchers, and reformers.

3. The numbers have varied across the four years from 32 to 45 participants, including both school and university teachers. Begun in 1988 with three schools, the Seminar has expanded to include participants from five others.

4. The Ethnography and Education Forum is a three-day national conference held annually in February at the Graduate School of Education, University of Pennsylvania. Since 1986, there has been a special emphasis on Saturday as Teacher Research Day, intended to bring together teacher researchers from across the country to share their classroom and school-based research with their colleagues in schools, programs, and universities.

5. Parts of this chapter are adapted from a series of papers written for a symposium about the Seminar in Teaching and Learning presented on Teacher Research Day at the Ethnography and Education Forum, University of Pennsylvania, 1991.

6. This framework comes from Cochran-Smith and Lytle (1992a).

REFERENCES

Branscombe, N. A., Goswami, D., & Schwartz, J. (Eds). (1992). *Students teaching, teachers learning*. Portsmouth, NH: Boynton-Cook Heinemann.

Brown, S. (1993). Lighting fires. In M. Cochran-Smith & S. Lytle (Eds.), *Inside/outside: Teacher research and knowledge* (pp. 241–249). New York: Teachers College Press.

Campbell, B. (1989). *Sweet summer*. New York: Putnam.

Carini, P. (1986). *Prospect's documentary processes*. Bennington, VT: The Prospect School Center.

Cochran-Smith, M., & Lytle, S. L. (1992a). Communities for teacher research: From fringe to forefront? *The American Journal of Education, 100*(3), 298–324.

Cochran-Smith, M., & Lytle, S. L. (1992b). Interrogating cultural diversity: Inquiry and action. *Journal of Teacher Education, 43*(2), 104–115.

Cochran-Smith, M., & Lytle, S. L. (1993). *Inside/outside: Teacher research and knowledge*. New York: Teachers College Press.

Cone, J. (1990). *Untracking advanced placement English: Creating opportunity is not enough*. Research in writing: Working papers of teacher researchers. Berkeley, CA: Bay Area Writing Project.

Crichlow, W., Goodwin, S., Shakes, G., & Swartz, E. (1990). Multicultural ways of knowing: Implications for practice. *Journal of Education, 172*(2), 101–117.

Duckworth, E. (1986). Teaching as research. *Harvard Educational Review, 56*(4), 481–495.

Goswami, D. (1991). Teachers as researchers: Building a new agenda. *The Quarterly of the National Writing Project and the Center for the Study of Writing and Literacy, 13*(4), 16.

Goswami, D., & Stillman, P. (Eds.). (1987). *Reclaiming the classroom: Teacher research as an agency for change*. Portsmouth, NH: Boynton-Cook.

Kingston, M. (1975). The girl who would not assert herself. In *The woman warrior: Memories of a girlhood among ghosts*. New York: Knopf.

Lather, P. (1991). *Getting smart: Feminist research and pedagogy with/in the postmodern*. New York: Routledge.

Lytle, S. L., & Botel, M. (1988). *The Pennsylvania framework: Reading, writing and talking across the curriculum*. Harrisburg: Pennsylvania Department of Education.

Lytle, S. L., & Cochran-Smith, M. (1992). Teacher research as a way of knowing. *Harvard Educational Review, 62*(4), 447–474.

McLaughlin, M. (1991). Enabling professional development: What have we learned? In A. Lieberman & L. Miller (Eds.), *Staff development for education in the '90's* (pp. 61–82). New York: Teachers College Press.

Oakes, J. (1988). Tracking in mathematics: A structural contribution to unequal schooling. In L. Weis (Ed.), *Class, Race and Gender in American Education* (pp. 106–125). Albany: State University of New York Press.

Orwell, G. (1954). *Animal Farm*. New York: Harcourt, Brace & World.

Sion, F. (1991, February). *The seminar in teaching and learning and staff development*. Paper presented at the Ethnography and Education Forum, University of Pennsylvania, Philadelphia.

Zumwalt, K. (1982). Research on teaching: Policy implications for teacher education. In A. Lieberman & M. McLaughlin (Eds.), *Policy making in education: 81st yearbook of the National Society for the Study of Education*. Chicago: University of Chicago Press.

11
Language Inquiry and Critical Pedagogy
Co-Investigating Power in the Classroom[1]

BOB FECHO

Laura Green, a urban African American student in my secondary English class, did a research study on profanity among her peers. She did this study because, as she puts it, "I myself don't use . . . slang or profanity, but I thought it would be good to know why my friends use it . . . because I'm in this environment everyday." As I talked to Laura about her work, she commented:

> Some people use profanity because they feel powerful. . . . And my one girlfriend . . . she use profanity because she put effort into it, she put stress into it because people are scared of her when she talk like that. She don't get in too many fights by her mouth. She can talk her way out of it, or talk her way into a fight, or talk somebody out of wanting to fight her, because of the way she speaks. She uses a lot of profanity and slang and that'll make a person think that she's from the streets and knows how to fight, so you really wouldn't want to mess with her.

Laura's comments are about language and power, and how the two interact in the lives of her classmates. Her comments are also problematic in that she considers herself both a child of her community and someone who is setting herself apart from that community through her language choices. While her words proclaim that she is attempting to remove slang and profanity from her day-to-day speech, her tone—not conveyed by a flat transcript—indicates a pride in her friend's ability to control life via clever and intimidating language.

Although Laura's conceptions of both language and power may differ from my own or that of academia in general, it is evident that she has given their definitions careful thought. To the students of Laura's study, language and access to power interact daily in ways that teachers or researchers need rarely consider in their own lives. Yet a teacher such as myself, who, as Delpit (1988) puts it, teaches "other people's children," must also confront questions of practice and theory that revolve around the ways my students construct their understandings of language and power, and how they interrelate. Additionally, for a teacher involved in a massive restructuring of an urban school, issues of language and power percolate to the surface with increasing frequency. Subsequent decisions about those issues have repercussions not only within one classroom, but throughout the school as a whole. Concerns about whose voice gets preference, what role language plays in all classrooms, and what access to power education provides get considered, defined, and acted upon as teachers work in groups to rethink the conception of their school.

In this chapter, I pursue three objectives. First, I attempt to chronicle what my students know, understand, and wonder about the relationship between language and power. Particular emphasis is placed on representing their actual words and voices in that effort. Second, I trace my own involvement with these terms because I believe that one characteristic that distinguishes research done by a teacher is how that teacher is placed within the study. Finally, I develop a description of how inquiry is supported by a prevailing atmosphere of reform. These three objectives are woven throughout this chapter, as discussions within one area often cross the boundaries into the others.

For sake of clarification, when I refer to the term *power*, I will be speaking about both an individual's sense of relative worth within the community and the individual's ability to effect change within him- or herself and also within the larger community. As Freire and Macedo (1987) remind us, considering questions of education is impossible without also considering questions of power.

THE TEACHER IN THE STUDY

Rather than providing a general review of the literature that places the current study within the body of past research on the topic, this section instead locates the teacher within the current study. The reason for the switch derives from the nature of teacher research and the reasons teachers embark on inquiry. Most teachers, and I am generalizing from myself and my colleagues who are teacher researchers, begin systematic research because they are unhappy about some aspect of their own practice. They then often go in search of theory—either through conversations with peers, readings of educational literature, or attendance at public forums, such as conferences and seminars, that speak to their problem. Using this theory as a foundation, these teachers go about adapting it to the conditions within their classroom, coping with the many variables, such as teaching styles, learning styles, accepted policy, and so forth. They gather data on the change, readdress the theory, and then continue to refine practice.

Given the nature of the search—that it begins within and is interested in theory and research that contributes to an understanding of a local problem— I feel it is more important in teacher reporting of research to trace the path of that search than to show exactly where the study lies in the larger research context. By tracing the literature that most affects the research, the teacher researcher invites the reader to understand the actual process that led to the research rather than to read through a listing often created after the research has begun and containing titles of works with only fringe effect on the study. In other words, what I read about pedagogy and what I observed in my classroom directly shaped my study. Knowing this trail of influence aids in informing the data analysis. In addition to knowing the literature trail, knowing about my classroom and my approach to teaching further enhances any interpretation of this presentation.

Starting with the latter, my classroom might be considered a whole-language classroom, despite that movement's primary school emphasis. My students read, write, talk, and self-reflect by themselves, in pairs, as small groups, and as a whole class. We read literature from the traditional canon, an example from this year being *Hamlet,* while also incorporating many works from less acknowledged sectors of our culture. Again, an example from this year would be Zora Neale Hurston's (1992) "Sweat." Work on this literature rarely resembles the traditional assignment in which students answer questions after reading the story. Instead, my students are asked to transact with and connect to literature and the world around them in a variety of ways that emphasize moving from the personal to the academic. For instance, my classes researched the Harlem Renaissance, based upon their own interests in the varied aspects of that time period, but were not asked to submit traditional research reports. Their goal was to re-create the time period, and the research was needed in order to realize a Harlem church or nightclub in full swing. What I try to establish in my classroom is an atmosphere where learning is valued, is connected to the lives of the students, and is viewed as a means for accessing power as they bridge their lives beyond their local communities.

The theories that drive my classroom, particularly as they relate to the accessing of power, have been assembled from a variety of sources. In an interview published in *Language Arts,* Delpit (1991) said the following:

> But power code literacy gives you access to the world outside of yourself and your immediate circle of intimates. For some children these two literacies are virtually the same. Their circle of intimates consists essentially of those who hold power in this society, so finding their own way into literacy will lead them to power. For other children whose intimates are not part of the culture of power, personal literacy will not give them access to the codes of power, and teachers must provide instruction for them to gain that access. (p. 543)

This is the sentiment that led me to consider how language is taught in my classroom and the motivation my students have for acquiring the power code literacy to which Delpit refers. While I am using a fairly recent quote to illustrate my concerns, Delpit's (1986, 1988) earlier work in this area, published as two articles in the *Harvard Educational Review*, spurred me to reflect upon my practice. What were my students' conceptions of language? What was important to me about the teaching of language? How could power code and personal literacy exist within the same classroom?

While I was encountering Delpit, I was also reading other researchers and theorists. Three in particular—Shor, Ogbu, and Gee—forced me to shed my shell of illusory neutrality and to consider the political implications of my work. Gee (1987) writes:

> English teachers are gatekeepers: Short of radical social change, there is no access to power in the society without control over the discourse practices in thought, speech, and writing of essay-text literacy and its attendant world view. . . . Like it or not, English teachers stand at the very heart of the most crucial educational, cultural, and political issues of our time. (p. 743)

As a teacher of African American students, it was difficult for me to ignore Gee's cry that to see the teaching of language as apolitical in nature is to play into the hands of a power system that deems otherwise.

Having heard and accepted Gee, I searched for a comprehensive approach to implement a curriculum that considered language and power as transactional forces worthy of inquiry. It was the work of Shor and his interpretations of Freire that pointed the way. As Shor (1980) writes: "The teacher surrenders the mystique of power and expertise while using his or her conceptual understanding of reality to provoke critical consciousness in the students, through which they reject their own class character" (p. 84). The idea of sharing power, defining power, and discussing power with my students became key to my creating a course where issues of language and access to power could be raised.

Despite these influential writings, it took Ogbu's examinations of race and education to rattle my basic philosophical foundation enough for me to launch myself into an examination of just what language study meant in my classroom. I, as perhaps most teachers, had believed that one benefit of education and/or literacy was access to the power that comes with gainful employment. But employment is not always a direct result of literacy or education, nor is honest employment always a venue to power. As Ogbu (1987) writes:

> Rather, the real issue is twofold, namely, first, whether or not the children come from a segment of society where people have traditionally experienced unequal opportunity to use their literacy skills in a socially and economically meaningful and rewarding manner; and, second, whether or not the relation-

ship between minorities and the dominant-group members who control the
education system has encouraged the minorities to perceive and define acquisition of literacy as an instrument of deculturation without true assimilation.
(p. 151)

In my own classes I had seen how my students could recite the litany of "We
go to school to get a good job"; but I could detect, in their lack of commitment
to the tasks of schooling, a grave doubt that school, employment, and power
were related in any way. Ogbu's work had forced me to reject economics as a
viable reason for gaining literacy and sent me in search of a replacement, a
search that, to some extent, still continues and has potential to be an ever-
evolving concept in my professional life.

After I had read the thoughts of these writers on language and power, an
incident occurred in my classroom that cleared the last hurdle to my study.
While teaching Nikki Giovanni's poem "Beautiful, Beautiful Black Men" and
trying to emphasize how I thought the poem celebrated African American culture and language, I was pulled up short by my students. They were offended
by the dialect used by Giovanni in the poem and felt she was ridiculing the
language of blacks. A discussion ensued, and suffice it to say that my classroom has not been the same since. What I learned through the incident was
that my students had well-defined conceptions of language and were both
capable of and interested in discussing the connections power had to language. If students were to investigate the power aspects of literacy, what
would happen to the classroom and how would my role as teacher be rede-
fined?

It was at this juncture that I constructed a study to allow me to access my
questions. In most English classrooms, language is a tool for studying literature or for creating written works. Rarely is language studied as a subject unto
itself. What often passes for language study is the skill and drill of grammar
books decontextualized from the rest of the curriculum. What I sought for my
classroom was to describe and analyze what would happen if language were
brought to the forefront and truly investigated for its import. Particularly, I
wanted to know what my students' conceptions of language were and how
they perceived the relationship of language and power. My students would be
studying their own language and the language around them, attempting to
make sense of its impact on their lives. I, on the other hand, would be documenting their process and the concepts they discussed. Together, we would
be studying language, trying to identify how it functioned in the classroom, on
the streets, and in the venues of power.

The reform efforts across the city create an atmosphere in which risk taking and reflection are not only encouraged, but facilitated. Consequently, a
study such as mine has a greater chance to be heard beyond the walls of my

classroom because an outer call for change has been made to match the inner call already in effect.

STUDENTS' CONCEPTS OF LANGUAGE AND POWER

In order to set the tone for language study, I filtered all my lessons for a year through the lens of language. For example, the school within a school of which I am part selected "How does learning connect you to your world?" as a year-long essential question. This question set a thematic issue across the curriculum in our program, one that encouraged students and teachers to constantly view the curriculum in terms of relating it to that question. Thus a chemistry teacher might focus on the chemical impact of pollution or medicine. I concentrated on how the learning of language connected students to their world. Out of the possibilities of our bookroom, I chose readings such as *Fences* (Wilson, 1986), *The Miracle Worker* (Gibson, 1956), and *For Colored Girls Who Have Considered Suicide/ When the Rainbow Is Enuf* (Shange, 1975) because of what they said about and how they used language. Students wrote autobiographies that stressed their own language use and eventually researched their own questions about language. In short, little occurred in the classroom that did not connect to the intentional, systematic investigation of language by both me and my students.

As the year progressed what most captured me was what I learned from the students about how they conceive of language. In particular, I want to concentrate on the way students perceived language and its relationship to power. My data consist of transcripts of class sessions and panel interviews, along with collections of student work such as the autobiographies and research reports already mentioned. These data were collected periodically over the course of one school year. An attempt was made to document work in all four classes that I taught, hoping to come to some compromise between depth and breadth. The data are analyzed in traditional modes of qualitative analysis, focusing on inherent themes and discrepant episodes. What follows will give a glimpse of what my students have been considering about relationships of power and language. In addition, in order to focus this chapter even more and somewhat control the impact of gender, all student examples will be taken from females in my classroom. Future work will feature males' conceptions of language and power, with a resulting comparison between the sexes.

As the quote by Laura Green that opened this chapter indicates, the urban-raised African American students in my classes first equate language and power in terms of the street. In addition, the power of language is seen as coming from its ability to create a persona that identifies the user as someone "you wouldn't want to mess with." The friend Laura mentions uses profanity and slang as a weapon to characterize herself as a person who must be tough because the language she uses seems to indicate toughness. This power is then used as a shield to control volatile situations, not so much by logical persuasion as by frontal intimidation.

On the other hand, we also know through Laura that not everyone chooses this type of language to achieve power. Laura herself has made a conscious decision not to fall into patterns of slang and profanity. As she writes in her autobiography, "As time went on, I found myself not liking to speak this street slang any longer. I felt as though I could accomplish more with an intelligent background and I must say that I have accomplished more." While she acknowledges that at one time in her life speaking street slang had advantages in terms of her peer group, she now states that "my knowledge [of standard English] helps me in life, whereas their ignorance hurts them."

Laura, however, comes from a literate background. As she tells us in her autobiography, her mother is always taking her to "fancy places, seeing and meeting people of higher intellect and life styles." She also describes her grandfather, a minister who pushes her to read and watch PBS. It is easier for Laura to equate language success with rises in financial security, social status, and community empowerment because she has witnessed these results in her own life. While Laura and students like her may directly connect change in social status to language, others in my classes are unclear about what language might mean in terms of the acquisition of power in society.

At the start, students were not quick to acknowledge the connections. Early entries in my audio notes (on-the-spot field notes dictated into a handheld cassette recorder) indicate that students resisted the concept of connecting language to power. Over the course of the year, however, our conversations turned more and more to power and what language contributes to the acquisition of power. But like all our conversations about language, little that we said was simple and straightforward.

Students mentioned that standard English seemed to be the ticket into the business world. As one of my students, Jeannette, put it, "For instance, if you go on a job interview and you use black English, they're gonna say that you don't really know how to talk properly. So you'll have less chance of getting a job." However, within the same panel interview, Sherita, another student remarked, "I be wonderin' why when people go to interviews and there's like a white person interviewin', why do . . . most white people . . . expect you to speak standard English? . . . I mean it's not like you disrespectin' them. Long as you answer the questions they ask you in a respectful way. It's nothin' wrong with it, but some people just want you to speak standard English, the way they talk."

Both comments were acknowledged by nods of agreement from the other participants in the discussion. On one hand, students are aware that standard English is the language of the business world. On the other hand, they do not accept all the arguments that privilege standard English. This ambivalence carries into other areas. From one perspective, my students believe that speakers can switch from dialect to standard English and suggest that the job of the English teacher is to, as Sherita says, "teach [standard English] as though . . . like when they go to job interviews and they want certain jobs." Once again, however, she qualifies her commitment by then saying, "'Cause then I think if a person change they way that's not used to speakin' standard English, it's gonna feel uncomfortable," later commenting, "'Cause I feel as though I gonna speak what I want to speak, how I want to speak it."

Aside from power in the mainstream, my students also are aware of the personal impact of language, primarily as a negative force to be used against enemies. Their autobiographies are filled with stories of how language was used to hurt. Student writers tell of parents who told them that they "were no good and would amount to nothing." Much like Countee Cullen's (1971) poem "Incident," my students recount episodes in which racial slurs destroyed times of fun or celebration.

Another story by a young woman harkens back to the conception of language as power on the street. Having lost a cousin in a car wreck, she writes about lashing out at a survivor of that crash who was teasing her unmercifully. As she relates, "Since I couldn't hurt him physically, I figured I'd try to hurt him mentally. . . . One thing I'm sure got to him. That's when I said, 'It should have been you [that died] and not my cousin.' At the time, I was so mad I meant what I said. I was also satisfied that he was hurt because of my words." Later in the conclusion to the autobiography chapter she relates, "I think from now on he will be cautious toward me. He will take pre-caution for things said and done to me in the future." As this story and the others point out, language is part of the offensive and defensive arsenal of getting by on the city streets.

Underneath all matters of language for my students lies the tension among three considerations—choosing language that lets you be who you are, choosing language that lets you be who you want to be, and accepting language that forces you to be someone you are not. The thread running through all this is the idea that somehow language and power transact with each other; such transactions resonate in very real and integral ways for all speakers in general and dialect speakers in particular.

IMPLICATIONS

As mentioned earlier, I am a teacher who is immersed in a context of reform that stresses reflective practice. Consequently, I read Ogbu, Shor, Gee, and Delpit because I was part of a network of teachers who routinely read and discussed such work. I was open to the concerns of my students about language because I had colleagues who periodically investigated children's work. I was able to amass and analyze data because I met regularly with teachers who were amassing and analyzing their own data. I was able to see my classroom as a site for inquiry because, as one of the founders of our school within a school, I had made an investment in my practice that would now resonate through seven other teachers voluntarily partnered to me. While it is true that I would still be a reflective teacher without an atmosphere of reform around me, it is equally true that the atmosphere of reform deepens and broadens the intent and consequence of my inquiry.

For at least this teacher researcher, then, it has become important and perhaps even necessary to broaden the audience. The nature of my work—that of a teacher investigating his students as they investigate language—has implications that directly affect my classroom but also resonate to the classrooms of other teachers as well. It is hard to speak of the one without mentioning the other.

For myself, coming to a deeper understanding of how my students connect power and language has brought about specific change in my practice. First of all, language can never again slip into the background within my room. Our discussion of the aforementioned story, "Sweat," centered around Hurston's use of standard English for narrative and dialect for dialogue. The issues addressed ranged from how Hurston's contemporaries were divided on the use of dialect through who has the right to write dialect and on to the uses of language in the television programs "Good Times" and "The Cosby Show." What this example represents is that once language is opened to scrutiny, it remains so and continues to color the sense-making of students.

From this study, I have also decided that part of my role is to present options to students. Discussions about language must be clear about the possibilities, consequences, and benefits language variations present. This is a touchy area for a European American male teacher of African American students. When Delpit says that black students need to learn power code literacy in order to access the power of society, black students probably perceive this as useful advice from someone of their culture. When I say the same thing, it can be read as someone ostensibly from the power culture looking to create lockstep conformity. I need to further inquire into how my students receive this message and what in my presentation affects such conveyance.

For the present, I am convinced that the issues surrounding personal and power code literacy must be elevated into classroom discussion in order for my students to make informed choices about language.

While my own classroom is affected by these discussions, so are those of the other teachers within my program, seven other teachers who grapple with language in their practice even though their subjects may be chemistry or math. Sharing my data with these teachers opens up discussions about the nature of language use across the curriculum. Rather than searching for a quick fix, teachers in my program generate discussion that enhances how they view their own classrooms, specifically in regard to language use. Instead of relying upon knowledge to trickle from the outside in, we construct our own knowledge and use that knowledge to further refine practice and spark new questions.

A recent example of this centered around our discussions of a senior project. In attempting to create an assessment that reflected what our seniors had learned, the teachers of the program were forced to confront their own beliefs about language and standards of usage in writing and speaking. The need to access power code literacy, the difficulties of code switching, the politics of language—all became issues as we sorted out this means of assessment. These teachers—of different genders, races, and generations who teach different subjects—held a wide range of viewpoints that needed to be developed into a consensus about language in order for an adequate assessment to be created.

Moving out one layer, I co-lead a teaching and learning seminar in which classroom inquiry is a key element. My experiences, both generally as a teacher researcher and specifically as an investigator of language, have been woven into the frame of our sessions. Either through the sharing of my data, discussions of my written work, or conferences about research in process, teachers in the seminar have accessed my research and I, in turn, have benefited from critique and self-evaluation. Once again, talk in these professional development sessions revolves around issues and process, not how-to's or staged models.

During the development of this chapter, I received an article about women, dialect, class, and race from a colleague who teaches pregnant and parenting teenagers. She also conducts her own investigations into gender and classrooms. Knowing I would be interested in the piece, she sent it my way. This alone is not uncommon or noteworthy. Concerned teachers have always shared resources. What is worthy of note is that we are part of a national network of urban teachers, linked by modems and the common background of the National Writing Project, who routinely share articles, data, writings, and support.

Of particular importance, the diverse racial composition of this group of teachers has made it possible for my data to be viewed from a variety of perspectives with a variety of implications. Earlier this year, this group read the transcript in which Laura Green gave her views on language. Among their comments was the point, described herein, that Laura saw power on the street and power in the larger society as different realities. This work sparked a series of discussions in the research group on language and urban teaching. Once more, what had begun as a question of interest within my classroom had widened to include a greater audience of teachers. What may have gone down as one person's perspective had been enhanced by the views of a diverse group of concerned educators whose classrooms were all affected by the subsequent discussions.

It is important for me to note that despite the positive context within which my practice resides, all is not conducive to my conducting research. Teachers who work actively at research are the exceptions rather than the rule. A research-friendly teaching schedule, one that allows flextime for teachers to record data, is a rare occurrence. Existing school district and labor union hierarchies and divergent goals often combine to make reform and research into that reform difficult or even fruitless. Teachers, too often victims of educational fads and administrative whims, are suspicious of movements—whatever the source—that require more work for unclear ends. Finally, it often seems easier for me to travel across the country to present at conferences in order to gain support and critique for my work than to share data within my own building.

Despite these obstacles, research can occur because enough is in place to allow it to happen. That positive context, at least for now, is enough to displace the negatives and allow me to inquire and analyze. As I continue to sift the data, I will continue to access and inform these teaching communities. What I learn about my classroom I will funnel back into my discussions with other teachers. What my students say about language will affect how I approach my classroom. The questions I am asking now will generate new questions in the future. These are givens, for me and for all teacher researchers. What we need to do, as a research community, is to find ways to broaden these discussions to include those in our local context and the wider discourse community as a whole. Access to this broader research community must be gained because much can be learned from a collaboration of the academy and the classroom. As we are reforming classrooms, so must we reform the ways those classrooms are researched. The ideas here hopefully will move us all one small step toward that greater good.

NOTE

1. This chapter was originally prepared for the American Educational Research Association Conference in San Francisco, California, April 20, 1992. This work was partially supported by the Urban Sites Writing Network of the National Writing Project with a grant from the DeWitt Wallace–Reader's Digest Fund.

REFERENCES

Cullen, C. (1971). Incident. In D. Randall (Ed.), *The black poets* (p. 157). New York: Bantam.

Delpit, L. (1986). Skills and other dilemmas of a progressive black educator. *Harvard Educational Review, 56*(4), 379–385.

Delpit, L. (1988). The silenced dialogue: Power and pedagogy in educating other people's children. *Harvard Educational Review, 58*(3), 280–298.

Delpit, L. (1991). A conversation with Lisa Delpit. *Language Arts, 68,* 541–547.

Freire, P., & Macedo, D. (1987). *Literacy: Reading the word and the world.* South Hadley, MA: Bergin & Garvey.

Gee, J. (1987). Orality and literacy: From the savage mind to ways with words. *TESOL Quarterly, 20,* 719–746.

Gibson, W. (1956). *The miracle worker.* New York: Bantam.

Giovanni, N. (1971). Beautiful, beautiful black men. In D. Randall (Ed.), *The black poets* (p. 289). New York: Bantam.

Hurston, Z. N. (1992). Sweat. In J. C. Oates (Ed.), *The Oxford book of American short stories* (pp. 352–364). Oxford, UK: Oxford University Press.

Ogbu, J. (1987). Opportunity structure, cultural boundaries, and literacy. In J. Langer (Ed.), *Language, literature, and culture: Issues of society and schooling* (pp. 149–177). Norwood, NJ: Ablex.

Shange, N. (1975). *For colored girls who have considered suicide/ when the rainbow is enuf.* New York: Macmillan.

Shor, I. (1980). *Critical teaching and everyday life.* Chicago: University of Chicago Press.

Wilson, A. (1986). *Fences.* New York: New American Library.

12
Girl Talk: Creating Community through Social Exchange

DIANE R. WAFF

The profound life problems involving drugs, teenage pregnancy, sex, and other societal pressures are taking student attention away from academics. Many students are unable to focus on their work, their attendance is sporadic, and they are not seeing a connection between school and life. These observations certainly apply to the students I teach at DuBois High School, comprised of racial and ethnic minorities whose lives are circumscribed by racial, social, and economic oppression.

I teach adapted English and remedial math in the Leadership House, a program for mildly handicapped special education students. The Leadership House is one of the small semiautonomous schools within the school, created to disrupt the anonymity of the larger school structure. Unlike the larger charters servicing 200 to 400 students, we service over 80 students with a core group of 5 teachers. The students cycle among me and four other primary-subject teachers. There are 22 girls and 80 boys. The girls consist of 11 Latinas, 10 African Americans, and 1 Irish American. This uneven gender distribution exacerbates the problems faced by female adolescents struggling under oppressive special education labels and the peculiar burdens of being African American and Latina young women. It is in this context that I struggle to engage students who are, for a wide range of reasons, disengaged.

THE INQUIRY PROJECT

My participation in the Seminar in Teaching and Learning put me in the company of 35 other beginning teacher researchers who wanted to become teachers who empowered their students to make changes in their lives. Every other Monday afternoon we would break into journal groups, debate the merits of articles read, relate the readings to our individual classrooms, and reflect on our classroom pedagogy. Words like *connections, essential questions, community building*, and *meaning making* became the grist for reflective conversation and heuristic journal writing.

I began to realize that the reason I was not being successful with my students was largely due to my insulated middle-class lifestyle. I was losing the opportunity to help them because I did not invite their realities, their experiences into my classroom. Every time my students attempted to introduce their private lives into the structure of the classroom, I managed to silence their voices quickly with words such as, "We have a lot to cover, let's get back to work" or "This sounds like something you should discuss with the counselor." My classroom was teacher-centered, and the students had little or no input into what was "covered" or discussed. Assertions like, "My mom's boyfriend is always . . . My boyfriend is always . . . My dad is always . . . Those people in the shelter always . . . " made me uncomfortable.

I had grown up in the inner city, attended a predominantly black high school, and lived in a neighborhood similar to that of my students. Yet I still felt a tremendous sense of separation from the students in my classes. I did not understand how they could come to school without books, paper, or pencils. Their school performance was a sign that they did not give a damn about their education. Detentions, reprimands, and lectures were not able to reverse an "I don't care" attitude. My students just could not identify with my words, and I could not understand theirs.

When I was invited, along with my colleagues in the Seminar, to do an inquiry project on some pressing classroom issue, I chose the one that seemed to reverberate throughout my journal writings: *Students want and need the chance to make their voices heard.* I discussed the project with Cozette Ferron, the Leadership House coordinator, and we agreed that our students needed the chance to raise those issues and concerns that we do not address in the traditional classroom setting. We decided to accomplish this by establishing a mentoring program. Our initial goal was to invite mentors, role models from the community, to team up with small groups of students and engage them in reflective dialogue. The students would have the opportunity to discuss issues, reflect on them, and, where possible, take steps to alter their individual situations. We sent out letters to parents, area churches, and concerned members of the community. We engaged the services of the Uncommon Individual Foundation to train 15 volunteer mentors who responded to our invitation.

Out of the 15, only Barbara A. Ash, Esq., an African American attorney, came consistently. We were faced with the dilemma of how best to utilize the services of our only volunteer. After a conference with Barbara, "Girl Talk" was born. We decided to have her meet with our girls to give them a chance to use her as someone to talk to, as a shoulder to cry on, and as someone to give them a push in the right direction when possible. We were there to provide Barbara with moral support and to clear the way with our school administrator so that Girl Talk would become an ongoing facet of the Leadership House program. Barbara met with the girls twice a month during the school day for two periods in a small, vacant classroom adjacent to mine. The four other teachers in Leadership House cooperated fully. They willingly excused the girls from class for Girl Talk.

BEGINNING GIRL TALK

I encouraged all the girls to make personalized journals, which they unanimously decided to name "Girl Talk." The girls made their journals out of manilla folders and lined paper. They took a lot of time decorating them, using stencils, colored markers, and crayons. They really enjoyed working on their journals because, for the first time, this was a school activity that had some relationship to their daily lives. Each girl agreed to store her journal in a locked cabinet in my classroom to insure privacy and to be certain she would have her journal on hand for Barbara's visits.

I asked the girls to record their impressions at the end of every Girl Talk session and to jot down ideas or topics they wanted to discuss in future sessions. I assured them that I would only read their journal entries with their permission. On some occasions no entries were made. Girl Talk is not a class, so the girls wrote only when they had something to say. Their observations and suggestions became the text for their Girl Talk sessions. They were writing a curriculum that was truly reality-based.

I also kept a journal, where I recorded observations of the girls' reactions to their sessions and changes I observed in the group's evolution. In addition, I held regular, informal interviews with the girls on their views of the sessions, and I made audiotapes of group interviews I conducted at various times during the year. I also recruited representatives from the African American and Latina girls who were regular participants in the sessions to act as confidantes and to feed me data for my ethnographic research. The use of confidantes gave me a window into the actual workings of the sessions from both black and Latina perspectives. The students who participated in my small-group interviews became my research collaborators. As we examined issues underlying some of my research questions, we developed a close relationship built on trust and respect, and we became true co-learners and co-explorers.

I transcribed most of the material on the tapes and pulled out the girls' responses to the most frequently raised student issues. These included the use of obscenities in group, reaction to "sex talk," and student suggestions on ways to alter Girl Talk to make it responsive to the needs of the most reticent girls. The transcriptions, along with girls' journal entries and our conversations together, also revealed much about the kind of forum that encourages the expression of these issues and the changes in student perceptions with regard to the sessions, the mentor, and one another. They also reveal the students' emergent recognition that they do possess the power to alter things in their environment.

THE MENTOR

Barbara was able to develop an open, caring relationship with the girls. She made a pledge to maintain the girls' confidentiality, with the caveat that she would break her vow of silence if they told her of matters involving child abuse, substance abuse, illegal acts, or anything she viewed as detrimental to their well-being. Surprisingly, despite her warning, the girls were anxious to share.

I monitored their journals and asked questions about Barbara and her facilitation of the group. I also asked the students how they perceived Barbara and why they felt comfortable in sharing their stories with her. This excerpt from Valerie's journal reveals student attitudes towards their mentor:

I like this program because Ms. Barbara will tell you up front and she don't hold nothing back. You can tell her anything and she won't be offended. You can tell her your mind. She is really cool.

Barbara, unlike their teachers, allowed the girls to express themselves in forbidden ways, and the freedom to use obscenities was a hot topic when Girl Talk began. Boys and girls alike whispered about "the really together lady" who was just like one of them. Obscene language was Barbara's passport to acceptability. Once she had gained their acceptance, she succeeded in winning their hearts.

During a group interview, I told the girls that I had heard some people say they could not wait to get to Girl Talk so they could curse:

MYRDIS: Yes, they're just there to cuss and call Ms. Barbara bitches and all that stuff.

CARRIE: It's just a way to express themselves. They get it from their parents, the street, and whoever they hang with. If you hang around the wrong person, you'll be doing the same thing they do. I don't think they need to curse. But it is how some people talk.

TAMMY: Ms. Barbara, the first time she met us, told us we can curse.

MYRDIS: Everybody said, "All yeah! we can cuss, we can cuss!"

TAMMY: We're just taking advantage of her and I think it's wrong. She said we could call her a bitch, so they say things like, "Look, bitch!" I think that's wrong, even though she said we can call her that and she won't get offended. How do we know? She doesn't have to show her feelings. Even though she said we can curse. I don't curse.

MYRDIS: I'll respect her like she's my own mom. I might say a curse and then talk the rest of the way. I don't say "Yeah, this bitch, I don't like this bitch." I don't do that.

MS. WAFF: Is it most of the girls or some?

TAMMY: Some of us have the same problems, but we don't express our feelings the same way. When I was small, I was raised by my grandparents. My grandmother told my mother she's not setting an example for us cursing all the time. I listen to my mom, but I don't respect her much.

I spoke to Barbara regarding her views on this subject. She said:

I didn't want to come to the girls as a lawyer, someone who was so far removed from their reality. I wanted to be one of them. I needed to establish a rapport with the girls, so I told them they could curse if it fit the occasion. I wanted them to feel they could say anything, anyway they wanted, without fear of repercussions. If they were really upset about something, they could say "I'm going to fuck that bitch up" and I did give them permission to curse me by saying, "Look, bitch." Once the excitement wore off, the cursing virtually stopped.

Barbara also gave the girls a place to share and to process experiences with their peers. Rosita wrote in her journal:

The girl talk sessions got me closer to all of the girls. Things that we can't share with our sisters or mothers we share here. Our problems are we don't feel good about ourselves but we don't have anyplace to go and talk. A lot of us are curious about boys, worried about school, our family, and trying to find work. We learn from each other, bad and good.

Barbara echoed Rosita's sentiments.

I offered the girls a chance to talk and to air their problems. I offered no solutions to their problems. I can't get anybody out of a shelter. Often, the only thing I offered them was a, "What do you think about this?" or "How do you feel about that?" Sometimes a question at just the right time would lead one of the girls to see a particular course of action. I gave them a place to cry, a chance to drop the tough facade, the "I can handle everything" stance.

She talked about Tammy, a perfect example of the tough kid. Obscene language, constant fighting, and a defiant attitude marked her interactions with peers and authority figures. During one session, the girls finally confronted

Tammy about her behavior, and in an intensely emotional moment, she confided that she had no one who cared about her. Her grandmother's death had left her with aunts who did not care, an alcoholic grandfather who could not care, and a crack-addicted mother who, earlier that day, had sat on a bus in a crack stupor, oblivious to Tammy's existence.

This moment was an epiphany for Barbara and the girls. One session explained away a year of Tammy's hostile inaccessibility. Collectively they made a breakthrough and began to see themselves as a family unit. Each girl assured Tammy that she cared and that she would always be there for her. Barbara reports that there was not a dry eye during that session. A phenomenal change was noted in Tammy's behavior and overall school performance after a very short period of time.

Barbara found that when their talk turned to the future, many of the girls did not set high goals for themselves. Their parents were painting negative pictures with such words as, "You can't be that . . . You'll never go to college . . ." Their parent's short-sightedness clouded their visions for the future. They did not even have the confidence to dream big. Barbara was able to offer the girls hope. If someone wanted to be a cosmetologist, she planted the entrepreneurial seed of shop ownership. Barbara told the girls of her own climb from the ghetto, and they looked at her and said, "Hey, maybe I can do it, too."

LISTENING TO STUDENT VOICES

As I talked to the girls, read their journals, and observed the changes in them, I began really to listen to what they were saying. In an interview with a student, I received a painful lesson about how I as a teacher shut down meaningful exchange in my classroom. Marsha told me she enjoyed Girl Talk because it allowed her to talk using her own words. She did not have to worry about getting into trouble for cursing, and she got a chance to talk without worrying whether she used good grammar or three-syllable words. Her comments led me to see the "silencing" effect of my overcorrection of grammar mistakes (Delpit, 1990), and I began to encourage the students to enter class discussions using their preferred style of discourse.

I also stopped trying to interpret their lives by using my own as a backdrop. The girls' journals gave me a lens on a wide variety of personal issues that were not being addressed in the formal classroom setting. Juanita and her sister Iris, two Latina girls, were poor attenders and chronically late to school. They were not behavior problems, but when they came, I knew I had to spend time fitting them back into the class routine.

When I read their journals, I was able to listen as they shared their hearts. Juanita wrote:

When I met Jose I was afraid to look at him. I was scared to talk to him, and I was scared to kiss him. I've kissed him and I've loved him. Now I'm going to have a baby and I'm scared I'm going to lose him. My mom says I might lose my baby too. My sister Iris has a baby and she's not going to take care of two babies plus my sisters and brothers. I'm really scared.

Her sister Iris wrote:

We talk about boys today and pregnant. I talk to her I have a babe. I miss school because I have to care of my babe.

As I read their journals, I also learned that Juanita and Iris had lost everything they owned in a house fire. Once I learned about their struggles, I understood why they were always absent and unprepared. Buying paper and pencils would not be a high priority item for me either.

Myrdis frequently came to class with such a foul body odor that the students and I were forced to open windows. She became the butt of cruel jokes and insensitive remarks. She revealed her feelings on this subject in a journal entry detailing a painful Girl Talk session:

Today the girls said somebody in the group stinks. I knew they were talking about me. We don't always have hot water and by the time I get to use the bathroom my brothers use up all the deodorant. I don't have the money to buy any.

Here is an excerpt from my journal:

The students have been cruel to Myrdis particularly the past two months regarding body odor. I wanted to find a way to delicately talk to her about the importance of good hygiene. I got my chance today because of her journal entry. Now I know she needs and wants help. I gathered together soap, sample perfumes, and toilet articles and presented them to her in a little Lord & Taylor shopping bag. She was so happy, she rushed down with Mrs. Johnson, the non-teaching assistant, to the nurse's office to wash up. We were shocked when she showed the gifts to her classmates.

Myrdis functions on a third-grade level in math and is reading on a second-grade level; division is particularly frustrating for her. Before my gift, she came to class and promptly feigned illness or went to sleep. Now she is alert more often and struggles to do classwork. Her personal hygiene is markedly better, and she is permitted to use the nurse's office to freshen up with her own toilet articles. Myrdis has subsequently brought me her own gift—flowers. She still sees me as a teacher, but now she sees me as someone who cares. One small act of kindness transformed my relationship with this student.

As I have listened to my students and gained more insight into their lives, I have been more willing to relinquish absolute control of my classroom. It had always been important to me to have a quiet, well-run classroom. I always had the desks in orderly rows, the goal clearly displayed on the board, and all my students on-task in a well-planned, teacher-directed lesson.

During a math problem writing lesson, I was observed by the vice-principal and a visiting teacher. The class was nothing like the above description. The chairs were arranged in a circle, and the students were buzzing with conversation. They had been asked to write and solve their own original math story problems and then share these problems with peers in small, cooperative groups. When the vice-principal entered the room, I was tempted to restructure the lesson quickly, take control, and orchestrate all activity. I decided to be a risk taker and chance a bad evaluation. I really did not know if the students would stay on-task or if their collaboration would disintegrate into name calling or private conversations totally unrelated to math.

Students who share their feelings see one another more humanely. They are more willing to help one another, and they work together as a class to reach a common goal. The girls, who quickly assembled into small groups, went to the board and cooperatively problem-solved. This cooperative spirit was contagious. The boys in the class, who had not benefited from the Girl Talk sessions, began to join in. The student-developed problems were difficult for some group members, and each problem poser served as the teacher/coach. Students were able to get their peers to verbalize the steps necessary to problem-solve. The student-centered classroom was more effective than the teacher-centered one. All the students were engaged, and there was an enthusiasm for learning that is not evident when I am in sole control.

DISCOVERING THE POWER OF STUDENT VOICES

The Girl Talk sessions represented a disruption of the girls' usual stance of sitting around silently accepting the status quo. They began to articulate their concerns and develop the mental attitude to problem-solve. After school and during our common lunchtime in my classroom, I met with the girls to discuss the sessions. We split hoagies, shared sodas, and focused on a wide range of issues and concerns. Tammy, an African American, and Rosita, a Latina, talked about the ways they felt the sessions could be improved:

TAMMY: We're in the ninth grade. We should act more mature. We need to make the groups smaller. You'll get more answers and questions from the girls like Sonia and them.

ROSITA: Sometimes we feel uncomfortable in a large group. In a smaller group we'd have more confidence sharing our secrets and problems.

They told me that in large-group sessions a few girls were monopolizing the discussions, and others who were less vocal did not get the opportunity to share. Latinas, especially, were not as vocal as their white and African American classmates.

When I questioned the girls about issues they talked most about in their sessions, they became quite animated and revealed much insight into group dynamics. They were able to identify a vocal group of girls who appeared to dominate the sessions with intimate details of their sexual relationships with boys. A significant number of girls wanted to discuss other topics, but their voices were silenced.

ROSITA: The other girls feel uncomfortable. They're real quiet and don't say nothing. I want to share my feelings about museums, about painting our nails, and how we do our hair. We could talk about going to the mall or to the movies.

TAMMY: We don't have to talk about sex every Friday. It's three or four people controlling the conversation. She should ask what we all agree to talk about. She's not doing that.

I shared this information with Barbara, who made an effort to invite participation from the girls who were less vocal. New discussions opened up on school, parents, and the future. Eventually, Barbara was able to arrange to spend additional time at school, and we divided the girls into groups of four or five. The girls responded favorably to the smaller sessions and indicated an appreciation that their suggestions were followed. By having a direct hand in shaping how the sessions were run, they discovered the power of their own voice.

Rosita, in one of our many private conversations, expressed her pride in being a Puerto Rican and her frustration that the school had no books by Puerto Rican writers, no Puerto Rican teachers, and no real sense of Latino culture in the school. She said she did not want to appear like a racist or a separatist, but the Latinas really needed to have a group of their own. She said they would share more and they could understand one another's problems better.

Rosita was making an impassioned plea to see herself reflected in the world in a real, positive way. I began to search for a Latina role model, and I found one in Agnes Collazo, a University of Pennsylvania doctoral candidate and a practicing engineer. She began working with the girls and has been able to communicate with them from a cultural framework they understand. She has also been able to shed light for their African American and white teachers on reasons for the girls' chronic absenteeism, lack of career aspirations outside the home, and familial attitudes toward school. Agnes learned the girls are expected to miss school to take care of younger brothers and sisters. She also learned that the girls primarily see their future as mothers who do not work outside the home. The Latina girls, in turn, expressed surprise at and a deep sense of pride in Agnes's accomplishments. They confided that they did not have anyone like Agnes in their families or in their communities.

I began to notice a change in the girls as the suggestions they made had a direct impact on how Girl Talk was run. Other girls began to stop in and share their opinions with me on the Girl Talk sessions and on other issues as well. As soon as the girls realized that someone was really listening to them, they were empowered to see themselves as people who mattered. They knew they had the chance to have a direct impact on their lives. They became more vocal about everything.

I got suggestions on ways to alter my classroom so it would be more responsive to their needs. The girls expressed a desire to read different kinds of literature. They were sick of reading books by men about men. *Huckleberry Finn, Tom Sawyer,* and *The Call of the Wild* were books featuring male heroes, and they wanted to see women in starring roles. "We want books written by people like us," they told me. "We want to read some books with romance, love stories."

As an immediate response to their request, I introduced the work of female poets and the rap poems of lady M.C.'s (rappers) into my English classes. I had students write poems imitating the style of Maya Angelou, Nikki Giovanni, Emily Dickinson, and others. We also juxtaposed the voices of women with the voices of male bards. Kool Moe Dee's "A Cool Black Man" and Walt Whitman's "Song of Myself" lost out hands down to the strong, powerful voice of Sister Souljah's "360 Degrees of Power" and Angelou's smooth, sassy, and confident voice in "Phenomenal Woman." Males and females alike began to realize that regardless of gender or color, everyone has a voice that deserves to be heard.

The girls decided to make their voices heard in yet another area of school life—discipline. They expressed dissatisfaction with the way discipline was handed out by the male who filled in whenever our female disciplinarian, Ms. Hoxter, was absent. All the girls—Latina, black, and white—marched down to Ms. Hoxter collectively because they were not satisfied with the way her substitute had handled their complaint that a boy had tapped one of the Latinas on the behind. Ms. Hoxter promptly met with them and the boy, and she suspended the young man for three days. She discussed sexual harassment and cautioned that harassment would not be tolerated whether it was perpetrated by males or females. This explanation placated the boys, but the girls knew they had won a major victory.

The girls' collective action demonstrated a bond that had developed among them across racial and cultural lines. They were finally looking out for themselves and one another. They were elated and visibly triumphant. They spoke of times in other schools when their complaints had been ignored or when they were disciplined for overreacting to what was labeled "playful behavior."

I talked with my Leadership House colleagues about the girls' perspectives on the harassment issue. We now see that many of our "discipline problems" are really cases of sexual harassment. Now whenever a girl walks into the classroom and the boys jeer or make inappropriate comments, I immediately redirect their behavior and open the floor to discussion on why women find their behavior offensive.

I no longer hold a "boys will be boys" approach to classroom discipline. I am beginning to address the harassment problem in a curriculum chosen to stimulate critical inquiry into the area of male/female relationships and to present positive images of women through classroom literature. Hopefully, this change in curriculum will encourage boys and girls to view one another in new ways and foster more harmonious male/female interaction. I took this initiative as a response to requests from the girls. The girls had developed a collective voice, and it was powerful.

CONCLUSIONS

There is a hierarchy of inequality faced by the Leadership House girls experienced through the lens of race, gender, and power. They lack power as a racially defined group, they lack power as adolescents, and as young females they lack power in relation to their male counterparts. Their perceptions of themselves and the world they live in, as well as their notions of womanhood and manhood, are contextualized by these factors.

Heilbrun (1988) writes: "Power is the ability to take one's place in whatever discourse is essential to action and the right to have one's part matter. This is true in the Pentagon, in marriage, in friendship, and in politics"—and in the classroom (p. 18). The adolescents who participated in Girl Talk were empowered by the sense of community that was established through their ongoing social exchange. If "learners enter into the process of learning not by acquiring facts, but by constructing their reality in social exchange with others" (Wallerstein, 1987, p. 34), then the Leadership House has accomplished this through mentoring. The reflective dialogue—students sharing stories, examining and questioning, developing their own strategies for bringing about constructive change in their world—was valuable. Once the girls were able to see that their voices were valued by their peers and their teachers, they began to believe in themselves. This self-belief gave them the power to fight for change in school discipline and class curriculum. It also affected how they negotiated relationships both inside and outside school.

My research on Girl Talk has also caused me to reexamine the attitudes and perspectives that I bring into the classroom. I have developed insights into lives I saw before in only the most superficial way. These young people, urban poor, are leading the lives of adults in the bodies of children. Many of them are parents, have had one or two abortions, live in shelters, or all of the above.

The possibility of students' becoming empowered is evident from the success of Girl Talk. Teachers who listen to the voices of their students are able to construct classrooms responsive to the needs of the students they seek to serve. Brown and Gilligan (1992) write of the importance of listening to student voices in their analysis of "authentic relationships"—relationships in which girls and their female teachers listen to one another, share life experiences, and begin to explore their responses to one another. Teachers and students develop—awkwardly at first—power-sharing behaviors. Their discourse is an effective way to explore issues, resolve them, and develop attitudes of understanding and mutual respect. The benefits of the integration of reflective dialogue and students' personal stories in the mentoring situation points to the wide possibilities for its use in the traditional classroom.

REFERENCES

Brown, L. M., & Gilligan, C. (1992). *Meeting at the crossroads: Women's psychology and girls' development.* Cambridge, MA: Harvard University Press.

Delpit, L. (1990). Language diversity and learning. In S. Hynds & D. L. Rubin (Eds.), *Perspectives on talk and learning* (pp. 249–250). Urbana, IL: National Council of Teachers of English.

Heilbrun, C. G. (1988). *Writing a woman's life.* New York: Norton.

Wallerstein, N. A. (1987). Problem posing education: Freire's method for transformation. In Ira Shor (Ed.), *Freire for the classroom* (pp. 34–35). Portsmouth, NH: Heineman.

Afterword
Transforming Urban Schools:
Building Knowledge and
Building Community

ANN LIEBERMAN

Finding somewhere to stand in a text that is supposed to be at one and the same time an intimate view and a cool assessment is almost as much of a challenge as gaining the view and making the assessment in the first place.
Clifford Geertz, 1988, p. 70.

School and university educators who are taking on the challenge of restructuring schools and school systems in urban areas are involved in nothing less than the transformation of existing bureaucracies, bureaucracies that have had the power to control what is taught and how schools are run. Many of the ways in which school bureaucracies have created organizational conditions that have alienated and "silenced" students, parents, and teachers are deeply rooted in the regularities of the school's everyday life. In the process of changing these conditions, educators come to confront the necessity of substantially changing how students are valued and challenged. Accomplishing such profound changes involves a fundamental rethinking of the role of teacher and student, both parties becoming active participants authentically involved in dealing with emotional and intellectual commitments to learning and teaching.

In addition to changing the relationship between teachers and students, organizational structures that make possible real community may also become a challenge to the larger bureaucracy of which they are a part—since issues of power and control that challenge hierarchical dominance inevitably surface. The struggle to transform schools is central to the process of working on and working through the difficult problems that face a society in social and economic transition, a society that seeks to realize a new meaning of community and that includes and gives voice to those who have long been silenced, ignored, or invisible.

LESSONS ABOUT COMPREHENSIVE CHANGE IN URBAN SCHOOLS

The history of the Philadelphia Schools Collaborative documents the attempt to transform all 22 comprehensive high schools through the creation of small communities, called "charters," within these existing schools. The chapters in this book reveal larger issues that are embedded within this specific history. These include the necessity to rethink practices that support teaching and learning, with special reference to new and expanded meanings of research and inquiry as ways of building knowledge for positive change; the possibility of changing roles and relationships between and among all participants within the school community; and a deeper and more profound understanding of the magnitude and complexity of the problems involved in the process of transforming schools and school systems in urban America. These are important learnings that reach far beyond this city, learnings that can make a significant contribution to understanding the process of change in general, and within schools in particular.

RETHINKING PRACTICES THAT SUPPORT TEACHING, LEARNING, AND COMMUNITY BUILDING

Central to the effort to improve high school education is the breaking down of large schools into smaller units with the intention of transforming troubled high schools into small communities that are nurturing and supportive, both intellectually and emotionally. Councils made up of teachers and parents become the governing group of these small communities, these charters. Several charters may exist within a school—each building its own curriculum, pedagogy, and instructional practices and each governed by its own council. Students, teachers, and parents meet together, learning how to unlearn years of anger, rage, and blame, and participate in becoming family groups that connect students' lives to their academic learning. Techniques such as action research are used to inquire into, and help reveal solutions to, expressed needs of the charter; ongoing professional development and learning, which provide the means to continually build the capacity of the teachers to make changes in themselves as well as their students, are an integral part of the process.

CHANGING THE MEANING OF RESEARCH AND INQUIRY

At the heart of the Philadelphia Schools Collaborative is an approach to research that involves both university- and school-based educators, and it involves them in ways that are enlarging the margins of both academic and school communities. Academics involved in doing collaborative and critical ethnography find themselves working as organizers of teacher and parent groups, collaborators in helping to develop classroom-based performance assessments, co-constructors of written work documenting the process of change, advocates for decentralized professional development, learners attuned to parent, teacher, and student questions and challenges, and teachers raising issues that aim at fundamental reform. Academic work means being involved in charter meetings, ethnography groups, and teacher seminars; but it also means collecting data, feeding back information, and writing about it—making sure that what is public has the consent, input, and sometimes authorship of fellow collaborators in schools. These academics are co-creators of knowledge *and* critical analysts of the content and processes of change. Although they are passionately involved in reform as advocates, they continue to inquire into their own, as well as others', processes and practices in schools.

School-based educators are involved with research in their own classrooms, but they are also using action research techniques to collect and use data to better understand their communities, to help restructure their schools, and to gain further insights into their students' culture, commitments, and concerns. Some schools are in the process of becoming centers of inquiry, as the entire school learns how to acquire and use information that best serves the interests of its students. From critical conversations, such as discussions of literature analyzed from feminist perspectives, to teacher research, which informs professional knowledge and practice, teachers are using, creating, and constructing knowledge, blurring the line between research and practice. Both university- and school-based educators are involved in building knowledge even as they are building community.

CHANGING THE ROLES AND RELATIONSHIPS
IN THE EDUCATIONAL COMMUNITY

An important characteristic of the Philadelphia Schools Collaborative is the willingness to examine systematically and systemically the roles and relationships that have heretofore protected the status quo. Charters make demands on everyone to change. District personnel must examine centralized control over many decisions about resources, personnel, and evaluation at the school site. The teachers union must deal with hard-fought issues of seniority and selection, expanding its purview to include not only protecting teachers economically but also supporting and expanding teaching and learning. Teachers accustomed to working alone must learn to work together because in essence charters are small communities struggling to practice democracy through shared decision making, thematic academic work, and social concern. Principals who develop leadership in others find themselves sharing what was formerly sole decision-making power. Department chairs, in learning how to work across subject-matter boundaries, are helping to craft interdisciplinary themes. Parents, long estranged from the organization of schooling, are participants on school councils—learning, supporting, and helping to shape a new meaning of community. Researchers, who in the past have been content to describe dispassionately what schools are like, are intimately involved in and committed to a collaborative view of knowledge creation, as they struggle to find a voice that sensitively captures both the insider's and outsider's view of reality. When charters gain the commitment of their constituent group, no role is left untouched, no relationship unchanged.

UNDERSTANDING THE MAGNITUDE AND COMPLEXITY OF TRANSFORMING SCHOOLS AND SCHOOL SYSTEMS IN URBAN AMERICA

The ongoing story of the Philadelphia Schools Collaborative may become our first primer, teaching us basic lessons for radical reform in urban schools. From the initial "public conversations" about the possibilities for transforming schools, to the creation of small groups of teachers, students, and parents, we learn that all parts of the community, regardless of role or position, must be involved individually and collectively in shaping the future of schools. In a sense everyone is "at risk," yet everyone has something to gain from a system that works for all its participants.

Perhaps the greatest lesson from this reconstruction of the first three years of the Collaborative is that a new view of community is being crafted: one that takes place not only inside the charter but outside as well, that respects diversity and confront differences, that represents a sensitivity to and engagement with the whole life of adolescents as they live it. Most important is the creation of a learning community for all its participants: a community that includes rather than excludes, that creates knowledge rather than assuming that it is all produced by others, that expects controversy and conflict to be part of the educative process, and that, while accepting the boundaries of subject and the authority of knowledge, encourages a constant construction and reconstruction of these boundaries and this authority in the spirit of a democratic and humane society.

REFERENCE

Geertz, C. (1988). *Works and lives: The anthropologist as author*. Stanford, CA: Stanford University Press.

About the Editor and the Contributors

Michelle Fine is Professor of Psychology at the City University of New York Graduate Center and senior consultant at the Philadelphia Schools Collaborative. Recent publications include *Beyond Silenced Voices: Class, Race and Gender in American Schools* (SUNY Press, 1992); *Disruptive Voices: The Transgressive Possibilities of Feminist Research* (University of Michigan Press, 1992); and *Framing Dropouts: Notes on the Politics of an Urban High School* (SUNY Press, 1991).

Essie Abrahams-Goldberg has taught English at Abraham Lincoln High School for twenty-four years. A fellow of the Philadelphia Writing Project, she also serves as the charter coordinator of the Temple Connection and is currently involved in an authentic assessment pilot and in the Re: Learning initiative.

Jolley Christman is Director of Research for Action, a not-for-profit research and evaluation organization that specializes in helping educational institutions and programs develop their capacity for assessment and reflection. She is Associate Faculty at the University of Pennsylvania, Graduate School of Education.

Richard W. Clark is a senior associate of the Center for Educational Renewal, University of Washington, and a senior researcher with John Goodlad's Institute for Educational Inquiry. He has worked with the National Network for Educational Renewal from its inception, serving for five years as a regional coordinator. He is a team leader on the School Change research study with the Coalition of Essential Schools at Brown University and the principal investigator on a grant to IEI from the Pew Charitable Trusts to study and assist in the reform of this school district. Clark was a teacher and administrator for thirty years and also taught at three universities. He has worked as a consultant on site-based management and on teacher and program evaluation, written high school language arts textbooks, and authored articles and chapters of books on curriculum, professional development schools, and school-university partnerships. Clark's Ph.D. is from the University of Washington.

Jody Cohen is a consultant with the Philadelphia Schools Collaborative and Research for Action, working with teachers and students constructing inquiry into education. She holds a doctorate from the Language in Education program at the University of Pennsylvania and has taught English and Social Studies in urban high schools for ten years.

Joan Countryman is head of Lincoln School in Providence, Rhode Island. She taught mathematics for twenty-three years at Germantown Friends School in Philadelphia, where she also served as assistant head and director of studies. Her book for teachers, *Writing to Learn Mathematics*, is published by Heinemann Books.

Shirley Farmer has taught English in this school district for twenty-three years and is a writing fellow of the University of Pennsylvania Writing Project (Philwp) and the Pennsylvania Writing Project (pawp). She is currently serving as secretary to the Executive Board of the Delaware Valley Association for Supervision and Curriculum Development (dvascd).

Bob Fecho has been teaching secondary English in this school district since 1974 and is a staff member of Crossroads, a school-within-a-school conceived by himself and two colleagues, at Simon Gratz High School. A teacher consultant with the Philadelphia Writing Project since its inception, Bob is founder of two of that group's publications—"The Update" and "The Voice." Recently he was appointed to the advisory board of The National Writing Project. His writings appear in several books on educational reform including *Inside/Outside: Teacher Research and Knowledge* edited by Cochran-Smith and Lytle.

Ann Lieberman is Professor of Curriculum and Teaching and Co-director of the National Center for Restructuring, Education, Schools and Teaching (ncrest) and is Editor of Professional Development and Practice Series, published by Teachers College Press.

Susan L. Lytle is Assistant Professor of Education in the Language in Education Division at the Graduate School of Education, University of Pennsylvania. She is also director of the Philadelphia Writing Project and of the master's and doctoral programs in reading/writing/literacy. She is co-author of several books, including *Inside/Outside* (Teachers College Press, 1993), as well as many articles on literacy and teacher education. She is co-holder of the Joseph L. Calihan Chair in Education.

Pat Macpherson has worked for two years as an ethnographer for a charter formed under the Philadelphia Schools Collaborative. She taught English at Germantown Friends School from 1973 to 1986. Her publications include *Reflecting on Jane Eyre* and *Reflecting on the Bell Jar* for the Routledge series, *Heroines?* She has co-authored two articles on adolescent girls with Michelle Fine, "Over Dinner" and "Hungry for an Us."

Bernard J. McMullan is vice president at the Center for Assessment and Policy Development, a policy analysis organization that addresses issues in educational programs and policy, social interventions for disadvantaged populations, and systemic reform in the delivery of services to children and families.

Dina Portnoy has been a teacher in public schools for fifteen years. She has also been a part-time instructor of English at Community College of Philadelphia since 1984. She is an active member of the Philadelphia Writing Project and a participant in the high school restructuring process of the Philadelphia Schools Collaborative.

Linda Powell is a lecturer at Harvard University's Graduate School of Education, organizational consultant, and psychotherapist in private practice. She is a founding partner of Millenium, a consulting group that focuses on issues of power in organizational change.

Fran Sion teaches English and Language Skills in this school district. She has been a staff development consultant, a leader in the Seminar in Teaching and Learning, and a member of the Philadelphia Writing Project.

Virginia Vanderslice is president of Praxis Associates, a Philadelphia-based consulting firm that provides a full range of legal, financial, organization, and educational services to employee-owned companies. She also works with schools that are involved in restructuring. The author of several articles on organizational change, she teaches in the Dynamics of Organization Program at the University of Pennsylvania.

Morris J. Vogel is Professor of History at Temple University, where he has taught since 1973, and senior consultant at the Philadelphia Schools Collaborative. His books include: *The Invention of the Modern Hospital; Still Philadelphia; Philadelphia Stories;* and—most recently—*Cultural Connections: Museums and Libraries of Philadelphia and the Delaware Valley.* Vogel has been editor of the "Pennsylvania Magazine of History and Biography."

Diane R. Waff is a special education teacher, a Philadelphia Writing Project Teacher Consultant, Family Group facilitator, seminar leader, and doctoral student at the University of Pennsylvania. Her article, "Open All Night," was published in the October 1977 issue of "Philadelphia Magazine."

Nancie Zane is a Ph.D. candidate in social psychology and works as a senior research associate at the Center for Workplace Studies at the University of Pennsylvania. Recent publications include *In Their Own Voices: Young Women Talk About Dropping Out* and *"Bein' Wrapped Too Tight: When Low Income Women Drop-out of High School,"* co-authored with Michelle Fine.

Index

Teamsters Union, 23
Temple University
  Carnegie Corporation proposal of, 50–52, 62
  professional development school program and, 48–52, 57–61, 62
Things Fall Apart (Achebe), 56
Tracking, 7, 23, 27, 28, 36, 40, 170
  charters versus, 69–70
  teachers' discussion of, 163–164
Truancy, before charters, 7
Turnover, student, 71, 132

Uncommon Individual Foundation, 193
Unger, Roberto, 24
Unions, 11, 33, 38, 39, 44, 54
University of Pennsylvania, 153–155

Vanderslice, Virginia, 83, 85–97, 88, 97 n. 1, 137
Vassa, Gustavas, 57
Violence, Values, and Justice in the Schools (Bybee and Gee), 133 n. 1

Vogel, Morris J., 47–62, 49, 53–54, 59, 60
Voucher systems, 38, 44

Waff, Diane R., 155–156, 192–203
Wallerstein, N. A., 202–203
Walton, Mary, 45 n. 3
Wehlage, Gary, 6, 18, 63, 64
Weiler, K., 98
Weinstock, Lee, 102, 103
Whole-group discussions, 164
Whole-language approach, 182
Wilson, A., 185
Wolf, Wendy, 43, 45 n. 3, 63
Woman Warrior (Kingston), 169
Women
  authority of, 145–146, 157–158
  classroom discipline and, 201–202
  mentoring program for female students, 193–203

Zane, Nancie, 84, 122–135, 137, 144, 145, 149, 150
Zucker, Lynn, 24
Zumwalt, K., 160